Connecting
Hearts and Minds

Also by Greg Nees

Germany—Unraveling an Enigma

Connecting
Hearts and Minds

Insights, Skills, and Best Practices
for Dealing with Differences

Greg Nees

Vagus Publications

Published in the United States of America by
Vagus Publications
PO Box 1445
Longmont, CO 80502.

Vagus Publications is a trade name of The German Connection, Inc.

Book and cover design by Natalie Bolton

ISBN: 978-0-9965729-9-6

Library of Congress Control Number: 2015910827

Printed in the United States.

In memory of my grandparents

Contents

Note to the Reader

Whenever I introduce a person by first name only, it is a pseudonym I am using to protect the actual person's privacy. Conversely, when I use both a person's first and last name to introduce them, it indicates this is their real name.

In the spirit of inclusiveness, I have alternated the gender of third person pronouns that refer to generic persons. Odd-numbered chapters use feminine pronouns. For example, "If the reader wants to know why, *she* should..." Even-numbered chapters use masculine pronouns, as in "If someone comes by, tell *him*..."

Part One

Introduction

No great improvements in the lot of mankind are possible, until a great change takes place in the fundamental constitution of their modes of thought.

—J.S. Mill

Introduction

Ironically, being personally happy requires that we greatly expand our narrowly defined individual preoccupations. We are built to be a "we"—and enter a more fulfilling state, perhaps a more natural way of being, when we connect in meaningful ways with others.

—Daniel J. Siegel

Life unfolds in the most surprising ways. As a young man, I felt lost and had no idea what to do with my life. Looking back with the advantage of hindsight, I see how one small event rippled through time, transforming me and putting me on a better path. Back then, I was living in a small commune in the woodlands and hills of central Germany.

Frank Steinmeier and I had both moved in a few months earlier, but had not gotten to know each other well. Partly it was because we had different jobs. He was apprenticing at a local farm and I was helping friends in a woodworking shop. Partly it was because I was envious. At six foot six, he towered over most people, had a deep voice, and was Hollywood-handsome. Women gazed at him with bedroom eyes and men respected him. Whenever he was around, people turned their attention toward him and I felt like I was standing in the shadows, which I didn't much like. I found it easy to remain aloof.

One sunny July afternoon, we found ourselves in the kitchen both wanting coffee. Being young men, our talk soon turned to women. We both agreed they were the key to our happiness, but somehow we kept losing the key. That conversation took place well over thirty years ago so I won't tell you I remember it like it was yesterday.

What I do remember is that Frank told me his parents were going through a painful divorce. His mother was suffering and he was angry at his father for leaving her for a younger woman. Before that moment I had only seen him from the outside and what I saw made me envious. Afterwards, I saw him as another human who also suffered, faced challenges, and was trying to find the same happiness I was seeking. After that conversation, Frank became my friend and our friendship remains strong to this day.

What I also remember is that I had just ended an unhappy relationship with a woman in Berlin and I was hurting and unsure of myself. Splitting up had been agonizing. Powerful emotions were tossing me about like a small boat in a storm. Even acknowledging to myself how little control I had over my feelings seemed dangerous, so I surprised myself when I began talking about my situation to Frank.

I remember that when our conversation was over, something inside me had shifted. I felt happier than I had for months, perhaps years. Our talk had unburdened me and I felt a sense of ease and lightness. I also felt less conflicted and more connected to the people around me. That would have been more than enough, but in many ways it was just the beginning. When that conversation took place, I had no idea of the role culture was playing, nor did I know that in less than a year I would return to college to study German and end up becoming a professional interculturalist.

Culture and mind fit together like hand and glove and both influence the way we communicate. You can't understand a mind without understanding culture because minds, like chameleons, adapt to their surroundings. And you can't understand culture without understanding how the mind works, because minds create cultures in the first place. Because communication styles reflect both minds and cultures, the way we talk exemplifies how these function, especially when we talk with someone from another culture who sees the world differently.

For example, I grew up in a blue-collar family in Pennsylvania at a time when it was common to believe a man should not talk about his feelings. Feelings were private and meant to be contained. While it might be okay for women to talk about them, for a man it was, well, unmanly. So I was caught off guard when Frank spoke so openly about his family and the pain of his parents' divorce. By talking authentically, Frank had implicitly given me permission to do the same.

Like a pebble thrown into a pond, the waves of that conversation rippled out, prompting me to begin thinking more deeply about my own family, who I was, what I wanted to do with my life, and countless other questions, both big and small. In retrospect, I see how my beliefs about manhood had conspired with my communication style to keep me trapped inside a prison. To be more precise, it was the things I learned not to talk about that ensnared me, keeping me unaware of what was going on inside me. What has stuck with me in the years since that conversation is this: If I have the courage to open up and talk authentically, I will discover things about myself that will surprise and liberate me.

Talking and awareness are like two sides of a single coin. When I wasn't able to talk about what was real for me, my thoughts and feelings raced around inside me like a dog chasing its tail, getting nowhere. All I could see was a blur. But when I was able to speak truthfully about my thoughts and feelings, I gained clarity, became more aware of who I was, and the dog became calmer.

To be truthful with ourselves is to risk becoming aware of things we'd rather not know. Our minds have been conditioned by the cultures we grew up in. They are filled with assumptions, beliefs, conclusions, opinions, excuses, and other forms of thinking we use to justify who we are and why we do what we do. When we are willing to think and talk truthfully, we become aware that we are more than the social roles we play and we can begin to transcend our conditioning.

Talking is much like breathing. Although we engage in both constantly, we usually don't think about them unless something goes wrong. Until our lungs become ill, or until we get caught in an unpleasant conversation, we don't notice how essential these two activities are for our well-being. Just as breathing provides us with the necessary oxygen, talking provides us with connections, outlets, and pleasure. We are social beings and without the meaning and connections our conversations provide, we shrink and wither.

What happens, then, when we converse with people who see the world differently and who share meaning with different communication styles? What happens when we must live and work with others whose assumptions, morals, and world views differ from our own? Historically, such personal and cultural differences often resulted in misunderstandings, conflicts, and violence, but using violence for settling differences is becoming less tenable as our world becomes a global village and warfare becomes more deadly.

Our differences are not about to disappear, but we are now more interdependent than ever and the daunting problems facing us as a species are complex. Conflicting interests and different points of view will always need to be reconciled or managed. The writing is on the wall and the message is clear: The earth is small, essential resources are finite, and more and more humans want a share of those resources.

The premise of this book is just as clear: The world needs more people who are adept at connecting hearts and minds to bridge our differences. To solve the problems facing all of us, wise, coordinated action is more than desirable, it is essential for our safety and well-being. This is just as true for individuals as it is for large organizations and nation-states. And to coordinate wise actions, we need to develop better, more satisfying ways of talking with one another.

While the challenges we face are great, resources are becoming available to meet them. New domains of knowledge from many different disciplines, not least from neuroscience, psychology, and communication, are becoming widely available. For example, scientists have shown the efficacy of mindfulness to improve performance and well-being, while at the same time, mindfulness practices have been spreading rapidly, including in the business world. As more and more people learn how our brains, minds, and cultures actually function, new possibilities emerge. Seeing this bigger picture allows our personal identities to expand as we become more skillful at managing our differences. By taking an interdisciplinary approach,

Connecting Hearts and Minds helps make sense of the ocean of human diversity that exists today.

I am well aware that trying to integrate the findings from many different fields is a risky undertaking. For one thing, it requires me to paint with a big brush and thus leave out important details. For another, our studies of the brain and mind are in their infancy and there is still much we do not know. Nonetheless, the newest findings about the workings of the brain and mind are encouraging and they offer new answers to such age-old questions as who we think we are and what it means to be human. My own belief is that the more we understand the answers to these complex questions, the better our chances for achieving peace, compassion, and justice for all on our small blue planet. At the same time, this knowledge can improve our personal relationships and help us lead more satisfying lives. If my belief is true, it is more than enough reason to attempt such a risky undertaking.

There is a clear developmental arc to the book's contents. Part one introduces the challenges facing us when we communicate with people who are different. Part two provides basic insights into how brains work, allowing us to understand better the nature of our minds, a core competence for communicating successfully. Part three shows why cultures are so different and how communication styles reflect the values and world views of a particular culture. Part three also explores how cultures and emotions interact to structure our identities. Part four expands upon this theme, showing how understanding the mind can help us grow our identities to achieve more personal well-being, better relationships, and professional success. Whether you aspire to be a professional interculturalist or just want to learn more satisfying ways to communicate with people who are different, *Connecting Hearts and Minds* will raise your awareness and present the skills and best practices you need. As you will soon discover, learning to think like an interculturalist can help you better manage many of the challenging situations you face, both in your personal life and in the workplace.

One

Mind Distance

*Culture hides more than it reveals, and strangely enough what it hides,
it hides most effectively from its own participants.*

—Edward T. Hall

Just before his departure to a summit meeting in Washington, D.C.,
Prime Minister Sato of Japan announced that "Since Mr. Nixon and I
are old friends, the negotiations will be three parts talk and seven parts
haragei."[1] Diplomats were caught off guard by his unusual statement.
The context was clear: It was 1970, Japan and the United States were
trapped in a trade conflict, and negotiations between President Nixon
and Prime Minister Sato were intended to create a new trade policy
and relieve escalating tension. But what was *haragei*?

In Japanese, *hara* refers to the belly and, translated literally, *haragei*
means the "art of the belly." But in the traditional Japanese world view,
the *hara* is more than just a region in the body, it's a primordial energy
center and is what an English speaker might mean with words such as
soul, heart, or intuition. Such a view can make *haragei* seem mysterious
to an American, and even the Japanese have trouble defining it in words.[2]

The renowned Japanese psychiatrist, Takeo Doi, once used the
following example to explain *haragei* to a Westerner: If two traditional
Japanese gentlemen had not seen one another in a long time, the
friends, upon meeting again, would probably sit side-by-side in
silence. They might not speak more than a few formalized words of
greeting in the first five or ten minutes. Instead of peppering each other
with questions and sharing what they had done in the last few years,

the two would be, according to Doi, trying to intuit how the other was feeling and, based on that, ascertain what essential changes had occurred since their last meeting.[3]

While the people of the United States are characterized by their diverse cultural and ethnic backgrounds, Japan is a close-knit society characterized by homogeneity. Possibly as a response to its diversity as well as its use of English as a common language, good communication in the United States is equated with a concise, pragmatic speaking style. In contrast, because the Japanese share history, common values, expectations, and behavioral norms, they do not speak as directly as Americans. Instead, long meaningful pauses, subtle nonverbal signals, and indirect allusions are common in Japan, and *haragei* is one example of this.

While this intuitive style of communication is familiar to the Japanese, it's not clear how well the American diplomats understood the ramifications of Sato's remark. After huddling among themselves, they decided the Prime Minister was assuring President Nixon he understood the threat Japan's trade policy posed. When the talks were over, Nixon assumed new export quotas from Japan would be forthcoming. When they did not appear, he was furious. And when Sato learned his well-intended words had unleashed a new wave of American hostility towards Japan, he felt guilty for the harm he had caused his country.[4] Both men were dissatisfied and distressed.

Understanding Mind Distance

If you have ever lived or worked with people from other countries, you know how cultural differences can create confusion. And if you have to communicate with people who do not speak your language well, you are familiar with the challenges of a language barrier. Both cultural differences and language barriers can cause misunderstandings and stress that harm our performance, our relationships, and even our health and well-being. Despite their teams of expert advisors and abundant resources, Nixon and Sato were not immune to the misunderstandings and stress caused by the mind distance they faced.

Mind distance is any difference in the subjective experience of two human beings.[5] A simple thought experiment makes this abstract idea more concrete: Imagine creating a perfect replica of yourself who not only has all your genes, but all your memories and life experiences. Between you and your double there would be zero mind distance. Now imagine an extra-terrestrial being from another galaxy who has a different body, different sense organs, a different way of communicating, and different past experiences. If there is zero mind distance between you and your clone, there would be infinite mind distance between you and the extraterrestrial. This difference between zero and infinite mind distance forms a theoretical continuum on which we could locate any two humans on the planet. Everything else being equal, the greater the mind distance, the more difficulty two people will have communicating with each other.

Mind distance is created by the different perceptions, physical sensations, and emotional reactions people have to the same event or situation. It is exacerbated by differences in ideologies, values, identities, beliefs, and assumptions about reality, oneself, and other humans. In short, it's a lack of shared experience and meaning. As will become clear, creating shared meaning is an effective way to reduce mind distance and promote understanding. But all too often we focus on superficial similarities and gloss over the underlying mind distance.

In the case of Sato and Nixon, the mind distance between them was huge, highlighted by the confusion among the Americans when Sato mentioned *haragei*. In essence, these two men came not only from different geographical regions, but also came from different sociocultural and psychological realities. Given the different cultures in which they were raised, it is not surprising they failed to communicate well.

Even when two people from the same culture sincerely intend to create a win-win situation, mind distance can lead to misunderstandings. But when people from different cultures try to communicate, the mind distance makes it that much harder. Better intercultural skills would have helped Sato and Nixon. These same skills will become even more essential for personal well-being and professional success in the global village of the twenty-first century.

Differences Seem Wrong

Have you ever wondered why it is harder to communicate with someone who is different from you? Differences can seem superficial, such as the way we are addressed: "Why does she insist on calling me Madame Brown when I've asked her to call me Sue?" Or they can be profound, as in the case of contradictory world views: "How primitive of them to think the universe is alive and that a supernatural power controls their destiny. Every intelligent person knows the universe is inanimate and we are simply a cosmic accident resulting from random chemical reactions." Regardless of type or degree, differences have the ability to upset and confuse us, forcing us to spend valuable time and energy figuring out how to deal with them.

Even worse, differences often seem wrong. Humans are emotional beings who can, on occasion, think and communicate rationally, not rational beings who happen to have emotions. When we notice someone behaving differently, we are not inclined to rationally categorize the behavior as "different" or "unexpected." Instead, our brains evaluate the difference intuitively, and it ends up becoming stupid, wrong, dangerous, or evil.[6] These rapid, autonomous judgments are often based on our cultural conditioning, and this is true even for people who are intellectually aware of the world's cultural diversity and who would prefer not to react in such a judgmental manner. Nonetheless, when our expectations are violated, our initial reaction is often judgmental.

Our expectations are learned as part of the enculturation process we go through as we grow up and, as a result, differences are often perceived as threatening, which triggers the brain's ancient fight-or-flight response. When this happens, we are flooded with stress hormones, making it all the more challenging to deal with differences in a reasonable manner. Expecting others—consciously or un-consciously—to be other than they are is an elementary stumbling block when interacting with people who are different.

To avoid misunderstandings, good interculturalists learn to "hit the pause button" and test relevant assumptions before over- or under-reacting. For example, when we find ourselves upset by another person's behavior, it is often because we are making, either consciously or unconsciously, assumptions about that person's intentions. If we are able to pause and question this assumption by seeing the situation from the other person's point of view, we often discover the person has a different motive than we first assumed. By assuming valid reasons for why the other person is behaving as she is and then, like a good detective, trying to understand them, we are able to respond in a more appropriate manner.[7]

The Trap of Similarity

When I left the United States in 1976, I had no idea I was on my way to becoming a professional interculturalist. I thought I was just taking a year off to see the world, but a series of serendipitous events led me to live and study in Germany. What started out as a gap year in my professional development turned out to be fourteen years abroad that transformed me from a naïve, culture-bound young man into a fuller, freer human being.

Learning to think and communicate in a new language triggered profound, not always pleasant, changes in me. I was lost and looking for direction when Professor Heinz Göhring, a sociologist and interpreter, took me under his wing. At that time I was studying German and Spanish at the University of Mainz and earning my living teaching English. While attending Professor Göhring's intercultural communication seminars, things began to fall into place for me. Without realizing it, I was taking the first step towards developing the knowledge and skills I would need as an interculturalist. When he offered me the opportunity to work as his teaching assistant, I was glad to accept. I was also glad to accept his offer to move to a first-name basis, which in Germany is considered an honor and a sign of friendship.

While Heinz taught me many lessons about intercultural communication, one of the most important was the role expectations play in our lives. Expecting people to be other than they are is one of the most fundamental errors we can make. With his help, I became aware of the role growing up in the United States played in forming not only my expectations, but also my personality traits. Thanks to him, I began to see how internalized expectations were the source of my misunderstandings with German friends and colleagues. Part of my problem arose from the many external similarities Germans and Americans shared. Because of these I failed to notice subtle but important differences.

While obvious external differences can disappoint our expectations and lead to upset and fear, unrecognized mind distance is a hidden pitfall that makes intercultural encounters even more challenging. Like the bulk of an iceberg lying in wait for an unsuspecting ship, the less obvious differences are misunderstandings waiting to happen.

For example, when two people use the same word without noticing it means something different to each of them, they have fallen into the trap of similarity. Maybe the word is *freedom,* or *love,* or *vacation.* No matter what the word, if the two parties use it without noticing how it means something different, misunderstandings are bound to arise.

Or imagine a young, third-generation Japanese-American woman who has grown up speaking English in the United States and then moved to Japan as a young adult. Many of the Japanese she encounters will be caught off guard if they try to speak to her in Japanese. They will discover that her Japanese is rudimentary and her thinking more like an American. This illustrates the problem: The trap of similarity can be subtle, appearing in many different guises, but in each instance a person fails to notice some underlying mind distance. Instead of seeing a person who is different, we see a copy of ourselves that seems defective.

One way to reduce mind distance and avoid the trap of similarity is to become aware of, and distinguish between, differences and commonalties on three levels: A universal level on which we are all the same; a cultural or group level on which group members exhibit certain similarities and tendencies; and an individual level on which each person is unique. We can visualize these three levels as a pyramid with the universal level as the foundation, the cultural in the middle, and the individual at the top.

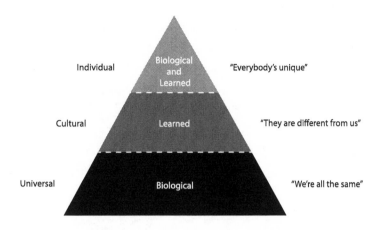

Figure 1.1 — Three Levels of Human Diversity

Human behavior always represents some combination of all three levels. Take smiling as an example. People everywhere smile. Even babies who are born blind smile when happy, although they have never seen another human smiling. Smiling is innate to all of us. At the same time, cultures have unwritten rules about when it is appropriate to smile and how to interpret it.

For instance, people who are familiar with both Germany and the United States will agree that Germans, in general, smile less than Americans, especially in public settings. And those who know the Germans well also know that people in Germany who smile a great deal are often thought of as naïve or a bit slow on the uptake. The cultural meaning of a smile would thus be represented on the middle level.

But if we zoom in and focus on individual differences, we discover a wide diversity among individual Germans and Americans as to how often, when, and why they smile.[8] Some Germans smile much more than others. A similarly wide range of diversity exists in the United States. If we measure frequency of smiling, we will notice a number of Americans who smile less than many Germans, while there are a number of Germans who smile more than many Americans. These individual behaviors are represented by the top layer of the pyramid.

When we say people everywhere are the same, we are right because we are emphasizing human nature or the universal level. When someone else says people from other cultures are different, they are also right because people from different cultures do exhibit different patterns of behavior. When others say we are all unique individuals, they are also right. All three viewpoints contain a part of the truth and we need to consider all three to get an accurate and comprehensive understanding of human diversity. Like the zoom lens on a camera, these three levels of analysis provide different degrees of detail. Good interculturalists take all three levels into account when dealing with other people because ignoring any one of these levels can distort our perceptions.

While the trap of similarity can mislead us, so, too, can over-generalizing. For instance, if we only know one or two people from another culture, it is easy to assume everyone in that culture is similar. This points to an important fact: Often there is more mind distance and diversity within a single culture than between different cultures. If we, purely as a hypothetical example, use the normal curve to represent some given trait that varies between cultures, such as emotional expression, the distribution within two cultures might look something like this:

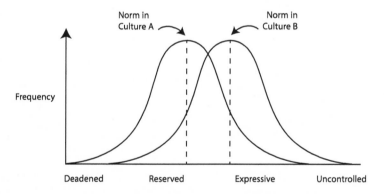

Figure 1.2 — Distribution of Emotional Expressivity

But because of our limited experience with the other culture, we often fail to notice its diversity. So, while we see the individual differences in our own group, "they" all seem to look the same. Such stereotypical thinking distorts our perceptions and can lead to less-than-optimal behaviors when interacting with "them."

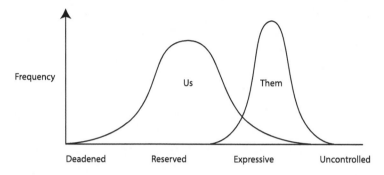

Figure 1.3 — Biased Perceptions of Us and Them

As I learned in my first months in Germany, superficial contact with people from another culture does not guarantee better communication and cooperation. That requires increased understanding to reduce mind distance. If it was Professor Göhring who began to free my culture-bound mind, it was Dr. Arnold Mindell who helped me learn to reduce mind distance by switching points of view more skillfully.

Reducing Mind Distance

Living in a new culture and confronting my expectations encouraged me to explore areas of my life I had never ventured into before. During these explorations, I chanced upon Mindell's *Dreambody – The Body's Role In Revealing the Self.* I was intrigued by its cross-cultural, interdisciplinary exploration of the so-called mind-body problem, which has bedeviled Western philosophy for centuries.[9] In this short book Mindell, a renowned psychotherapist, links the mind's dreaming process with illnesses and physical symptoms as well as with disciplines such as yoga and tai chi. I was so fascinated I drove to Switzerland to participate in a workshop he was organizing.

Mindell is not your average psychotherapist. He started out studying engineering and physics at MIT, where he graduated with a master's degree. He was doing graduate work in physics at the ETH (*Eidgenössische Technische Hochschule*) in Zürich, when he met Franz Riklin, then head of the Jung Institute. What started as a friendship developed into a therapeutic relationship and he changed careers, leaving physics to become a therapist.

Today his clients and students—to whom he is affectionately known as Arny—come from all corners of the world. His empathy and curiosity about how others see the world make him a natural interculturalist who excels at building trusting relationships across cultural boundaries. Trust is, of course, one of the pillars upon which relationships everywhere stand or fall.

Arny has the courage of an explorer, an essential trait for any interculturalist. Thanks to his intense exploration of his own psyche, as well as thousands of hours of work as a therapist, he has developed a deep understanding of human nature. For example, his hypothesis that the same forces underlying individual behavior could also be observed in group dynamics allowed him to become an expert facilitator for large groups in conflict.[10]

Such insights, plus his extensive investigation of other cultures' ways of understanding human nature, culminated in his creation of Process Work. Process Work draws on insights from both modern science and the wisdom traditions as well as diverse schools of psychology. The advantage of this synthesis is its ability to understand humans everywhere on the personal, cultural, and universal levels. Arny's success in creating an intercultural community of fellow explorers from around the world—Europe, Asia, Africa, and the Americas—testifies to the efficacy of this approach.

After that first workshop in Zürich, I felt more optimistic, vibrant, and alive than I had for quite a while. Over the course of the next few years, I participated in a number of workshops that Arny and his associates organized. During those years, I discovered the degree to which mind distance can exist among individuals and the problems it can cause. I also began to realize I can only understand another person to the degree I understand myself. When I deny, repress, or dissociate parts of myself, not only do I make my own life more difficult, I also end up causing more problems for everyone around me. To my surprise, I discovered that to understand myself better, I needed to become more empathic.

Self-Awareness

One under-appreciated component of empathy is the ability to notice how our own words and nonverbal signals are affecting the other person. Arny is not an expert on Japanese culture *per se*, but his consummate skill at self-monitoring helps him communicate well with people from around the world. For example, once he was working with a man in Japan who kept turning away from him. At the time Arny was not yet aware of his unconscious assumption that direct eye contact was a sign of good communication. Because this assumption was still unconscious, he kept trying to make eye contact and the man kept turning away.

Arny was not sure why the conversation felt so awkward, but rather than blame the man for being shy or defensive, he focused on his own behavior. By noticing his own nonverbal signals, he guessed it might be his eye contact that was causing the man to turn away. Being a good scientist, he tested his hypothesis. He began looking down and away from the man and in no time the two men were having a fluid, productive conversation.

Arny says one key to his success as a therapist and group facilitator is the intense work he has done to raise his awareness of the nonverbal elements of communication. He has trained his attention to notice the signals his body, face, and voice are sending while also noticing what's going on in the outside world. By monitoring the feelings and sensations in his own body, he is able to create congruence between his body language and his words so as not to send contradictory signals. He points out that when our words and nonverbal signals are not congruent, we trigger resistance and misunderstanding in the other person, which can derail the conversation.

The ability to self-monitor and switch points of view go hand-in-hand. Both are essential skills for communicating well with people who have different perspectives and expectations. For example, Arny was once working with a new client from Ghana who told him she didn't know why she had come to see him.[11] It was her first visit and Arny assured her that was fine and encouraged her to relax. She did so and began staring at a large tree outside the office window. One of the things Arny does best is to connect with people by noticing what they are paying attention to. Following his client's lead, Arny switched his attention to the large tree and sat silently, letting his imagination play.

After a few moments he said, "What an amazing tree, so green and so tall." The woman kept staring silently at the tree and then said suddenly, "Yes, it's magical, can you imagine speaking with a part of the tree as if it was an advisor for you?" Without missing a beat, Arny joined her reality, replying, "I don't do that kind of dreaming often, but I need such advisors, and should speak to trees more often. What does the tree say to you?" At that point the woman began telling Arny what the tree was advising her about a serious problem she was facing in her life. That advice was useful to the woman and she thanked Arny profusely for helping her understand what she now needed to do. She explained that belief in the wisdom of trees was important to her people, and that living in the West had encouraged her to forget this ancient knowledge. By remembering this belief, she was able to access a part of herself she had marginalized, and this gave her a new perspective on the problem she was facing.

Notice both what Arny did and what he did not do. He didn't tell her she was delusional, nor in any way imply she was the victim of a superstitious world view. He did have the courage to take her point of view and, at least temporarily, join her reality. This ability to switch viewpoints and join the other's reality is an essential component of all successful communication.

We all, both as individuals and as groups, have our ways of understanding reality. These different world views are at the heart of the mind distance that can cause so much suffering. By paying attention to what others are attending to, we take a step towards reducing mind distance. This empathic move towards experiencing the world the way the other experiences it is a prerequisite for developing trust. Without some degree of trust, our conversations are exercises in futility as we bounce words off each other's defenses.

Noticing what other people are attending to may sound simple, but it's not. Being willing to step into the other's reality and see the world the way they do is like a leap into the unknown, an act of courage requiring deep confidence in one's own view of reality. Every time we are willing to see the world through someone else's eyes, we run the risk of discovering how our own point of view is more limited, more distorted, or more erroneous than we realized. Such empathic connection with others, especially with others who are radically different, is not for the faint of heart. But it is our empathic connections that provide us with some of our most fulfilling moments. Poets and sages have been saying as much for millennia and science is now confirming it.

One of the most exciting areas of current scientific research is the field of interpersonal neurobiology and the growing body of evidence indicating that our brains are designed to attune to one another.[12] In the last ten years, neuroscientists have been able to observe living human brains as they engage in recognizing faces, experiencing emotions, processing language, making music, meditating, and more. The results are clear: Not only are our brains designed to connect, it turns out the structure and functioning of our brains gets shaped by our relationships.[13] As Daniel Goleman, author of the ground-breaking book, *Emotional Intelligence*, puts it: "Our social interactions operate as modulators, something like interpersonal thermostats that continually reset key aspects of our brain function as they orchestrate our emotions...To a surprising extent, then, our relationships mold not just our experience but our biology."[14]

While genes predispose growing brains to develop in particular ways, who we become is influenced by the enigmatic interaction between our genes and the web of social relationships we grow up in. When our relationships with others go well, we tend to be happy and healthy.[15] When they go wrong, we get stressed and sick. In other words, not only are our brains hardwired to connect, the way we connect has huge consequences: Healthy relationships nourish us, while bad ones upset and distress us. They can even damage our immune system and impact our health.[16]

But if we are hard-wired to connect, and if our health and well-being depends upon developing and maintaining good relationships, why are misunderstandings and bad relationships so common, and why is the history of our species filled with violence and wars? A large part of the answer is the mind distance that separates us, mind distance that is exacerbated by the various ways in which different cultures have constructed their social realities.

The Ethnography of Communication

I first met Dr. Kristine Fitch, a professor of communication studies, when I arrived at the University of Colorado in 1990 to complete my graduate studies. Professor Fitch's academic specialty is the ethnography of communication. She studies the way a culture's assumptions, values, and norms are reinforced by the everyday language of particular speech communities. The ethnography of communication provides a valuable toolkit for better understanding cultural differences, and Kristine was happy to share her skills and knowledge. Not only was she adept at clarifying complex communication patterns, she was also passionate about understanding the interaction between language and culture.

Studying with Kristine enabled me to investigate the way a group's language mirrors and corresponds to its culture, as well as how the group's culture is maintained and passed on to future generations via its communication patterns. Understanding the relationship between language, communication patterns, and culture is essential for every interculturalist, and it's an argument for learning as many languages as possible.

Like all of my best teachers, Kristine found ways to shake me up and make me look at the world anew. One of her favorite ways of doing that was to write WEDTM?, short for, "What exactly does that mean?", in the margins of my papers whenever my thinking became sloppy.

Kristine's phrase was my constant companion during the years I studied with her. It has now become internalized in my mental life. This simple question has challenged me over and over, forcing me to become not only clearer about what I am thinking and saying, but also illuminating how limiting language can be when we try to express what moves us most. It also made me a better, more active listener as I sought to really understand what others meant, rather than be satisfied with just their words. This question has also driven home just how much of our thinking and talking mirror the socially constructed worlds in which we live.

While social constructions create much of the diversity which challenges us, studying the way we communicate also allows us to explore the universal level of human needs. When we are able to understand the deeper needs motivating people's behaviors, we have a tool to bridge the mind distance that separates us on both the cultural and individual levels.

As we will see in chapters eight and nine, all cultures face fundamental dilemmas they must manage if they are to remain viable. These challenges are part of the human condition and can't be avoided. By studying the fundamental dilemmas facing all cultures and their members, not only can we better understand the great diversity of socially constructed realities, we can also use this knowledge to reduce the mind distance that separates us.

For instance, if President Nixon and Prime Minister Sato had better understood each other's communication style, they would have better understood each other's intentions and perhaps have reached a more satisfactory outcome at their summit meeting. When communication styles collide, the results are confusion and distress.

What I learned while working with Kristine was the important role communication styles play in helping groups generate collective intelligence. Because a common communication style provides a shared platform to exchange and manage meaning, it promotes social cohesion. This book will explore both the surface features of different communication styles as well as the deeper needs underlying them. By understanding both kinds of differences, we become more able to better communicate with people from cultures everywhere.

How Deep Is the Rabbit Hole?

Since the time of Socrates, good teachers have used questions to guide their students. I combined Kristine's question, "What exactly does that mean?", with another powerful question to create the subject for my doctoral research. I can still remember the day Professor Göhring asked what it was that made a conversation satisfying. I was thirty years old and had never thought of asking such a question. I was blind-sided and embarrassed as my mind went blank. What *does* make a conversation satisfying? What makes one conversation so energizing and fulfilling, another so dreadfully boring, and a third so emotionally intense it leaves us upset for hours afterwards? The more I reflected upon this question, the more I realized just how profound it was.

Equipped with the ethnography-of-communication tool kit I had acquired under Kristine's tutelage, I returned to Germany in 1994. My goal was to discover what made conversations satisfying for Germans. For nine months, I conducted interviews in all regions of the country. I took notes while engaged in countless social events and conversations as a participant-observer. I also visited German schools and businesses to understand what it was Germans were doing when they were talking with each other.

Having spent the better part of fourteen years in Germany— speaking German, living and working with German friends and colleagues, and graduating from a German university—I was not expecting to learn much new. I could not have been more wrong. In retrospect, I think I learned as much in that fifteenth year as I had in my first year abroad, showing me once again the power of my own expectations to deceive me. While humans everywhere use assumptions and expectations to guide their thinking, if these assumptions and expectations are inaccurate, they make mind distance all that much more difficult to master.

People often assume they understand their own culture and its people better than they do, and certainly better than any outsider. For example, many of the Germans I interviewed wondered why I was asking so many strange questions about their ways of talking. I explained I wanted to understand the prevalent communication style in Germany, whereupon a number of them informed me there was no such thing. Bavarians told me they communicate differently from the Prussians, and Rheinlanders insisted there was no comparison between the way they talked and the way Swabians did. When I suggested there might be nationwide similarities, some became insulted, insisting their region's style was unique and my undertaking hopeless.

They were both right and wrong. They were right in proclaiming regionalism to be a major force in Germany. Different dialects, identities, and subcultures abound. But important common elements tie together the way Germans communicate, elements many of my interviewees weren't aware of. Their inability to switch perspectives blinded them to the commonalities among Germans in general.

I am happy to report that those Germans who have read the book based on my research, *Germany – Unraveling An Enigma*, are enthusiastic about what I wrote. One reader thanked me, saying it was as if I had given him a mirror to look at himself in a way he had never seen before. This same reader also said he now realized increased awareness of one's own cultural conditioning is essential for improved communication with other cultures. Conversely, becoming more aware of the ways in which cultures differ allows us to develop more self-awareness. Seen from this perspective, cultural differences can serve as mirrors, allowing us to discover more about who we are.

Much wisdom can be found in first seeking common ground to build our relationships upon. Being able to switch one's point of view and see the other's perspective is one way to achieve this common ground. But at some point, we will also be faced with the challenges presented by the ways in which we are different. When that happens, we need to have ways of thinking and talking that allow us to manage the mind distance that separates us. Such conversations require skill and courage, but when done well, they allow us to switch points of view and grow the mutual trust essential for good relationships. Without a respect-filled, truthful way of talking about our differences, they get pushed under the table where they sabotage our best efforts.

Human well-being depends upon our ability to communicate. Whether it is an intimate conversation with a loved one that gives meaning to our lives, a business discussion that allows a team to develop a new technology, a coaching session with a mentor that helps us develop our potential, or an international meeting to address poverty and social justice, we need to be able to talk together successfully. If mind distance is our challenge, the development of mindsight, which we will explore in the next section, is the solution.

Part Two

Brains and Minds

The mind is its own place, and in itself can make a heaven of hell, a hell of heaven.

—John Milton

We are all capable of believing things which we know to be untrue, and then, when we are finally proved wrong, impudently twisting the facts so as to show we were right. Intellectually, it is possible to carry on this process for an indefinite time: the only check on it is that sooner or later a false belief bumps up against a solid reality, usually on a battlefield.

—George Orwell

Two

Opening Pandora's Box

One of the greatest truths in psychology is that the mind is divided into parts that sometimes conflict. To be human is to feel pulled in different directions, and to marvel—sometimes in horror—at your inability to control your own actions.

—Jonathan Haidt

Bruce pressed his body into the bottom of the foxhole as the enemy approached. His heart was pounding as he tried to melt into the ground and become invisible. When his comrade arrived, Bruce grabbed him by the ankle, pulled him down into the hole, shoved a weapon into his hand, and whispered, "Shoot them if they come to get us."

The history of our species is soaked with the blood of men using violence to settle their differences, but this particular battle took place in a man's mind. Bruce, a patient in a Veteran's Administration hospital, was hiding under his bed when he grabbed Dr. Daniel Siegel's ankle, pulled him down, and shoved a broom into his hands, saying, "Shoot them if they come to get us."[1]

At the time, Dr. Siegel was a young psychiatrist at the start of an illustrious career and Bruce was a Vietnam veteran suffering from post-traumatic stress disorder. Dr. Siegel's mind raced to make sense of this bizarre situation. He knew he was in the VA hospital in Los Angeles, but where was Bruce? Somehow Bruce was back in Vietnam, involved in a life-or-death struggle with his enemies. Although these two men were members of the same culture, the mind distance between them could hardly have been greater.

How is such a highly subjective state of mind possible? How could Bruce mistake a broom for a rifle, a hospital room for the rice paddies of Vietnam, and the area beneath his bed for a foxhole? More importantly, what do such distorted perceptions have to teach us about the subjective nature of our minds, and the importance of this subjectivity when we are dealing with people who see the world differently? While we will never know for sure what Bruce was experiencing as he pulled Dr. Siegel under his hospital bed, recent advances in psychology and neuroscience allow us to make some educated guesses. The mind distance between the two men can be likened to what engineers call a "black box problem", because trying to understand what is going on in any other person's mind is like trying to see what is happening inside a closed, opaque box. We can see the outside of the box (the person), but we cannot see what is going on inside (the mind). We see what goes into the box (the stimuli) and we can see what comes out (the behavior), but we can't see what happens in between.

In the case of a veteran with PTSD who drops to the ground when a car backfires, we can represent the black box problem like this:

Car backfires
(stimulus)

?

Veteran drops to ground
(response)

Figure 2.1 — The Black Box Problem

Our inability to see what is going on in another person's mind is a problem that has fascinated and frustrated people everywhere and in all epochs. It is also a problem interculturalists must face because we are continually dealing with people whose minds are—to one degree or another—different from our own. While most people's perceptions may not be as different from our own as Bruce's were from Dr. Siegel's, understanding the subjective nature of perceptual differences is essential for every interculturalist.

Mindsight

Various methods have been proposed for overcoming mind distance and discovering how the mind works. Classical behaviorists suggested we could never know the subjective nature of another's mind, and shouldn't waste our time trying. They suggest focusing on what we can see and measure: stimuli and behavior. Others, such as neuroscientists, suggest the mind and the brain are one and the same and that by studying the brain, we can learn all we need to know about the mind. They point to the recent advances in knowledge provided by functional MRI scanners and other new technologies that allow us to observe healthy brains in operation. Others, such as cognitive psychologists, suggest that by careful study of both stimuli and responses we can use a reverse engineering approach to gain insights into what happens as the brain processes information and energy. Still others suggest we need only ask a person what he is thinking and feeling to get valuable insights into the workings of his mind.

Another approach to understanding the mind is introspection, or turning our attention inward to explore the workings of our own minds. Many people avoid introspection, fearing what they might find. Others, in an effort to protect their self-esteem, avoid deeper self-knowledge. Unfortunately, remaining blind to the workings of our own minds can have negative consequences. Not only does being mindblind keep us from developing the mindsight we need to lead authentic, healthy lives, it also encourages self-deception, and can even make us afraid of the outside world.[2]

Mindsight, as defined by Dr. Siegel, is a "kind of focused attention that allows us to see the internal workings of our own minds."[3] It encompasses not only the insights necessary to understand our own minds and the minds of others, it also promotes empathy.[4] If mind distance creates barriers between people, mindsight enables us to bridge those barriers. All of the above approaches offer valuable ways for the interculturalist to understand the mind. If we use them all, we get a more accurate and holistic picture of human nature, thus increasing our mindsight.

That encounter with Bruce left Dr. Siegel shaken. After he came out of Bruce's room, a nurse asked him where he had been and all he could say was, "I don't know." Meeting later with his supervisor, Siegel asked about the incident and was told it was a "flashback." While having a label for Bruce's symptoms was useful, it was not satisfying, so he scoured the literature for more information. He found nothing to explain how a flashback might occur. Because Bruce was not his only patient who experienced flashbacks, Siegel set out to understand how the past could distort perceptions of the present.

Because mindsight is a combination of empathy and insight into the inner workings of the mind, it is a prerequisite for both the emotional and social intelligence that every good interculturalist needs. The good news is that even if we don't have this intelligence to the degree we would like, we can develop it if we so choose. One step in developing more mindsight is to understand some basic facts about how the nervous system works.

The Inner Team

Our nervous system can be compared to a large, complex organization made up of teams of specialists who carry out different tasks. When these different teams cooperate and are doing their job well, they are contributing to the well-being of the entire organization, helping it survive and thrive. If the nervous system is the entire organization, the brain is the headquarters, comprised of diverse departments with different functions. If we extend this metaphor further, the CEO of the organization is our sense of being a conscious self. Like executives everywhere, the "I" must make decisions to ensure the health and well-being of the entire person.[5] But in a large organization, an almost infinite number of decisions need to be made for the company to function well. Imagine the gridlock that would occur if every decision had to be made by the CEO.

Running diverse, parallel networks allows the brain to quickly process a wide variety of information. These autonomic networks are connected in complex feedback loops that support each other. To avoid gridlock, much of this processing occurs without conscious awareness. Here's how Timothy D. Wilson, a professor of psychology at the University of Virginia, describes it:

> The mind operates most efficiently by relegating a good deal of high-level, sophisticated thinking to the unconscious, just as a modern jumbo jet is able to fly on automatic pilot with little or no input from the "conscious" pilot. The adaptive unconscious does an excellent job of sizing up the world, warning people of danger, setting goals, and initiating action in a sophisticated and efficient manner.[6]

The capability of the brain to function both consciously and unconsciously is often referred to as the dual-process model.[7] This ingenious construction enables rapid reactions to routine situations we face in our daily lives. Notice, for example, how fast you pull your hand back from a hot stove. No conscious thought was required. In fact, your hand was already pulling back before the feeling of pain reached conscious awareness. Thank specialists on your inner team for that quick reaction.

The dual process design also gives us the flexibility of conscious choice, allowing us to reflect upon and adapt to a changing environment. Our conscious mind is good at reflective decision-making, but it has a limited capacity. Our job as CEO is to ensure that the overall functioning of our inner organization and our relationships with the outside world are going smoothly. We cannot be aware of everything that is going on inside ourselves at any one time. That's where dual processing comes in. For example, it is essential that your body's internal temperature be maintained within a narrow range for the cells in your body to thrive. But it would be a waste of your time and resources as CEO to be concerned with micro-managing temperature. This vital job is delegated to specialists who are trained to keep the body in homeostasis. But if homeostasis is disrupted by illness, you are notified that all is not well. Then you as CEO must decide whether or not to take time off from work to recover.

As we will see throughout this book, unconscious processing affects not just our physiology, but also our perceptions, feelings, and thoughts. As Wilson makes clear, much high level processing occurs out of conscious awareness. Our inner team is impulsive and biased, but it is also the source of lightning fast action, brilliant inspiration, and powerful intuitions that aid creative problem-solving. Its power to process masses of complex and ambiguous information is nothing short of amazing. But to harness this potential, we need to understand how our brains learn.

The Secret Life of Sea Snails

Before beginning his research, Nobel Prize-winner Eric Kandel took time to choose his subject. After several attempts with other creatures, he focused on the sea snail, *Aplysia californica*. Each adult sea snail measures more than a foot long, weighs several pounds, and feeds on seaweed. It is also a creature with an astounding sex life. These snails are hermaphrodites. They can, and do, have sex as male or female and sometimes both simultaneously. Groups of *Aplysia* have been observed forming long copulatory chains in which those in the middle act as both male and female for the ones in front of and behind them.

But it was the simple nervous system, not the exotic sex life of *Aplysia,* that persuaded Kandel to base his research on the snails. *Aplysia's* brain consists of only twenty thousand neurons instead of the approximately one hundred billion in a human brain.[8] In addition, *Aplysia's* neurons are quite large and many can be seen with the naked eye, allowing Kandel to study the cellular processes that enable the snails to learn.[9] Kandel spent many years studying *Aplysia* and his research forms the basis for much of what we now know about the anatomy of memory. That's because neurons, although they come in an array of sizes and shapes, function basically the same throughout the animal kingdom. Thus the difference between a snail's brain and a human brain resides more in the size and complexity of their neural networks, not in the individual neurons. As Kandel writes: "The cellular mechanisms of learning and memory reside not in the special properties of the neuron itself, but in the connections it receives and makes with other cells in the neuronal circuit to which it belongs."[10]

What Kandel discovered is that the structure of the synapses—the connections between neurons—change in response to experience. Each of the billions of nerve cells in a human brain is connected to countless other nerve cells.[11] In just one second an individual neuron can receive hundreds of signals. In the time it takes you to read this paragraph, the neurons of your brain will have exchanged billions of electrochemical signals.[12]

Networks of neurons are living electrical circuits. When a neural network is activated on a regular basis, it begins to change its physical structure. Using a series of ingenious experiments, Kandel was able to demonstrate that changes in *Aplysia's* neural structures corresponded to the three types of learning studied by Pavlov and other behaviorists: Habituation, sensitization, and conditioning—also called associative learning.[13]

When neurons fire at the same time, it strengthens the connection between them. At its simplest, memory is an associational process that links neurons together. Or, as neuroscientists like to say, "neurons that fire together, wire together."

Scientists refer to the brain's ability to change and adapt to new environments as "experience-dependent plasticity," which is a technical name for what we refer to as learning and memory. While instincts and other fixed patterns of behavior are reliable ways to respond quickly to a stimulus, they are too rigid to adapt to a complex, changing environment. With increased memory capacity comes the ability to learn and adapt to change. While learning is present even in simple animals, in humans it reaches a new level, giving us the ability to use languages and think symbolically.

By showing that habituation, sensitization, and associative learning were accompanied by changes in the neural structures of the snails, Kandel provided us with an understanding of how the simplest forms of memory are encoded. Of course, no one thinks the sea snails were remembering the way humans do, but as we now know, humans have two basic types of memory, implicit and explicit. This is a crucial point in understanding the workings of our minds. What Kandel's groundbreaking research explained has come to be known as implicit memory, the first layer of memory, which differs from explicit memory in a number of important ways.

For starters, implicit memory is evolutionarily much older than explicit memory. When nature comes up with a good invention it is retained or, as biologists like to say, conserved. Implicit memory provided such a powerful way to adapt to a changing environment that nature has used it for millions of years and spread it to most of the animal kingdom. Structurally, implicit memory is simple. In contrast, explicit memory is newer, more complicated, and requires additional brain circuitry. In humans, when all is going well, implicit and explicit memory work together as a team with perceptions, emotional states, and behaviors first encoded in implicit memory.

Implicit memory is sometimes called procedural memory because it allows us to learn complex behaviors such as walking, riding a bicycle, dancing, and more. Learning such activities takes time and after each practice session, neural connections in the brain change so that we gradually increase our skill level. That such unconscious learning is at work in human development has been known for a long time, as the following quote from Aristotle makes clear, "We are what we repeatedly do. Excellence, therefore, is not an act, but a habit."

Explicit memory is a more advanced, integrative process that links implicit memories together. This allows us to form ever larger chunks of memories, from small facts to whole narratives. While implicit memory is already functioning by the time we are born, explicit memory does not develop until we are around eighteen months old. At this time the hippocampus, one of the brain's specialized structures, has matured enough so it can begin linking different implicit memories together. We can think of an explicit memory as the result of a construction process that uses implicit memories as building blocks to create the house of memories in which we live our lives. In this metaphor, the hippocampus is the mason that lays and cements the bricks to create our house of memories.

Explicit memory is sometimes called declarative memory because it provides explicit knowledge that we can express in words. One type of explicit memory is called factual memory, a specialty of the brain's left hemisphere, where we store the impersonal, timeless knowledge of dates and facts. Another type, autobiographical memory, allows us to remember events from our own past and assemble those memories into the images we have of ourselves, a specialty of the right hemisphere.[14]

Memory Is Distributed

Implicit memories are not stored in any one location, but are scattered throughout the brain. Where each element is located depends on what type of information it encodes. For instance, imagine a two-year-old child encountering a puppy for the first time. The child will see, smell, and hear the puppy. Each of these perceptions will be encoded in the area of the brain responsible for that particular type of sensory information.

If the dog is small and not threatening, the child may feel excited to see such a furry playmate. What a strange and wonderful creature! The puppy captivates the child's attention. Maybe the child also feels affection for this small, playful creature. All of these different subjective perceptions, feelings, and urges to touch are correlated with neural firing patterns in different areas of the brain. But because these different neural firing patterns are being activated simultaneously, the brain is linking them together into a whole that will be available in the future.

At the same time, imagine that the child's mother is telling him that this warm, fuzzy creature is called a dog. The child's brain will be laying down implicit memories of the sound of this word as well. All of these different implicit memories are the building blocks which get linked together to form an explicit memory so the child can later remember what a dog is. As the child grows and has other experiences with different dogs, its concept of what a dog is will grow, generalize, and become more complex.

Using the construction metaphor, we can say the child has built a mental edifice out of many implicit memories (the building blocks) by using his hippocampus (the mason) to link them all together. So every time he hears or sees the word *dog*, these different neural networks get reactivated and the child remembers what a dog is. Or, conversely, when the child sees or hears a real dog, the same networks get activated and he knows that the creature causing those images and sounds is called a dog. All of this remembering happens in milliseconds so the child has the immediate sense of knowing what this furry creature is.

Not only do these connections between and within different neural circuits get activated every time the child encounters the animal or the word, they also strengthen with each activation. As we will soon see, this is an essential insight into understanding how cultural differences get internalized in individuals and institutionalized within groups.

Remembering

Whenever an explicit memory gets activated, we have an internal sense of "I am remembering this." We intuitively know this is a mental event, i.e., we have some sort of awareness of seeing, hearing, or feeling something that we know is from the past and not a perception of now.[15] For instance, if I ask you what you did yesterday, as you recollected what you did you would know you are remembering something from the past and not experiencing it in the present.

This sense of remembering only occurs with explicit memory. In contrast, when an implicit-only memory is activated by something in our current situation, there is nothing to indicate this is a memory and not something we are seeing, feeling, or doing right now. Because there is no conscious intent to remember, nor any internal sense of, "I am remembering this," there is also no awareness that what we are perceiving or feeling is coming from the past. Instead, the memory floods the mind as if it were happening right now. Understanding this difference between implicit-only and explicit memories helps us understand the nature of flashbacks and why they can seem so real.

What Siegel suggests is that in flashback situations, a person's current perceptions become conflated with implicit-only memories from the past, thereby causing distorted perceptions and a bizarre reliving of a past event in the present.[16] Such flashbacks point to an extreme lack of mindsight. In essence, the person experiencing the flashback does not realize he is conflating implicit memories of past events with perceptions of the present. When intense and vivid, implicit-only memories of perceptions and emotions can create major challenges, causing us to behave inappropriately.

Trauma, electric shocks, and too much alcohol all have the ability to disrupt the functioning of the hippocampus. When this happens, it cannot process and link implicit memories to create the explicit memories necessary for future recall. But the implicit-only memories of perceptions, feelings, and action impulses are nonetheless being encoded in the neural networks of the brain. In effect, they are like a ticking bomb, just waiting for a later stimulus to reactivate them, creating a flashback in which the person conflates the past with the present.

Bruce was only eighteen when he was severely wounded in a firefight and almost died. At the same time, his best friend, Jake, died in his arms as they were being helicoptered out. These intense implicit-only memories were seared into Bruce's brain, but probably never linked and processed by the hippocampus. As a result, they seem to have remained implicit-only. If a loud sound or fear startled Bruce, these unintegrated memories could be activated, leading him to believe he was back on the battlefield and that his life was at stake. We could represent it like this:

Figure 2.2 — Implicit Memory in Flashback

If we were to write off Bruce's behavior as simply a sign of PTSD, we would miss the larger message. Flashbacks of traumatic situations such as war, rape, abuse, etc., are extreme, but implicit-only memories affect many of our daily perceptions in ways we are rarely aware of. In this regard, Bruce's case is different only in degree from our own. What this means is that the subjective way we experience the world today is a direct result of the experiences we had in the past.

Brain Maps of Reality

Implicit memory has another important characteristic: It creates generalized representations of regularly occurring experiences.[17] This ability to generalize allows the child's growing brain to recognize patterns in the environment and adapt its behavior accordingly. Different researchers refer to these generalizations as brain maps, internal representations, cognitive maps, mental models, or schemas. Whatever we choose to call them, such generalizations are also at the heart of the stereotypes we have of other people and groups. For clarity, I will refer to them as either generalizations or brain maps.

We use these generalizations in the form of assumptions and expectations to help us navigate our way through life. In other words, implicit memories create expectations about what is likely to happen, as well as assumptions about why something is happening and how to respond to it. This system works fine as long as the generalization being activated is appropriate for the current situation.

Because the hippocampus does not become functional until a child is about eighteen months old, it is not possible for us to remember anything before that time. Researchers refer to this as infantile amnesia.[18] Nonetheless, implicit memories were being laid down and our brains were being conditioned by our physical and social environments even though we can't remember those experiences. This conditioning process is in full swing as mother and child bond and begin communicating nonverbally. Later, the child bonds with other members of the family, and then with individuals from its immediate environment.

If this description of memory sounds like the old "blank slate theory" where we are merely a product of our experiences, this is not the case. Instead, we are predisposed to learn some things easily, while others seem almost impossible: Some things, e.g., fear of snakes or being disgusted by the smell of rotten eggs, are easy to learn, whereas other things are far more difficult, e.g., learning to fear daffodils or being disgusted by sugar. This is important to remember because evidence shows that even our moral judgments are based upon predispositions we are born with.[19] If this proves to be true, then it is not just a question of how experience gets internalized, but now we must also ask, how do these predispositions get expressed and how do they vary from person to person and from culture to culture?

Brain maps in a newborn are like a rough sketch drawn according to instructions provided by our genes. This rough sketch is undifferentiated and lacks detail. But as the billions of neurons in the child's brain fire in response to experience, more and more details are added to the rough sketch so that clearer, more precise neural representations are formed.[20] It's as if the newborn's brain is filled with millions of small dirt roads. As "traffic" (our experiences) begins to flow through the brain, some of these roads get used while others do not. Those driven frequently soon become wider, then they become paved, and in no time they have become eight-lane freeways filled with speeding cars. At the same time, the unused roads become overgrown with weeds. In this way, the brain adapts itself to the environment in which the infant grows up. For example, all healthy babies are born with a neural predisposition to learn language. But which language a baby learns depends on its experience.

Because the brain remains plastic throughout our lives, we can always learn new languages and new behaviors, but our first experiences serve as the foundation for future learning. Take, for example, our ability to hear the individual sounds of a particular language. Each of the planet's more than six thousand natural languages are composed of a unique set of basic sounds called phonemes.[21] Phonemes are the consonants and vowels of a language and correspond roughly to the letters of a language's alphabet. These building blocks of sound can be combined in different ways to create an infinite number of words and sentences. Mastering a language requires us to be able to hear, recognize, and reproduce each of its particular phonemes. While there are hundreds of different phonemes used around the world, each language uses only a small subset of the total number. For example, most forms of American English use only about forty basic phonemes to create hundreds of thousands of different words.

Early in their lives, infants everywhere are able to hear and distinguish all phonemes of all languages.[22] At this point their hearing is more accurate than an adult's and they have the potential to learn and master any language. But because they grow up hearing only the phonemes of the language or languages spoken around them, their brains focus on those particular sounds. In doing so, they strengthen the neural pathways used to hear those specific phonemes, while pruning away unnecessary neural pathways. It's a case of use it or lose it, or survival of the busiest.[23] By the time an infant is one year old, it has lost the ability to distinguish between many of the phonemes it was previously able to recognize. The child is now well on its way to becoming culture-bound.[24]

For instance, both Japanese and American infants around four months of age can distinguish between the phonemes *l* and *r*. By the time it is a year old, an American infant is even more accurate and faster at recognizing the differences between these two common English sounds. But a one year-old Japanese infant has lost the ability to distinguish between these two sounds because they are not used in Japanese.

In effect, a year-old infant is no longer a citizen of the world.[25] It is no longer hearing reality as it is, but rather hearing through a set of filters. Because a Japanese infant is not developing accurate brain maps for the *r* and *l* sounds, it will later have difficulty if it tries to learn English as an adult. The result will be the typical accent of a Japanese speaking English, saying what sound like "flied lice" to an American's ears, instead of "fried rice."[26]

Mind Distance and Enculturation

As people everywhere grow from babies to adults, their brains are continually internalizing their experiences by creating brain maps to help them understand and navigate these experiences. The process of an individual internalizing his social and cultural environments to become a competent member of the group is referred to as enculturation by anthropologists.[27] Enculturation takes place in all areas of experience, from the sights and smells of our surroundings, to adapting to the sounds of our native language, to creating beliefs and expectations about our cultural institutions.

But because those environments are different, and because brain maps play a key role in perception, the process of perception is, to one degree or another, subjective. Just as the native speaker of Japanese has learned not to hear the distinction between the r and l sounds in English so, too, English speakers have learned not to hear the difference between *chi* and *shi* in Chinese. To the English ear both of these sound like "she."[28] To the Chinese ear they sound very different.

When we forget the learned, subjective aspect of our perceptions, i.e., when we believe our perceptions to be exact replicas of the external world, we are not only ignoring the conclusions of countless scientific studies, we are also impairing our ability to understand and empathize with others. Not only do we run the risk of confusing our perceptions of the world with the actual world, we are almost certain to dismiss people who perceive it differently as wrong or misguided. This natural tendency to confuse our perceptions of the world with the world itself is referred to as "naïve realism" or, more jocularly, the myth of immaculate perception.[29]

At this point, there is still much we don't know about the depth and breadth of human subjectivity and mind distance. Surely we will know more in the future, but for now, an awareness of our inherent subjectivity is essential for every interculturalist. Not only do people in other cultures sometimes behave differently, we often misinterpret these behaviors, which is a source of countless misunderstandings. When we recognize the influence of implicit memories on our perceptions, feelings, and thoughts, we become better able to manage our subjectivity and the resulting mind distance.

The process of enculturation relies upon the ability of our brains to create internal maps of our experiences. Every time a brain reactivates the firing patterns of a particular brain map, it reinforces that map, making it more likely to be reactivated in the future. At the same time, by repeatedly using the group's culturally sanctioned brain maps, each individual reinforces the group's shared memories. In this regard, a culture is not a finished product, it is an ongoing production.

Seen from this perspective, everyone who interacts with a young child serves as his teacher by continually representing the world to him, both verbally and nonverbally, until he can intuitively interpret reality in the ways his culture expects. This encompasses every relevant aspect of group life. It's learning when to speak and when not to speak. It's about learning to whom, when, and how to show respect. It's learning what counts as work and what counts as play. It's learning what counts as good work, what counts as bad work, and how much good work is enough. It's learning about relationships and what a family is, as well as how to behave in one's family compared with how to behave towards people who are not family. It's also learning the various social roles we may be expected to play and which social roles are off limits for us. It's learning how one should behave in different social situations, including how to communicate nonverbally, when to smile, how to gesture, how to walk properly, and even how to pose for a photograph. It also includes what to pay attention to and what to ignore as well as how to react emotionally. Almost nothing in a child's life is untouched by culture.

While the process of enculturation is often portrayed as a one-way street in which the child is taught the group's way of life, enculturation is actually part of the larger process of cultural evolution. Here's how Michael Tomasello, an American developmental psychologist, describes the larger process:

Human artifacts and behavioral practices often become more complex over time (they have a "history"). An individual invents an artifact or way of doing things that is adequate to the task, and others quickly learn it. But then if another individual makes some improvement, everyone, including developing children, tend to learn the new and improved version. This produces a kind of cultural ratchet, as each version of the practice stays solidly in the group's repertoire until someone comes up with something even newer and improved. This means that just as individual humans biologically inherit genes that have been adaptive in the past, they also culturally inherit artifacts and behavioral practices that represent something like the collective wisdom of their forebears.[30]

These ongoing processes of enculturation and cultural evolution can be represented visually as follows:

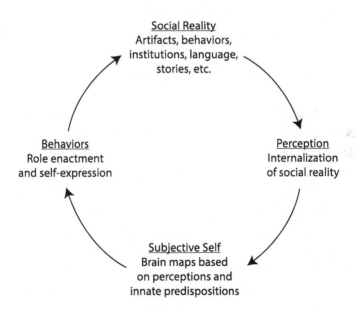

Figure 2.3 — Enculturation and Cultural Evolution

Conclusion

Understanding the differences between implicit and explicit memory helps us realize the degree to which our earliest experiences become the foundations for later psychological and social development. Understanding how memory conditions us to perceive and interpret the world in a particular way also helps us realize how we become "culture bound." Without this knowledge, much of a culture remains invisible, even to insiders who aren't aware of the role implicit memories are playing in their perceptions.

Implicit memories are the basis for the assumptions we take for granted because they seem as normal and unremarkable as heat on a sunny day. Because we don't notice them, we can't question them. In effect, implicit memory adds to the creation of a black box within ourselves, making it difficult to understand some of our own motivations and actions. As we will soon see, a lack of self-awareness can lead to self-deception, with all its attendant dangers. One of the advantages of encountering cultural differences is discovering that many of the things we once took for granted as natural and universal are, in fact, learned and local.

An infant's brain is pre-wired with built-in predispositions and it is the interaction of these predispositions with lived experience that creates the brain maps we use to make sense of our world. The generalizations we create from recurring events act like filters for our perceptions, i.e., our perceptions are more like paintings than photographs. And just as different painters create different paintings of the same scene, so too, cultures and individuals perceive the world differently. Because perceptions are constructed with the help of memory, we are not perceiving the world exactly as it is, we are perceiving the world the way we learned to perceive it. The same plasticity that enables us to adapt to a changing environment also enables our memories to become distorted and biased, a topic we will explore more in later chapters.

Our brains are continually mapping and adapting to changing environments, but brains are far more than just exquisite mapmakers.

As we will see in the next chapter, they are also self-regulators that work hard to help us maintain stable internal states.

Three

Test All Assumptions

The first principle is that you must not fool yourself, and you are the easiest person to fool.

—Richard P. Feynman

The seminar was running well and I was riding the smooth wave of exhilaration I sometimes experience when speaking in front of a group. The group was engaged and we were connecting almost effortlessly, giving me a strong sense of confidence. Knowing, in the back of my mind, that states of positive experience are good for my health only made the experience more enjoyable. For instance, Daniel Siegel notes that when we are in such optimal states, our brains are functioning as an integrated whole and we become more flexible, adaptive, coherent, energized, and stable.[1] Mihaly Csikszentmihalyi, the researcher who popularized the word *flow,* defines it as the enjoyable state of optimal experience in which our resources and capacity to act match the challenges we are facing.[2] Taking a more physiological approach, scientists at the Institute of HeartMath report that when people's brainwaves and heartbeats become synchronized, they experience a state of optimal experience during which they feel more energized, more at peace, and more able to think clearly. They refer to this state as coherence.[3]

Whether we call these states of optimal experience flow, coherence, being in the groove, the zone, or something else, people everywhere around the world describe them as an enjoyable sense of being more focused, more confident, and more energized than usual.[4]

They also express the desire to experience such states more often in the future. I was certainly hoping to stay in that state for the rest of the seminar.

I'm not a natural when it comes to public speaking and often suffer from stage fright. Whatever skills I have, have been developed through hard work and study. While I find public speaking challenging, I also find it exhilarating. This is doubly so when I am doing it in German, which I learned as an adult.

But that day my skills were up to the challenge and I was connecting well with my German audience. We had spent the morning discussing some basic ideas about what a culture is and then moved on to exploring the historical development of German and American values. When people understand why particular differences developed, they find it easier to accept those differences and to treat people from the other culture with more respect. In other words, another way to reduce mind distance is to show people why other cultures developed different values and norms.

At one point, I suggested that many of the earliest immigrants to the United States were optimists and risk takers. Who else would leave the security of their homeland and cross a treacherous, storm-filled ocean in small wooden vessels? These values influence the sometimes audacious behaviors and entrepreneurial spirit of many Americans to this day.

I was in mid-sentence when a participant interrupted me, contradicting what I had just said. I felt like I had been blindsided by a large truck. It happened so fast that even now I can't really describe exactly how I felt or what thoughts flashed through my mind. What I do know is that Wilma contradicted what I had just said and this set off an instant chain reaction in my mind and body. As she explained at length why immigrants to America were neither more optimistic nor more willing to take risks than the people who stayed in their home countries, I found myself becoming more and more impatient for my chance to refute her claims. I was so intent on figuring out what I would say that I was not listening well. As best as I can now tell, her argument was that immigrants to America were forced to leave home because the conditions they were living in had become unbearable.

This is a fair claim and I would have done better to listen more closely to what she was saying. But at that point I was already reacting impulsively and I interrupted back. "Certainly," I conceded, cutting her off in mid-sentence, "the external conditions played a major role in the choice to emigrate, but the fact is, there were lots of other people in the same situation and not all of them chose to emigrate. Some chose to stay, and...." I was beginning to recover my poise, but at that point Wilma interrupted again and a fearful sense of, "Oh no, don't go there," shot into my mind. I vaguely realized I was in danger of escalating to a place I did not want to go to, but I was already becoming stressed and not thinking clearly enough to know what to do about it.

The Ultrafast Inner Team

I was heading towards what Daniel Goleman calls an emotional hijacking in which evolutionarily older members of the inner team—the amygdala and other subcortical areas of the brain—mutiny and take control of behavior.[5] In normal states of consciousness, diverse areas of the adult brain work together as an integrated team under the leadership of the prefrontal cortex.[6]

In 1952 neuroscientist Paul MacLean proposed that the structure of the human brain is the result of evolution. He identified three major regions of what he called the triune brain.[7] The oldest region is the brain stem and spinal cord, which is sometimes referred to as the reptilian brain because the nervous system of reptiles exhibits a similar architecture. Atop and surrounding the older brain stem is the newer limbic system, which is sometimes called the mammalian brain. As its name implies, the basic elements of the limbic system are common to all mammals. Atop and surrounding both the brain stem and limbic system is the neocortex. Serving as the integrator of all three regions is the evolutionarily newest member of the inner team, the prefrontal cortex.

The prefrontal cortex is not only the newest part of the brain, it also takes the longest to develop, often not reaching full maturity in humans until a person is twenty-five years old. The prefrontal cortex is most associated with reflective thinking, conscious planning, and mature decision-making. However, during an emotional hijacking, the prefrontal cortex gets sidelined and we lose the integration that allows members of our inner team to work well together.[8]

In contrast to the slower, more rational prefrontal cortex, the amygdala and other parts of the limbic system make lightning fast decisions designed to ensure our safety. Because safety and security are such high priorities for our brains, the limbic system operates 24/7. When these older members of the inner team interpret something as dangerous, they become more activated. Subjectively, we experience such activation as anxiety, irritation, impatience, etc. It is during situations of perceived danger that the limbic system is more likely to stage an emotional hijacking. Like a rogue middle manager who is fed up with a large bureaucracy, the amygdala triggers the fight-or-flight response. At this point, listening empathically and thinking clearly become all but impossible.

I'd suffered enough emotional hijackings in my past to know I did not want to go there. Luckily, I was still present enough to try to listen to what Wilma was saying and I heard her use the word *intelligent*. That helped me hit the pause button and start thinking more clearly. I knew I had never used that word and I guessed she had taken offense. She thought I was implying that those who emigrated to the States were somehow more intelligent or better than those who chose to stay in their home countries. This was not at all what I had intended to say.

I explained I had never meant to say that early immigrants to the United States were more intelligent and this seemed to satisfy her. She graciously suggested there had been a misunderstanding, which allowed me to continue talking with little loss of face, but by that point my body was already filled with adrenaline that had no place to go. I was shaken by the close call, but also relieved we did not get into a longer argument that could easily have pushed me past my emotional speed limit.

Emotional Speed Limits

Although Wilma and I managed to de-escalate our misunderstanding, the exhilarating sense of flow was gone and I was now anxious and wary. At that point, more than anything else, I wanted to calm myself down and avoid acting in a way I would later regret. Then I remembered such interruptions and direct contradictions are common in Germany. Somehow, a part of my brain had ignored where I was. I had forgotten that unwritten rules regarding interruptions were different here than at home.

Remembering this helped me assume Wilma had not intended to attack me personally, but only to call a statement into question. This insight helped me further calm down my mutinous inner team. Calming myself down also helped me reconnect with Wilma and create an atmosphere of safety for both of us. We were back on track.

Calming myself down involved pulling myself back from my emotional speed limit and moving back towards my baseline of emotional arousal. I am using the term "emotional speed limit" to refer to the point at which my fight-or-flight response would have been triggered by increasing levels of emotional arousal. Had that happened, I would have become less able to continue communicating in an empathic manner. By moving back towards my emotional baseline, i.e., the amount of internal arousal I normally experience in daily activities, I was able to stay connected with Wilma and the other members of my audience.

Arousal states arise from the interactions of some of the oldest parts of our brains, including the autonomic nervous system.[9] There is still much to be learned about the complexities of arousal states, but the general consensus among researchers is that too much arousal can trigger the stress response, with all its attendant consequences. For our purposes, we can call the amount of arousal an individual experiences in normal conditions her emotional baseline. If the baseline is the usual amount of arousal we experience when functioning normally, the emotional speed limit refers to the point where any more arousal would trigger an emotional hijacking.

Colloquially, the area between our baseline and emotional speed limit is sometimes called our comfort zone, but this is misleading because we can remain functional and integrated while feeling discomfort, as my experience with Wilma shows. Siegel calls the range of experiences we are able to tolerate and still remain functionally integrated our "window of tolerance," and I think this is a better term than comfort zone.[10]

Experiences near our baseline are often a case of "no news is good news," meaning when I am not in pain or discomfort all is well, my needs are being met, and I can go about my business without worrying. At other times, when we are functioning well and getting our needs met, we experience more positive states of happiness and flow. The message from our limbic brain is then, "This is good, more, please."

But when something moves us away from the feelings of pleasure or neutrality toward the discomfort or pain of too much arousal, the message is also clear: "Pay attention, something may be amiss." Antonio Damasio, a leading neuroscientist and expert on emotional states, refers to these bodily sensations of pain and pleasure as primordial emotions and suggests that, "One cannot fully explain subjectivity without knowing about the origin of feelings and acknowledging the existence of primordial feelings, spontaneous reflections of the state of the body."[11] He views these primordial feelings in the body as the foundation for all other emotions.[12] Pleasure indicates that things are going well, while discomfort and pain are nature's way of telling me my life-sustaining homeostasis is disorganized and that I need to do something about it. Pain and physical discomfort are motivational states that send a clear message to the team leader: Something is not right, do something about it! Such states are often experienced as stress.

A similar view is expressed by Bruce McEwen, another well-known neuroscientist and an expert on the nature of stress. McEwen views desire as similar to pain and pleasure in that it is a primordial emotional signal that lets us know we have needs that must be met.[13] When our needs are not met, we experience the discomfort of stress.

Hitting an Emotional Speed Limit

When there is too much arousal, we experience states of anxiety or confusion, feeling frazzled and unable to think clearly. If the levels of arousal and discomfort increase and we do not move back toward more pleasurable areas of our window of tolerance, the limbic brain becomes increasingly likely to mutiny.[14] In other words, as our levels of arousal and discomfort increase, the subcortical areas of the brain will begin acting autonomously without the modulating influence of the team leader, the prefrontal cortex. When we are in states of stress, such as situations that demand more resources and skills than we have, we may be pushed out of our window of tolerance. We become prone to emotional hijackings and will often think, say, and do things we later regret. After we have calmed down, we say things like, "I don't know what came over me," or, "I wasn't in my right mind."

Actually, if Siegel is right, there is also a lower limit to our window of tolerance.[15] When the flow of energy and information in the brain sinks below a certain level, we tend to experience uncomfortable states of boredom, rigidity, or depression. The lower limit of our window of tolerance may be likened to the stall speed of an airplane. In order to reach the amount of lift needed to remain in flight, a plane must achieve a minimum speed. If the plane's speed falls below this minimum, it will stall and fall to earth. In the same way, if the level of arousal in our brain sinks too low, we have trouble functioning in a healthy manner.[16] According to Siegel, when we fall below the lower limit, our thinking and behavior tends to become more mechanical and we tend to use older, less functional patterns of behavior rather than adjust to the current situation.

In either case, the window of tolerance represents the range in which our brains are most integrated and functional. And somewhere in this window of tolerance is the flow we all desire to experience. A key to success in dealing with differences is discovering how to grow our window of tolerance.

The rest of that first day went smoothly. The participants seemed excited by the material we were covering and they engaged in many animated discussions about differences between Germans and Americans. I was still feeling uneasy about my reaction and was paying particular attention to how often they interrupted each other and seemingly thought nothing of it. I was also more careful about how I was expressing myself and intent on not getting blindsided again. By concentrating, I was able to stay within my window of tolerance and remain functional. Although I was telling myself that my interaction with Wilma was over, I couldn't shake the vague feelings of anxiety and guilt that had been triggered earlier. Part of my inner team was worried and the nagging feelings remained until I went to sleep.

When I woke up at 2:30 a.m. from an unpleasant dream, I knew it was only partly because of the jet lag. I also felt a visceral sense of anxiety. Lying in the quiet darkness, I noticed my chest was tight and I could feel my heart beating and the blood pulsing in my belly and legs. My throat was also tense and swallowing was uncomfortable. It felt like something inside me was expanding in slow motion and my body was too small to contain it. I was reminded of putting a car in neutral and then gunning the motor.

In my mind I saw images of the day's encounter with Wilma coupled with harsh judgments about my behavior. My mind was generating one judgmental thought after another, each one chain-reacting into the next. I tried to push them away and fall asleep so I would be fresh for the second day of the seminar. They wouldn't leave. I tried a breathing exercise to calm me down. It didn't help. I tried reminding myself that these were just thoughts and I didn't have to believe them. That didn't help much either. I found myself wanting food, drink, sleeping pills, anything to allow me to drift back to sleep. But I had nothing and soon my mind was doubling down on the urgency of it all: *Oh no, I can't sleep. But I need to sleep otherwise I'll be stressed out tomorrow and that will affect my performance. And stress is unhealthy. Maybe I'll get sick. Or do a poor job and lose this client. Oh no, I can't afford that. This could ruin my reputation and then...* On and on it went. I was, without wanting to, catastrophizing and in no time my mind made it seem plausible I would end up bankrupt and homeless. The mind's ability to create mountains out of molehills was evident once more and the strong, unpleasant sensations in my body reinforced my thoughts.

Focusing Inward

Finally I stopped trying to avoid these thoughts and accepted the inevitable. I was not going to slip back into sleep, and rather than try to avoid my anxiety or fight my worries, I intentionally turned my attention inward and focused directly on them.[17] I began by reviewing the details of the interaction between Wilma and me. My goal was to get a more objective understanding of what happened, as well as explore my beliefs and assumptions. If I could find the assumptions motivating my anxiety and guilt, I could check them for veracity and, if necessary, revise them. The ability to notice our thoughts without believing or identifying with them gives us the ability to check their validity, a key skill for anyone who hopes to liberate themselves from limiting beliefs.

In the previous chapter we saw that memory is a major factor in the subjectivity of our perceptions, but our brain's inherent subjectivity is reinforced by the many forms of defensive reasoning and self-justification we humans engage in. Self-justification is so prevalent in our lives that Cordelia Fine, a Canadian-British psychologist, has written an entertaining and insightful book on the subject called *A Mind Of Its Own – How Your Brain Distorts and Deceives*. As Fine points out, self-deception has much to do with our sense of identity:

> The brain is especially self-advancing when poor performance on the task could deliver a substantial bruise to the ego. People told that puzzle solving is related to intelligence are much more likely to be self-serving than those told that puzzle solving is just something that people who don't like reading books do on trains. The bigger the potential threat, the more self-protective the vain brain becomes. In a final irony, people think that others are more susceptible to the self-serving bias than they are themselves.[18]

Because the tendency to unwittingly engage in self-deception is so common among humans, "Test All Assumptions" can be thought of as a fundamental guideline for dealing with differences. That's what I wanted to do by focusing in on my thoughts and feelings. Were they really accurate and in proportion to the situation? That's what I needed to find out.

As I began intentionally exploring my memories of the incident with Wilma, my first insight was that members of my inner team were upset because I had violated one of my core communication principles. By not listening empathically to Wilma's objections and then interrupting her, I had repeated one of the bad habits I was trying to change. Members of my inner team were upset that I was still prone to such behavior and they were letting me know it. At the same time, by reviewing Wilma's actual response and the reactions of the rest of the participants, I decided my own behavior had not been optimal, but it was hardly so bad I should be generating this amount of worry. The intensity of my feelings were out of proportion to what had happened. Thinking rationally, I assured myself the incident was not worth this amount of distress, but I could still feel the waves of anxiety welling up in me. It was if my inner team was at war with itself. While a rational voice assured me there was nothing to worry about, an irrational sense of guilt insisted my behavior was indeed reprehensible.

The metaphor of an inner team helps us think about the complexity of our brains as well as the internal conflict we all experience at times. We all strive for the enjoyable internal states when our inner teams are cooperating, and we are all familiar with the unpleasant mental and emotional stress created by internal conflict. According to Leon Festinger, the American social psychologist who first proposed the term "cognitive dissonance," it is the distressing state of tension we experience when we try to maintain two or more contradictory attitudes, ideas, or values at the same time.[19] The degree of dissonance we experience can range from vague discomfort to deep anguish. Because we all strive for internal consistency, and because dissonance is such an unpleasant state, we find it difficult to rest until we resolve the tension.[20]

Festinger's theory of cognitive dissonance has been confirmed by thousands of experiments and it has transformed our understanding of how the mind and brain function.[21] For example, functional MRI studies of the brain show that when we encounter beliefs we disagree with, our brains reduce their activity in the regions used for reasoning, but when we encounter beliefs that accord with our brain maps and consonance is restored, the positive emotion circuits of our brains light up happily.[22] What this means in practice is that once we have made up our minds, it is hard to change them. In other words, our brains seek out and prioritize evidence that accords with our current brain maps, while simultaneously ignoring and discounting evidence that calls them into question. This tendency, both conscious and unconscious, to seek out what we want to see and hear distorts our perceptions and is referred as confirmation bias.[23]

Because of our brain's dual-process design, we have, in effect, a black box in our own mind and are often unaware of the mental contortions our brains are going through to maintain a consistent view of the world. The writer Malcolm Gladwell refers to our inability to access much of the brain's unconscious processing as the "locked door of our minds."[24]

The brain's tendency to do much of its processing outside of conscious awareness and to present these results rapidly and effortlessly to our conscious self is sometimes referred to as "intuitionism."[25] Speaking of the thoughts and feelings generated by the inner team as intuitions can be misleading because this word means different things to different people. In this context, intuition does not imply some sort of telepathy or transpersonal insight. Rather, it refers to the almost effortless, bottom-up processing of information and energy by the brain and the ultra-fast presentation of the results of that processing to conscious awareness.

Used in this way, intuition differs from conscious reasoning that does require effort and intention, and which comes to a conclusion in a slower sequence of steps. Seen from this perspective, intuition, reflective reasoning, and even the appraisal of emotional meaning are simply different forms of cognition and the common-sense dichotomy between thinking and feeling turns out to be quite arbitrary.[26] What all these types of cognition have in common is that they help us navigate through an ever-changing world.

Priming

This intuitive processing of information and energy in the brain is nothing short of amazing. That we can do so many things so effortlessly is one of the inner team's great gifts to us. We don't need to think long when we find ourselves in the middle of the street and see a large truck rushing towards us. We intuitively move out of harm's way. Nor do we have to think long before knowing whether we like the person we just met or whether a new food tastes good. Part of intuition's power comes from implicit memory's ability to prime us, that is, to create expectations by anticipating the future based on the past.

Priming can be likened to changing your clothes so you are wearing the appropriate attire for a particular event. You would hardly wear your best formal clothes if you were going out to play tennis, nor show up at an elaborate wedding in cut-off jeans. In the same way, our brains change their states to accord with changing circumstances. By anticipating what is about to happen, brains prime us, i.e., they enter into what they assume is the appropriate mental state.

The power of priming has been shown in a number of clever experiments. Researchers at New York University scattered words such as *rude, impolite, aggressive, bold,* and *bother* into the text of what students thought was an experiment to measure their verbal abilities. [27] In the text given to other students the researchers interspersed words such as *polite, yield, patiently, courteously,* and *appreciate.* The supposed verbal experiment only took about five minutes to complete, and when the students left the testing room they thought it was over. Actually, it had just begun.

What the researchers really wanted to measure was how the students would now behave when they interacted with one of the experimenters who was stationed down the hallway. Students were instructed to approach this experimenter to get their next assignment. But whenever a student approached, the experimenter was always locked in conversation with another person. This other person was a confederate of the experimenter who was instructed to keep talking to the experimenter until the student interrupted. The results were astounding. On average, students who were primed with words like rude and impolite interrupted the experimenter after about five minutes. But the majority of the students who were primed to be polite did not interrupt the experimenter at all. They simply waited until the experimenter and confederate stopped on their own!

Priming is a powerful force. You can influence a young person to walk slower by interspersing words such as *Florida, retirement, old, gray, worried,* or *bingo* into a language experiment.[28] In the same way, people will tend to do better on a test if you tell them stories about high achievement before the test.[29] Priming is also effective when done subliminally by flashing words onto a screen so fast the person is not consciously aware of them.[30] These results indicate both how fast and how suggestible our brains are. They also show why enculturation, which occurs before we have developed critical thinking, has such a large impact on the way we perceive, feel, think, and behave.

Exploring the Worst Case

Like everything, priming and intuition have their downsides. As valuable as they are, they can lead us astray if our brains follow unconscious processes that were appropriate in the past, but which are now dysfunctional. As I continued to review the incident with Wilma, I became aware of something else. Before I was interrupted, my voice had been friendlier. After I was interrupted, my voice took on a harsher quality. From past experience, I knew this change usually occurs when I perceive my situation as dangerous. Somehow Wilma's interruption had triggered a fear reaction and that fear was still floating around inside me. As we will see in chapter five, because perceptions of danger can disrupt our ability to think clearly, they often have negative effects on our behavior and our relationships.

Still focusing inwards, I asked myself what I was most afraid of and why I felt so embarrassed. The answer came quickly: Some parts of me thought my disagreement with Wilma had exposed me as an incompetent hypocrite. How could I be teaching a class like this if I was still so susceptible to being emotionally hijacked? If I was the professional interculturalist advising people how to manage cultural differences more skillfully, I should be above such immature reactions.

Our emotional speed limits are not fixed, but vary in accord with our internal state and the external situation. While some people are quite adept at employing anger in socially appropriate ways, other people are easily triggered, shoot past their limit, and overreact. But the same person who can manage anger skillfully may become overwhelmed when she feels sad or is confronted with someone who is crying.[31] In other words, windows of tolerance vary from person to person and from situation to situation, allowing one individual to remain calm and function smoothly in one situation, but getting triggered and reacting poorly in another.

I knew I was sensitive to being interrupted which would explain why my reaction was out of proportion to what had happened. Happily, I also knew that my window of tolerance was now wider than ever before and would become even wider with more awareness and work. This encouraged me to continue focusing in on these unpleasant thoughts and distressing feelings. As I accepted and welcomed them into myself, the sense of immediate danger and urgency began to ebb and an inner spaciousness began to grow. By asking myself what was the thing I feared most, I had created a space for my fears and my inner conflict slowly began to ease. As it did, my body relaxed.

Consciously exploring the worst thing that might happen has another important advantage. It helps us determine if we are dealing with a real threat or if our minds are manufacturing unnecessary anxiety. Manufactured anxiety can result when implicit memories of frightening events from the past are reactivated. When combined with our imagination, these fears can take on truly irrational proportions. Learning to distinguish between manufactured worry and the fear signal that warns us of real danger is an invaluable skill.[32] But whether real or manufactured, fears can narrow our window of tolerance.

Assuming I was manufacturing my anxiety allowed me to re-evaluate my failure to listen empathically to Wilma. Instead of seeing it as a permanent character flaw, I accepted it as an under-developed skill I still needed to work on. If I were interrupted or contradicted the next day, I promised myself I would respond more skillfully. This resolution helped me further reduce the dissonance I had been experiencing.

Using the skills of concentration, sensory clarity, and equanimity we will explore further in chapter fourteen, I continued to work on myself until I noticed my breathing slowing and deepening. When I felt calm enough, I made some notes so I wouldn't forget the insights I had just gained. Then I went back to bed and drifted gently to sleep.

Reality Check

The following morning I was calmer and more confident. I arrived early to review my notes and get ready for the day's work. As luck would have it, one of the participants also showed up early and we began talking. Ursula was enthusiastic as she talked about what she had learned yesterday, so when she asked me how I was doing, I felt confident enough to divulge that I had not slept well. When I disclosed I had been concerned about the intensity of my interaction with Wilma, she expressed surprise. Her take was very different.

She had experienced my interaction with Wilma as just one of yesterday's many positive discussions. From her perspective, the fact everyone was so animated was a good sign, it meant they were fully engaged and found the topic interesting. This was what I had been telling myself, but hearing it from someone else was reassuring.

By doing this reality check with Ursula, I was able to make sure I was not deceiving myself. Doing reality checks to test our assumptions and avoid the confirmation bias is a necessary practice for anyone who hopes to build bridges across personal and cultural differences. But testing assumptions is difficult for several reasons.

First, many assumptions that drive our inner team's intuitions are stored behind the locked door of the mind. Second, even if we can unveil them, they may force us to see we are engaged in some form of self-justification that distorts our perceptions and keeps us from seeing the situation clearly. If my resolution to the previous night's insomnia had been self-deception on my part, and if Ursula said she found my behavior towards Wilma rude, it could easily have reactivated yesterday's unpleasant emotional cocktail of fear, annoyance, and embarrassment. In such situations, we often find it easier to believe our thoughts and feelings than do a reality check.

Luckily, in this instance I had not engaged in self-deception and my conversation with Ursula helped me feel even more confident. When the other participants arrived, we began where we left off the day before and the morning session flowed smoothly. I was focused, functional, and enjoying our work together. I wasn't in the exhilaration of a full-blown flow state, but I was moving in the right direction.

Communication Styles and Stress

In my German-American seminars I save exploration of communication styles for last because it pulls everything together in a neat fashion. Having already explored basic cultural concepts, demographics, national values, and various case studies, the stage is set for a deeper conversation about how stress can be triggered by different communication styles. The main message of the afternoon session is that it can be difficult, if not impossible, to connect empathically when the stress response is triggered.

I start by talking about differences in goals and attitudes that Germans and Americans bring to the table when they engage in workplace discussions. Then I explore their different assumptions that can cause both sides to leave a discussion feeling unsatisfied. Only then do I compare and contrast the differences in nonverbal signals used by Germans and Americans.

Nonverbal signals can trigger strong visceral reactions. When these go unnoticed, they can make conversations challenging. I point out that when Germans get deeply engaged in discussions they consider important, the intensity of certain nonverbal signals increases. Brows furrow and faces tighten, voices often take on a harder edge, and interruptions become more frequent. To Americans, these signals often make it look as if the Germans are engaged in an argument. But for the Germans, this is just normal discourse and they can talk at this level of intensity for hours without overreacting.

The same is true of interruptions. Most Germans will tell you it is poor form to interrupt another person while they are in the act of speaking. Most will also acknowledge that when people are fully engaged in a discussion, interruptions are quite common. Most Germans do not accord them much significance.

I help them realize that this ability to speak intensely and still remain within their window of tolerance is a skill they learned at home and in school. German teachers start guiding pupils at an early age in the art of discussing such topics as politics, religion, and sex. These are topics about which even children can become passionate, and German pupils learn to deal with confrontation and differences of opinion more openly and directly than many other cultures. By the time of high school graduation, a German student has had hours and hours of practice managing the emotional intensity a passionate discussion can trigger. Dealing with differences of opinion and controversial topics is an expected skill and most are adept at it. But what they often don't realize is that many cultures in the world do not train their children to speak so directly. They are also often not aware that some cultures view their direct style of talking as rude and impolite, or even childish and naïve.

For many Americans, such a direct, openly confrontational style can seem intense and argumentative. Due to our different upbringings, Germans and Americans, on average, have different expectations, emotional speed limits, and windows of tolerance with regard to interruptions, disagreement, and confrontation. As I was explaining how being interrupted can trigger a person who is not used to such a direct style, I used my reaction with Wilma as an example. I had not planned on doing this, it was a spontaneous impulse I chose to follow.

I disclosed it wasn't just that Wilma had interrupted me, but it was also her contradicting my statement which triggered me.

This hit a nerve. I'm not sure if the participants were more astonished I was speaking so openly about a personal experience or whether they were amazed I had such a strong reaction towards what they viewed as a normal discussion. Probably it was a mixture of the two. Some of the participants admitted how surprised they were to hear my perspective. For them it was a real eye-opener that their style of speaking might be stressful for some Americans. As we talked about our different emotional speed limits and windows of tolerance, it became clearer to all of us that communication is not just a matter of talking heads exchanging information, but rather a full-bodied experience that can have implications for our health and well-being, as well as our sense of who and what we are.

After the seminar ended and the participants departed, I sat down to check the feedback forms. All the participants had checked "yes" signifying they would recommend the seminar to others and the majority had rated the seminar as excellent. I was deeply gratified. That was more than enough reward to offset a sleepless night and send me on my way with a smile.

Conclusion

Behind the "locked door" of the mind, the inner team is hard at work, exerting a strong influence on all our thoughts, feelings, and actions. If we don't take time to get to know our inner teams, we remain mindblind and more prone to internal conflict that can push us past our emotional speed limits.

The rapid presentation of intuitive thoughts and feelings to conscious awareness helps us navigate the complex world in which we live, but our hard-working inner team provides us with more than just rapid recognition and intuitive insights. It also primes us for action by anticipating the future based on past experiences.

When communicating with people we are familiar with, we often anticipate their reactions accurately. But in dealing with people who are different, the brain's intuitive expectations can lead us astray. Unfamiliar situations and strange behaviors can push us past our window of tolerance into a state of anxiety and uncertainty. Not knowing what is about to happen next or whether we will be able to cope well can be unsettling, and this increased anxiety can make us susceptible to emotional hijacking. One way to manage this uncertainty is by developing more mindsight.

Developing mindsight helps us detect the invisible assumptions driving our behavior and then test their validity, a powerful way to offset the confirmation bias and self-deception that our brains use to help us maintain our self-esteem. When we can observe our thoughts simply as thoughts in the mind and not as incontrovertible facts, and when we can notice our feelings and urges as sensations in the body and not as infallible guides to action, we both widen our window of tolerance and increase our ability to hit the pause button.

With increased mindsight, thoughts and feelings become just thoughts and feelings and we have the option of following them or not, enabling us to behave more in accord with our higher values and principles. We also begin to realize more and more how uninvestigated thoughts and feelings automatically acted upon are one of the great sources of human suffering.

The intuitions and priming generated by our inner team always happen within a context. As we will see in the next chapter, to understand the workings of any individual brain and mind, we also need to understand the context in which that brain and mind are operating.

Four

The Unending Conversation

Choice does not exist for you if you don't see that you have it. It is only when you see that there are many possibilities in any situation and many possible reactions that you can consciously choose what you want.

—Frances E. Vaughn

One of my close friends was incredulous at the trick her mind had played on her. She had agreed to help me by reading a draft of this book. As she read chapter sixteen she found herself becoming upset at how naïve and Pollyannaish it seemed. How could I have written such sentimental drivel? She was going to have to give me the bad news: The final chapter was worthless and I would be best served by starting over. She knew the chapter held deep significance for me and was not looking forward to having to tell me this. But she had promised to give me her honest opinion.

After letting the draft sit for a few days, she called and we arranged to meet for dinner. She knew I would want specific details about what was wrong with the chapter and that calling it "sentimental drivel" was not going to satisfy either of us. So she sat down with pen in hand to underline all the spots that were characterized by over-the-top optimism and unsupported sentimentality. To her great surprise, she couldn't find any. How could that be? Just a week ago this chapter looked like unmitigated rubbish and now it made perfect sense. Try as she would, she could only find a few trivial points to underline.

Then she had a small epiphany: The night before her first reading, she had watched a bleak foreign movie where a couple's child died tragically and their lives began to unravel. Things went from bad to worse and in the end the couple divorced. Then the husband became an alcoholic and lost his job and the wife committed suicide. The film had been ultra-realistic in showing the hell that life can turn into when we are overwhelmed by events we don't know how to cope with. The stark images and the realistic portrayal of the couple's suffering had worked their way deep into my friend's mind and when she read my draft the following morning, it could only seem naïve in comparison.

What most amazed her was that she had not even realized how affected she had been. She didn't want to believe how much her perceptions were affected by her emotional state, nor how much her state was due to the movie she had watched. My friend is a highly educated, successful, tough-minded woman who prides herself on being grounded in reality. The idea that her perceptions were so susceptible to outside influences was disconcerting to her.

In this regard my friend is like most of us. We may be aware theoretically that external events can influence our perceptions, but we often ignore that insight, thinking it only happens to the other person. We reason that because we are intellectually aware of the effect context can have, we remain unbiased. This is rarely true. We are all impacted by the contexts in which we find ourselves. But we also have a self-serving bias that assures us it is other people's perceptions that are unreliable, not our own. This bias tells us that while other people may perceive things subjectively, we see reality just as it is.

The Role of Context

While many people discount the role of context in their perceptions, much evidence shows just how powerful a force it is. In the now-famous 1971 Stanford Prison Experiment conducted by psychologist Philip Zimbardo, the power of context to influence one's thoughts, feelings, and behaviors was clearly demonstrated.[1]

Zimbardo carried out this simulation to explore what happens when you put normal people in a bad situation. He wanted to know how much of an effect a person's surroundings would have on him.

Zimbardo and his assistants went to great lengths to make the experiment realistic, even to the point of hiring an ex-convict as a consultant. Zimbardo then chose healthy college students with normal personality profiles and randomly assigned them the role of either guard or prisoner.

At first, the students appeared relaxed and at ease as they went about playing their roles. But within a day's time, both "prisoners" and "guards" began confusing their roles with reality. It was as if they had forgotten they were voluntarily participating in a psychology experiment and their perceptions began to change. As they did, the situation became noticeably tenser. Some of the "prisoners" began experiencing extreme stress reactions that led to emotional breakdowns and the situation turned pathological. After only six days, Zimbardo was forced to end the experiment prematurely to ensure the safety of the participants.

Upon reflection, Zimbardo acknowledged that he, too, had become caught up in his role as "prison superintendent" and had neglected his actual role as a research psychologist. Zimbardo notes that this change in perception also occurred with many of the parents who had come to visit their sons in "prison." Somehow the context had blurred the line between role-playing and reality for almost everyone involved.

Speaking more recently, Zimbardo pointed out the clear parallels between the behaviors of the student "guards" in the Stanford Prison Experiment and the human rights violations by some of the American military guards at the notorious Abu Ghraib prison in Iraq. Zimbardo's conclusion is straightforward: Much of the power to influence our perceptions and our behavior resides within the social context in which we find ourselves and we ignore this power at our own peril.[2]

While the Stanford Prison Experiment may seem extreme, other classic experiments also show the power of social context to affect our thinking and behavior. In another famous study, Yale psychologist Stanley Milgram showed that a majority of ordinary Americans were willing to expose others to what they thought were painful electrical shocks if ordered to do so by an authority figure.[3] Despite reservations, many of the subjects were willing to override the dictates of their conscience as they followed orders. Milgram's obedience experiments took place in parallel with the trial of Nazi war criminal, Adolf Eichmann. The experiment was designed to shed light on whether Eichmann and his accomplices were morally convinced of the rightness of their actions, or if they were simply following orders.

A Fundamental Tension

While Zimbardo and Milgram's experiments demonstrate the power of context to influence people's behaviors, it is equally true that not all their subjects responded the same way. Some refused the orders to apply shocks to another human, and some of the guards in the Stanford experiment continued to behave in fair and humane ways towards the prisoners. In other words, it is not just context *per se*, but rather our subjective interpretation of that context that better predicts how we will actually behave.[4]

In *Man's Search For Meaning,* Viktor Frankl's moving memoir of his experiences in the death camps of the Holocaust, the author shows that our personal beliefs and expectations make up a significant part of the meaning we attribute to any given context. What Frankl showed, as have other heroes throughout history, is that individuals have a final freedom, the freedom to decide how they will interpret any situation. As Frankl so poignantly expressed it, "…everything can be taken away from a man but one thing: the last of the human freedoms—to choose one's attitude in any given set of circumstances, to choose one's own way."[5]

Our freedom to choose the meaning we attribute to an event or behavior can also help us avoid what is known as the "correspondence bias" or "fundamental attribution error."[6] While we often take external conditions into account when explaining our own actions, we are more likely to explain other people's actions in terms of internal character traits. For example, when explaining our own behavior we might say things like, "I didn't really mean to say that, but I was totally stressed because everything went wrong that day." Or, "I know I shouldn't have agreed, but I just couldn't stand to see her cry like that." Or, "I know I missed the deadline, but I needed to take my child to the doctor." Often our justifications for our actions are valid and not just clever tactics to maintain our self-esteem.

But why do we so rarely extend the same understanding to others? Why do we not ask ourselves, "What does this situation look like to the other person?" Or, "What has their culture or personal life history taught them that makes them see this situation differently from me?" Why, rather than assuming the other is a good person caught in a bad situation, is it easier for so many of us to attribute his behavior to bad character traits or malicious intentions? Sometimes it's because of stereotypical thinking, sometimes it's because we are just not aware of how powerful context is, and sometimes it's a lack of mindsight—we can't see the frame of reference the other person was using when he behaved as he did. If, for example, we are not aware that this person has had a terrible day in which everything seemed to go wrong, it would be easy to think or say something like this: "I can't believe he said such a mean thing, he must be a deeply troubled person." Or, "There he goes, caving in to her again, what a wimp." Or, "If he were as creative at doing his work as he is at making excuses, he'd never miss a deadline."

While we often take context into account to justify our own less-than-perfect behavior, we fall prey to the fundamental attribution error when we are not willing to do the same for others. The more we can see the situation from the other person's perspective, the less prone we are to make this error. At the same time, the more we understand the role that context plays in the way our brains process information, the more power we have to free ourselves from those influences. An important lesson to remember is that human perception and behavior always take place within a particular context. The context we find ourselves in will influence our perceptions and decisions and can be thought of as the frame of reference that surrounds us at all times. To help us remember this and avoid the fundamental attribution error, we can add this frame of reference to our image of the black box problem.

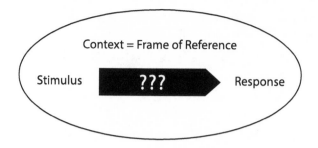

Figure 4.1 — Black Box in Context

Contextual Complexity

Contexts exist on many different levels and influence the way our brains process information in different ways. A neat thinker may imagine these different levels of contexts like a series of Russian dolls in which one is opened to find a smaller version, which is opened to find an even smaller version. This is somewhat true. But it is just as true that contexts are interwoven like a complex tapestry. They overlap and crisscross organizational levels and logical borders, making our understanding of any particular situation more difficult.

This inherent simultaneity of the different contexts in which we exist is a natural consequence of the interrelatedness of the world. Professor Albert-László Barabási, a leader in the new field of network science, says this about our interconnectedness:

Today we increasingly recognize that nothing happens in isolation. Most events and phenomena are connected, caused by, and interacting with a huge number of other pieces of a complex universal puzzle. We have come to see that we live in a small world, where everything is linked to everything else.[7]

We can illustrate this interconnectedness by imagining one particular engineer from Virginia and follow her to see how both her verbal and nonverbal communication varies as the context changes. One thing we notice immediately is that her way of communicating changes depending upon where the meeting takes place. When it is at a large conference table under the glare of the bright lights in the company's official meeting room, her body language becomes more constrained and less expressive than when she is meeting someone in her own office, which she decorated with soft, warm colors.

Her way of communicating also depends upon whether the people present are all peers or people of differing ranks. In addition, we notice differences between the way she behaves at meetings where only women are present versus meetings where she is the only woman. We also notice that her relationships with particular individuals influence the way she communicates in subtle ways. For instance, she likes and trusts Jan and she sits a little closer and leans in more when she talks to her than she does with Sally, whom she does not like or trust. We also notice that her choice of words changes depending on whether she is meeting with associates from her company, with a potential new customer, or with an established client. Generalizing, we can say that place, social role, gender, and relationship influence the way people communicate.

Then we decide to follow her around the world as she makes a business trip to visit other company sites. We immediately notice that meetings are conducted differently in different countries and so, because she is a good interculturalist, she does her best to adapt to the changing contexts. Because she lived in Japan for many years as a teenager and speaks fluent Japanese, she feels comfortable and finds it easy to fit in. We notice that here she is more quiet and reserved than she is during business meetings in the United States.

In contrast to Japan, this is her first trip to Germany and she is unfamiliar with German culture and its more direct communication style. Because she does not speak German, the meetings take place in English, forcing her German associates to use a language in which they feel less competent. Between the more direct style and the problems created by the language barrier, she finds herself feeling less comfortable and we notice that her body is stiffer and her smiles less frequent.

This seems complex enough, but then we decide to expand our observations beyond the context of her business life. We follow her home after work and observe her with her husband and children. Then we follow her to the fitness studio where she works out three times a week. As we expand the context beyond professional settings, we notice that her way of communicating changes in each new context. While there is a common denominator and style that connects them all, we also notice that each new context elicits changes, some subtle and some quite obvious, in what she says and how she says it.

If we had a time machine, we could expand this thought experiment a bit and watch our engineer as a child and compare her communication then and now. We would notice that as she matures, her repertoire of communication tools grows and she becomes more competent in playing the social roles expected of her. As she learns what works in a particular context and what doesn't, her brain is continually fine-tuning the internal maps it uses to help her master these various situations. At the same time, her sense of identity is developing in conjunction with the social roles her culture affords her.

Imagine, for example, how this same child would have developed had she been born in Virginia in 1750. Would she have grown up to be an engineer and participated in business meetings or would we more likely find her working as a seamstress or midwife? How would her surroundings have influenced the way she talked and acted? What if she had been born in Egypt in 2000 B.C.E? How would she have grown up and learned to talk if she were the daughter of a pharaoh as compared to the daughter of one of the workers who built the pyramids? And what if she had been born twenty thousand years ago to a band of hunter-gatherers roaming the great African savannahs?

Just as individuals develop through time and have their own personal stories, so too, cultures evolve and have histories. Any individual conversation is part of the larger web of conversations and historical events that have been going on since humans began communicating. We have been born into an unending conversation. That conversation is like a force field of shared meaning. Just as iron filings are held in place by an electromagnetic field, so, too, our perceptions, thoughts, feelings, and the way we act and talk are influenced by the contexts in which we find ourselves.

Just as cultures define the meaning of words, they also define contexts. These contexts include the social situations and roles we play, e.g., rabbi and young person to be initiated at a bar mitzvah; manager and employees at a business meeting; fans, coaches, and players at a football game; funeral director, priest, and family members at a funeral ceremony, etc. Such shared knowledge helps participants understand what is going on and what to expect; it thus helps them coordinate their behaviors in a socially appropriate manner, i.e., in a way that is appropriate for the context as defined by their culture.

Natural and Social Contexts

As we will see in more detail in chapter eight, the natural world has always been the meta-context out of which our social worlds emerged. As part of the current transitioning from the modern industrial age to what is often referred to as the post-industrial or information age, researchers in such diverse fields as linguistics, sociology, psychology, and more are discovering the ubiquitous role context plays for all forms of life.[8] Survival requires all living organisms to adapt to their changing environments—that is, to adapt to an ever-changing context. Context-sensitivity is thus a hallmark of life itself, but in humans, with our large brains, context-sensitivity has expanded to new heights and is present in all our sensory systems.[9]

The consequences of context-sensitivity for us humans, regardless of which level of existence we choose to study—the physical, biological, perceptual, emotional, mental, linguistic or socio-cultural—are becoming clearer as researchers delve ever deeper into the complex nature of what it means to be human. Here's what Robert Sapolsky, one of the world's leading neuroscientists and an expert on the stress response, has to say about the role of context for our physical well-being:

> There has been a revolution in medicine concerning how we think about the diseases that now afflict us. It involves recognizing the interactions between the body and the mind, the ways in which emotions and personality can have a tremendous impact on the functioning and health of virtually

every cell in the body. It is about the role of stress in making some of us more vulnerable to disease, the ways in which some of us cope with stressors, and the critical notion that you cannot really understand a disease in vacuo, but rather only in the context of the person suffering from that disease.[10]

Context influences even our most basic perceptions. Consider the influence of a picture frame. Not only does a picture frame serve as a boundary, letting us know where the picture begins and ends, the frame becomes part of the painting, adding to the visual impression we get when we look at the painting. Viewing the exact same picture in different frames—imagine a portrait of yourself in an ornate, gold frame from the Baroque era and then imagine that same portrait in a smooth, elegant black modern frame—seems to change the picture itself.

The influence of the frame can be further understood with another simple experiment. Take a small, red piece of paper and hold it up against a larger, green background. Observe the quality of the red. Then place the same red paper on a yellow background. If you observe carefully, you will notice that the shade of red seems to change depending on the color of the background. The background color frames and influences the quality of our experience.

This happens to all of our senses, not just sight. Here's a simple experiment you can try at home: Get three large pans and fill them with water. Put cold, almost icy water (about 40 degrees Fahrenheit) in one pan. Put lukewarm water (about 65 degrees Fahrenheit) in the second and hot water (about 110 degrees Fahrenheit) in the third. Then simultaneously put one of your hands in the icy water and the other in the hot water. Keep them there for about a minute and then, simultaneously, put them both into the pan with lukewarm water. You will have the unusual experience of seeing your hands in the same water, but each hand will have a different tactile experience. The hand that was in the icy water will feel very warm and the hand that was in the hot water will now feel cool even though both hands are in water of the same temperature.

The lesson is obvious: Even our most basic perceptions are relative, not absolute, and context serves as the frame of reference our brains use to interpret incoming sensory data. If such basic physical perceptions turn out to be so variable, how can our more complex social perceptions not be?

Culture as Context

Socially constructed events would seem to be more within the human locus of control, whereas events in the natural world seem less so. But there is a fuzzy, gray zone where it's not clear what is occurring naturally and what is socially constructed.

Take, for example, a common communication practice among office workers in South Korea. During the work day in a South Korean office, communication tends to be formal, hierarchical, and almost ritualistic.[11] But when the work day ends, the frame of reference changes from "at work" to "socializing with my group." The same people go out to eat and drink together. As they do so, they begin to loosen up and talk and behave less formally. The South Koreans do not say, "Because the context changed, it is now appropriate for me to say things to my boss that I would never dare say in the office." Instead, the South Korean belief system attributes the more direct and less formal behaviors to the alcohol, i.e., it is the alcohol that is talking and therefore whatever is said is to be excused and forgotten. Nevertheless, this informal, alcohol-laden communication practice allows the group to share important information that would not otherwise be communicated. Next day at the office, people will act as if whatever was said never happened. Using two different context-dependent communication styles is one way South Koreans manage the challenges that face all cultures: How can a group maintain social order, cooperate to produce wealth, and still build close emotional relationships that fulfill our needs for belonging?

But was it, you may wonder, only the alcohol that was doing the talking in those after-hour events, or was something more complex at work? It turns out that the effects of alcohol on men varies between cultures.[12] Recent cross-cultural research shows that in some cultures men tend to become more violent when drunk, while in others they almost never do. Similarly, in some cultures men become more amorous, but in others they don't. Same drug, different behaviors. In fact, research shows that context and correlated belief systems also affect the degree of addictiveness for not only alcohol, but also for tobacco and heroin.[13] Cultures and their shared belief systems are powerful contexts exerting strong influences on their members.

Regardless of where we are in the world, be it Korea, France, or Botswana, human conversations never take place in a vacuum. The shared meaning that allows people to interpret an event in a similar way is an integral part of the context. Seen from this perspective, culture is more than just a group's way of life, it is also a system for managing and sharing meaning that has grown and developed from generation to generation. This force field of shared meaning also creates mind distance when we communicate with people from different cultures.

But how is it my close friend was unaware that her emotions and perceptions were being influenced by the bleak film she had watched the night before? And why did normal college students who voluntarily signed up for a psychology experiment begin experiencing it not as an experiment, but as so real and dangerous it triggered extreme stress-reactions?

Part of the answer has to do with the mind-boggling complexity of the contextual cues that are impinging upon us during social interactions. As the leaders of our inner teams, we do not have enough attention to track all of them. When we focus on one, we ignore the others. Stage magicians and pickpockets are well aware that conscious attention is a limited resource and they use this knowledge to perform illusions or rob people by misdirecting their attention. For a convincing and entertaining demonstration of how easily others can direct our attention, go online and watch videos of Apollo Robbins. This master of misdirection uses his deft skills to pick people's pockets, steal their watches, and even remove their eyeglasses without them noticing.

But if our limited capacity for conscious awareness is easy to confuse, what about our brain's inner team? While the multiple circuits of a brain's unconscious processing allow it to deal rapidly with the complexity of our lives, our inner team is not infallible. As we saw earlier, our brains understand the present and anticipate the future based upon the past, making us vulnerable if our assumptions and expectations do not accord with the current situation. Understanding our brain's unconscious circuitry helps explain the power of context, but it does not explain the ability of some people to transcend the contexts in which they find themselves. Why did only some of the guards treat the prisoners sadistically in the Stanford experiment, and why did only some of the subjects follow the orders to administer dangerous shocks in the Milgram experiment? What gave Viktor Frankl the power to respond so heroically, while so many of his fellow prisoners succumbed to the hopelessness of their situation?

Growing Our Inner Power

For all practical purposes, all of Frankl's external power—his social rank, property, possessions, and even his liberty—was stripped from him as he was made to endure Nazi brutality, but he possessed strong internal power that enabled him to survive. As already mentioned, the foundation for that internal power was his ability to choose which meaning he attributed to his situation. This ability to reframe the meaning of a situation is a fundamental freedom all humans can develop.

As a general principle, we can say that while all humans are subject to the larger contexts in which they find themselves, they also possess some degree of personal power they can use to tame those contexts. An individual's personal power is composed of both external and internal power and we have the choice as to which we will develop. While some people view them as mutually exclusive, I believe we have the option to develop both our internal and external power if we so choose.

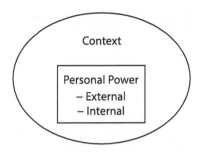

Figure 4.2 — Personal Power and Context

In addition to his power to choose the meaning of his situation, Frankl also wrote that he saw himself as serving a purpose higher than his own survival. He believed it crucial that he live to tell what happened so that such an horrific event would never occur again. Not only did his noble intention motivate his exemplary behavior during his time in the camps, it also served as a driving force for his long career as a psychotherapist and public speaker. As we will see in chapter eleven, our intentions and goals serve to reduce internal dissonance and unite our inner team, and thus have an enormous influence on the way our brains function and on what we are capable of accomplishing.

Another part of the inner power that allows people to manage themselves and the contexts they are in has to do with how much of our potential we have developed. All humans are born with great potential, but we are also born as helpless babies. As small children, we adapt to our environment to survive. As we develop both our sense of self and our innate potential, we gain more inner power to transcend and transform those contexts. Some individuals clearly have more inner power than others, but regardless of how much of our potential we have developed, these abilities and skills are the resources we use to survive and thrive.

To the best of my knowledge, there is neither a universally agreed upon nor a comprehensive master list of the key abilities and skills that constitute the inner power of a healthy, mature human. Nonetheless, developing certain potentials provides us with the resources we need to transcend contexts. Our intentions and our ability to choose what meaning we attribute to any situation are two of those key skills. Mindsight and clarity of perception are also essential if we hope to grow our inner power and stay in states of flow while managing challenging contexts.

Transcending contexts also requires the ability to manage our emotions. As we will see again and again in this book, the ability to understand and regulate these motivating forces plays a central role in developing the inner power we need for intercultural success.

But while growth of our inner power and personal independence is part of the process of healthy maturation, so, too, is our willingness to identify with and cooperate with the larger groups we belong to. Because humans are social beings *par excellence* and because we are, from one perspective, extensions of our families, communities, and cultures, our personal power and our survival also depends upon our ability to work together to solve the problems that threaten all of us. For this reason, we need the interpersonal skills that allow us to construct healthy relationships and satisfy our deep need for belonging.

As Viktor Frankl's behavior makes clear, we can choose to reflect before attributing meaning, or we can let our inner team and our conditioning automatically control our thoughts, feelings, and behavior. Frankl was a true hero and each of us has a right to aspire to such admirable behavior in our own lives. But to demand or naively expect others to be heroes is to ignore the power of context in their lives. People do the best they can with the resources and personal power they have, but not everyone has the same resources and personal power. It is easy to expect others to be heroes or to become disappointed and cynical when they are not. It is wiser and more noble to use our own resources to create better relationships and more humane social systems to bring out the best in all of us.

Conclusion

Humans base their decisions and actions on meaning, and our ability to choose what meaning we attribute to any given phenomenon is our fundamental freedom. Context is especially important for understanding the process of communication because the meaning of our words and actions is, in large part, derived from the vast historical network of contexts within contexts about which the individual often knows little. Nonetheless, the meaning we attribute to any given phenomenon will be influenced by those factors. Not having a single cause does not mean that there is no cause, it means we need to think about causality in a more sophisticated manner.

Consider some common synonyms we use for context: Background, circumstances, conditions, situation, setting, venue, historical era, environment, system, network, free market, field, and more. When you watch for these words, you will begin to notice they are ubiquitous in the assumptions that guide our day-to-day conversations.

Common contexts that frame our perceptions include time, place, relationship, social role, gender, rank, group membership, social event, language, culture and more. Thus, a prison guard may successfully be able to use threats, commands, and insults to coerce his prisoners, but he would be well advised to choose more deferential words and a milder demeanor with his supervisor. Similarly, a male medical doctor might find it easy to order a female patient to undress as part of a physical exam, but he would not find this effective with the woman he is courting. While this may seem obvious, it is crucial for us to understand the role of context when communicating with people from different cultures.

Understanding the levels and types of context in our lives helps us avoid the fundamental attribution error. Remembering that a person's actions are the result of character traits AND a function of the context as he perceives it, allows us to more easily hit the pause button and reflect before reacting in an unskillful manner. The more we are able to do this, the more we increase the odds of our success.

People behave differently depending on context. Some people may cheat and steal in one situation, but sacrifice their lives for a loved one in another. Put people in bad situations or inhumane social systems and it will bring out the worst in some and the best in a heroic few. We need only look at the behavior of many otherwise normal Germans when facing the Nazi dictatorship that had taken over their country like a cancer. While a few rose to heroic heights in fighting against the Nazis, most conformed and did their best to survive in a terrible situation. That's why creating safety, the topic of our next chapter, is so crucial for our success.

Five

Safety First

We have to face the fact that either all of us are going to die together or we are going to learn to live together and if we are to live together we have to talk.

—Eleanor Roosevelt

Are you the kind of person who likes to use your cell phone in public, talking in a loud voice as if to say, "Look at me, see how connected and important I am?" Or are you the kind of person who feels your blood pressure go up, your chest tighten, and your throat constrict as you restrain yourself from throttling such loud talkers? Or do you use your cell phone in public places so anyone within range gets an earful of your private dramas and why you think everyone of the opposite sex should be loaded onto the first rocket into outer space? Or are you in the shrinking minority of people who still don't use a cell phone?

While cell phone etiquette may not seem like anything to concern an interculturalist, it is. People around the world now have access to a cell phone and its use is growing daily. So are the rules—implicit and explicit—of cell phone etiquette to manage this modern technology. For instance, in Spain it is common for people to answer their phones in restaurants and in business meetings.[1] In Japan such behavior is frowned upon and people are expected to put their phones on "manner mode" (silence it) in trains, buses, and other public places.[2] This simple contrast points to a fundamental challenge facing interculturalists everywhere: In our fast-paced world, new rules are being co-created everywhere to manage the whirlwind of change and the differences in these new rules generate even more mind distance. Cell phones are only one example. From the etiquette of using Facebook to behavioral norms for remote virtual teams, people everywhere are being challenged. As if the blur of rapid social change were not enough, we are also faced with the backlash of resistance to the growing complexity in our lives.

What options does an interculturalist have to manage evolving cultural differences other than heading for the hills to live as a hermit? Two traditional approaches are available: The first is to take a big picture view of cultural differences and look for underlying patterns to make sense of them, and the second is to learn the details and specifics of the norms, values, and customs of particular cultures. Each has its strengths and weaknesses, and both are worth pursuing.

The Big Picture Approach

If you are dealing with people from many different cultures, the big picture approach is a good place to start. A number of researchers have distilled vast amounts of knowledge about cultural differences into simpler models, allowing us to locate a particular culture on various dimensions. One of the most well-known of these big-picture models was created by the Dutch social psychologist and organizational anthropologist, Geert Hofstede. Hofstede's current model of cultural differences uses six dimensions to compare and contrast cultures. These six dimensions are individualism-collectivism, power-distance, masculinity-femininity, uncertainty avoidance, long-term orientation, and indulgence-restraint. Four of these dimensions were created by statistical analysis of a world-wide survey given to employees of a large, international company.[3] Later, Hofstede and other researchers broadened this model by adding a fifth dimension, long-term orientation, to better reflect Asian values. More recently, they added a sixth dimension, indulgence-restraint, to further refine the model.[4]

Another universal model for measuring cultural differences, Moral Foundations Theory (MFT), was originally developed by psychologists, Jonathan Haidt and Craig Joseph. MFT assumes humans possess innate predispositions—what they refer to as moral modules or moral foundations—to feel, think, and act in terms of good and bad, right and wrong.[5] While these moral predispositions exist in all humans, they are given their final form by the cultures into which we are born. In other words, the moral compasses we use to guide our decisions are a function of both nature and nurture.

MFT postulates six fundamental moral modules shared, to a greater or lesser degree, by all societies and individuals.[6] These six are: Care, fairness, loyalty, authority, sanctity (avoiding disgusting things, foods, and actions), and liberty. At first glance MFT seems to bear little resemblance to Hofstede's model and a natural question is, "Which one is right?"

A better question is, "Can they both be true?" Based upon my reading, they both contain valuable insights to help us understand the human condition. In addition, a closer read of the two theories shows significant overlap. What MFT refers to as authority and fairness correlates positively with what Hofstede calls power-distance. And what Hofstede calls the individualism-collectivism dimension overlaps with what MFT is tracking as loyalty and liberty. Overlap also exists between MFT's "care" and Hofstede's masculinity-femininity dimension. That different researchers using different approaches show such correlation suggests we are on the track of underlying universals that can help us better understand how mind distance gets created.

Other researchers have developed different models to understand cultural differences. For example, the anthropologists Florence Kluckhohn and Fred Strodtbeck studied the value systems that cultures developed to master fundamental problems.[7] Another well-known anthropologist, Edward T. Hall, focused on the ways different cultures used time, space, and context to organize themselves,[8] while the sociologist Talcott Parsons developed a system that focused on the ways people relate to one another.[9] More recently, Fons Trompenaars and Charles Hampden-Turner developed a system of seven dimensions to show how societies deal with relationships between people, time, and nature.[10] These are just some of the most well-known systems.

Each of these systems provides an important perspective for understanding the various differences that exist around the world. Each system provides more resolution to our personal brain maps and there is no reason not to use all of them. The key is to choose the system that fits your purpose. Just as you would choose a topographical map and not a street map if you wanted to go hiking in the wilderness, so, too, choosing the right system depends on your purposes.[11]

Each of these big-picture models is a theoretical map of our social worlds and they all contain valuable insights that will help anyone who wants to understand cultural diversity. But, as useful as high-level generalizations are in getting the big picture, they often miss much of the specific differences that exists between cultures.

For example, let's return to cell phone usage and look at Japan and India, two cultures all researchers agree are highly communal, as compared to the more individualistic cultures of the West. In Japan, as already mentioned, use of cell phones in public places is frowned upon, and when asked, many Japanese will agree with cultural anthropologist Mizuko Ito: "In Japan your phone shouldn't be a nuisance to others...This means generally keeping it on manner mode when out of the house, and not taking calls in cafes and restaurants. If somebody's phone rings, they will be flustered and silence it or take a very quick call."[12] So in Japan, the importance of the individual fitting in to maintain social harmony is emphasized, a common precept in communal cultures.

But in India, another highly communal culture, cell phone use is rampant in public places, even in movie theaters. According to Kadira Pethiyagoda, an Indian doctoral student, "Indian society has a long tradition of tolerance, including in terms of allowing others to infringe on what those in the West would consider one's personal space." He adds, "This is why phone use in cinemas and crowded trains, is tolerated....Indian society is also more communal than the West, which, in part, leads to an increased importance of constantly staying in touch."[13]

These examples, taken from two highly communal Asian cultures, portray contradictory etiquettes to accommodate the use of cell phones in public space. Had we reasoned from the broad assumption that both cultures are communal, we would not have predicted such divergent behaviors. In other words, big-picture models try to measure cultural differences by using a number of abstract dimensions, which can interact in complicated, unpredictable ways. Such models are valuable in mapping out broad outlines of the human condition, but they require careful study to use them well. Many people find such models too abstract and prefer to focus on particular cultures.

The Need for Details

To compensate for the loss of detail inherent in high-level generalizations, it is useful to focus on in-depth, detailed studies of particular cultures. This approach is most useful if you are dealing with people from just a few cultures. Books, articles, films, podcasts, and more about the cultures of the world abound and, if you take the time to learn the specifics of a particular culture, you will have much pragmatic knowledge for use in everyday life and work.

But focusing on particular cultures is not fool-proof. Even at this level of generalization, it is still easy to fall into the trap of stereotypical thinking. Let's take our cell phone example once again and compare use in two areas of one country that are not far apart. In New York City, crowds of people, young and old, are on the move and it is common to see them in streets, buildings, and other public places with their cell phones clamped to their ears. Now drive just about a hundred miles out of New York City to Bird-in-Hand, Pennsylvania. The pace of life, style of conversation, and ways people interact with one another seem as different from New York City as they do from London or Berlin. And if you look around, you will notice fewer people using cell phones in public.

The problem with making broad generalizations about a particular culture is that it ignores the diversity in any given culture. Furthermore, those differences are not distributed evenly. Countries like Brazil, India, China, South Africa and the United States have so many different sub-cultures it becomes difficult to make accurate generalizations without falling into crass stereotyping. Factors—such as regional affiliation, rural versus urban, class and educational levels, as well as ethnic, linguistic, and religious differences—play significant roles in influencing people's beliefs, values, and behaviors.

Simplifying the Complexity

How should we manage this great complexity? Whether we study various big-picture models to understand cultural differences or try to study individual cultures, it's easy to become overwhelmed by the great diversity of humanity. Furthermore, while an intellectual understanding of our many differences is essential, intellectual understanding alone is no guarantee that we will achieve the success we desire. Is there not a more pragmatic and intuitive way to manage individual and cultural differences? I believe there is and it can be summed up in this simple mantra: Safety first, truth second.

Safety first, truth second is the essence of mutually satisfying communication because it is based on an aspect of human existence that applies everywhere: We all experience fear and we all yearn, at some deep existential level, for safety and security. Out of this universal experience comes a dimension that applies everywhere on the planet: Danger-safety. Because of its universal applicability, safety first, truth second can be used to reduce mind distance and guide us when communicating with people from all cultures and in all contexts. That's a big claim, so let's see why it's true.

First, the danger-safety dimension is a continuum with numerous gradations on it, not an either-or dichotomy. Where a person is on the continuum at any given time will depend, to one degree or another, upon her baseline level of anxiety as well as how she interprets the context she finds herself in. As we saw in chapter three, a situation can switch from seeming safe to appearing dangerous in the blink of an eye. That's because of the underlying neural mechanisms that are driving our perceptions.

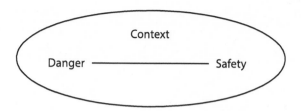

Figure 5.1 — Danger-Safety Continuum

The "danger-safety" dimension helps us understand human experiences everywhere because it corresponds to the functioning of the autonomic nervous system (ANS). The ANS, a major player on our inner teams, is composed of two main branches, the parasympathetic and the sympathetic, designed to balance each other, maintain homeostasis, and help us meet our needs.

Thanks to groundbreaking research by Stephen Porges, a professor of psychiatry at the University of North Carolina, we now know the parasympathetic branch itself also consists of two sub-branches that evolved at different times and which have different functions.[14] The older, more primitive section of the parasympathetic system is responsible for rest and digestion as well as for immobilization, the so-called freeze response. Imagine an animal frozen in fear in the glare of oncoming headlights and you have a vivid picture of the freeze response in action.

In contrast, the other section of the parasympathetic system is the newest part of the ANS in terms of evolution. Porges refers to this newer section as the social engagement system and he has shown it to be responsible for mediating the complex social and attachment behaviors we humans engage in. To do this, the social engagement system sends and receives signals to and from a variety of muscles and organs including the face, mouth, eyes, tear ducts, ears, vocal tract, heart, lungs, and more, all parts of ourselves essential for communication.[15]

If we compare the three sections of the ANS to three children in a family, the sympathetic branch of the ANS would be the middle child. In terms of our evolution as a species, it is younger than the parasympathetic section responsible for the freeze response, but older than the social engagement system.

The sympathetic branch of the ANS, this middle child in terms of evolutionary development, is responsible for arousal and mobilization of a person when conditions demand it. In particular, the sympathetic branch mediates the stress response when an organism perceives its situation as dangerous. The stress response—also known as the fight-or-flight response—causes the adrenal glands to secrete adrenalin and cortisol into the blood stream to elevate heart rate and blood pressure and prepare the body for action.

When the stress response is activated, our body's resources are mobilized to promote our physical survival, which means either running away in fear—in terms of communication, we leave the conversation, either mentally or physically—or going into fight mode with our anger turning us into search-and-destroy avengers. While we might have entered a conversation with the best of intentions, a person can flip into fight-or-flight mode in the blink of an eye. Such an emotional hijacking happens so fast to some people, they don't even notice it until they are sweeping up the pieces of a broken relationship. So keeping a situation safe and the social engagement system activated is a valuable skill because it allows us to use the resources of our entire brains, including our creativity, for clear thinking and effective problem solving.

Using the social engagement system has many advantages. For one, we tend to remain relaxed and this is inherently more pleasurable than being in the fight-or-flight mode. It is also less stressful on the body and allows us to remain within our window of tolerance. In contrast, chronic triggering of the sympathetic branch's fight-or-flight mode has adverse effects on our health and well-being.[16]

In addition to the effects on our health, when the social engagement system is activated, we have the highest chance of successfully communicating with another person. Not only are we able to think more clearly and use more of our brain's capacities in a healthy, more adaptive manner, we are also more able to create a safe context for the other person. If the other person does not feel safe, she will not trust us, and if she doesn't trust us, she won't listen to our point of view. So, safety first, truth second.

These three different neural circuits that comprise the ANS not only evolved at different times in our species' history, they are also activated in hierarchical sequence, rather than in a simple antagonistic system as was once believed. Which of the three circuits in the ANS is active at any given point in time depends on the brain's threat assessment system, which is constantly monitoring the environment for signs of danger.

Threat Assessment

Because we evolved in a world filled with potential danger, members of our inner team behind the locked door are constantly scanning our environment to ascertain whether the situation is safe or not.[17] Porges refers to this continual appraisal of a situation's potential danger as neuroception.

Neuroception helps explain why a baby smiles at its caregiver but may scream in distress when a stranger approaches. Neuroception also explains why we relax with people we know and trust but remain alert and tense around people we do not know. Understanding the role this innate threat assessment system plays in our lives offers us a broad and pragmatic way to take the other person's point of view and reduce mind distance.

When our threat assessment system perceives a situation as dangerous and triggers the stress response, the sympathetic nervous system is activated and the social engagement system goes offline. As it does, the part of our brains responsible for compassion, morality, and higher-level decision-making, the prefrontal cortex, is disconnected and the more primitive limbic system takes control.

As mentioned in chapter three, this is what Daniel Goleman refers to as an emotional hijacking, and when the prefrontal cortex goes off-line, we lose our ability to think clearly.[18] It's as if, in response to a crisis, we are sending the most skilled and resourceful members of our inner team on vacation and leaving the less talented members to handle the challenging situation. This might be the ideal strategy if we are being physically attacked, but in conversations with people who are just different, activating the stress response is counterproductive.

When the fight-or-flight mode is activated, it also becomes harder for us to listen empathically and understand the other person's point of view. In fact, as Porges has shown, when the fight-or-flight mode is activated, muscles in the middle ear that help us hear sounds in the frequency range of the human voice become deactivated, making active listening even harder. [19] Unless you plan on bludgeoning the other person into submission, getting the other person to listen to you is a prerequisite for generating trust, cooperation, and collective intelligence.

When our threat assessment systems perceive a situation as dangerous, we tend to diverge and emphasize the differences between ourselves and the other person. In other words, when we go into fight-or-flight mode, we are less likely to see the other person as a partner we can safely approach. To protect ourselves from the perceived danger, we tend to pull back and disrupt communication. On the other hand, if our brains perceive a situation as safe, we are more likely to remain relaxed, socially engaged, and able to use our entire brain.

We have all been emotionally hijacked at one time or another, but often have little awareness of what actually happened inside us. For example, in chapter three I described how I began to overreact when I was interrupted. It all happened so fast, I found myself reacting without much awareness. By carefully reviewing the actual experience, I was more able to recognize what had happened and to take responsibility for my actions. As we will see in chapter fourteen, when we pay attention to our emotions, we can grow both our mindsight and our window of tolerance.

The Social Motor

By taking into account the threat assessment circuitry and the functions of the ANS, we have a powerful tool for understanding how people everywhere react to situations they perceive as dangerous. Considering whether a situation is being perceived by the other person as safe or dangerous helps us begin seeing the world from that person's point of view. At the same time, knowing our own threat assessment system is always on the alert reminds us to self-monitor our inner states to notice when we begin going into fight-or-flight. If we can catch ourselves before the emotional hijacking gets going, we have a better chance of responding adroitly and avoiding a misunderstanding.

Understanding the central role the threat assessment system plays on our inner teams also gives us an important insight into why normal American college students began to behave in such an extreme fashion in the Stanford Prison Experiment. Things went well at first, but after the "guards" woke the "prisoners" up in the middle of the first night for a "count," things began to spiral out of control.[20] Until that point, the interpretation of the situation in everyone's mind seems to have been, "This is just another one of those odd experiments the psych department likes to run."

Waking people up from a sound sleep with loud noises and shouting, however, is not a normal event and it is one that can trigger deep fear and disorientation in a person. In a word, it can trigger the fight-or-flight response with all its attendant consequences. Because they could not flee, some of the prisoners chose to fight back. The next day they were less willing to go along with the guards' orders. Using our black box model, what happened looks something like this:

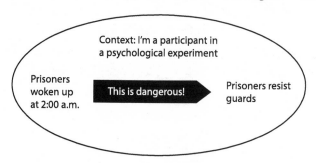

Figure 5.2 — Prisoner's Black Box

Then the guards were told by the experiment's director they needed to maintain their authority and not let the prisoners get the upper hand. While some of the guards continued treating the prisoners in a fair and humane way, other guards began using more harsh and authoritarian means to control the prisoners. Again, using the black box model, it looks something like this:

Figure 5.3 — Guard's Black Box

As the guards and prisoners continued interacting, their behaviors and their subjective interpretations of each other's behavior led to an escalation of aggression and culminated in the premature termination of the experiment. Combining the black boxes and the behaviors from one guard and one prisoner allows us to represent their interaction as follows:

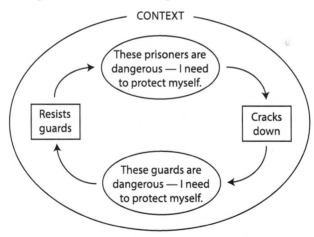

Figure 5.4 — Vicious Cycle Between Prisoners and Guards

Because neither the guard nor the prisoner was able to peer into the black box of the other's mind, their threat assessment centers could only evaluate the danger of the situation by interpreting the other's behavior. In other words, both the guard's and the prisoner's behaviors were determined by the decision-making process taking place in their minds, a process invisible to the other person. As we saw in chapter four, it is common to disregard the role of external factors when interpreting the actions of another person—the fundamental attribution error—while, at the same time, emphasizing how our own behavior is being driven by the external situation in which we find ourselves. But when we make the fundamental attribution error, we fail to recognize the ways in which our own actions are creating the very situation we find threatening. This is one of the great paradoxes and challenges of communication: We are often blind to the ways in which we are co-creating the very actions we find hardest to accept.

Not only are we all prone to such a biased view of other people's behavior, we are also prone to engage in self-justification to help us avoid the cognitive dissonance that occurs if our actions don't accord with our values. As we will explore more, this tendency to justify our actions to avoid cognitive dissonance can have major consequences, not just for our own lives, but also for the relationships and cultures we co-create with others.

This simple analysis of a complex social interaction does not present all the dynamics or insights we could glean from this classic experiment. If you are interested, those are available in books, articles, and online by searching for Stanford Prison Experiment. The point to remember is that all interactions between humans involve subjective assessments of safety or danger and this assessment will determine whether our social engagement system stays activated, or whether the stress response gets triggered, setting off an emotional hijacking.

Separating Evidence from Interpretation

Like the interaction between guard and prisoner, all conversations are comprised of both an external, objective component, which is empirically verifiable by observers, as well as an internal, subjective component, which occurs in the black box of the mind. If we generalize from the Stanford experiment, we get the following generic communication model I like to call the "social motor" because it distinguishes between both the objective dynamics and the subjective motivations of social interactions everywhere:[21]

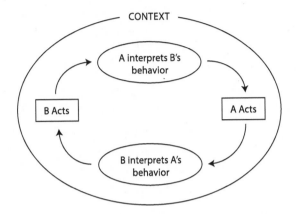

Figure 5.5 — Generalized Social Motor

To make the model more comprehensive, we can situate the social motor on the danger-safety continuum. For example, whenever a prisoner or guard resisted one another, the other's subjective sense of danger increased causing the social motor to move more and more into the danger zone. But remember, this was an experiment and there was no real threat of physical danger. But as the perceived dangers increased, reactions became more pathological. One of the prisoners even began experiencing a psychosomatic rash on his body, demonstrating that relationships are some of the most intense contexts humans can experience.

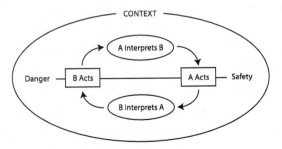

Figure 5.6 — Social Motor on Danger-Safety Continuum

In the give-and-take of our everyday conversations the social motor is turning, and, as it does, meaning is being created and shared. This meaning is the social glue holding our relationships and groups together or causing them to fragment. If we keep in mind that we are the context for the other person and thus influencing her thinking and feeling, we can avoid the fundamental attribution error, reduce mind distance, and increase the odds of having a satisfying conversation.

Of course, in an age of mass communication and social media, much meaning gets shared via other channels and we will look at the power of stories and other forms of shared meaning in later chapters. But this basic model of two people communicating is applicable everywhere and emphasizes how important our own behavior is in creating a safe atmosphere in which meaning can be shared satisfactorily.[22]

The Subjectivity of Danger

Staying in the safety zone is easier said than done, as is proven by the numerous arguments and conflicts we have all witnessed or been party to. Because our threat assessment systems operate below the level of conscious awareness, we are often the last to know our inner team has assessed the situation as dangerous. This would be challenging enough, but because of the way our brains work, we don't even need to encounter actual danger to trigger our fight-or-flight mode. Simply imagining or remembering a dangerous event will also do the trick. Danger, like beauty, is in the eye of the beholder.

Consider public speaking. For some people, the idea of having to stand up and speak in front of a large group is the stuff of their worst nightmares. Just thinking about standing in front of a crowd will trigger the stress response and have their hearts pounding and palms sweating. But for other people, this is not only an exciting opportunity, it is something so desirable they seek it out on a regular basis.

Even if there is an external trigger for our perceptions of danger, the mind, because of our ability to remember negative events from the past, has the ability to conflate the current trigger with those memories, thereby amplifying the intensity of the current experience. This ability to transform a relatively safe event into a dangerous one demonstrates how mind distance makes communication more challenging.

Distinguishing between our internal, subjective perceptions and the external, objective situation requires sensory clarity. This ability to distinguish between evidence and interpretation is a crucial part of being able to hit the pause button. It is also essential if we hope to understand the other person's point of view. Developing sensory clarity, a topic we will explore in chapter fourteen, enables us to see "just what is." This allows us to separate evidence from interpretation to avoid getting lost in our subjectivity.

For example, it counts as objective evidence if you see a person's brows furrow and the muscles of her face become more tense as she says, "Well, I'm not sure about that." It is evidence because it could be verified by anyone watching a recording of this event. But to say "she was angry," "she got upset about what I said," or, "she got scared when she heard what I said" are interpretations. These attributions may or may not be true, but if all observers don't come to the same conclusion, chances are we are dealing, to one degree or another, with a subjective interpretation, and subjective interpretations are at the heart of all mind distance.

This distinction between subjective and objective is represented on the social motor with squares representing objective evidence, i.e., those objective behaviors that can be seen, heard, or felt by any human present. In contrast, the ovals represent the subjective points of view, i.e., interpretations of what the objective behaviors mean for a particular individual.

One does not need to go to an exotic culture to see how subjective our threat assessment systems can be. In recent years, great advances have been made in understanding how past experiences influence our perceptions in general and the triggering of the threat assessment system in particular. We saw this in chapter two with Bruce's flashback. We now know people with histories of trauma can have their fight, flight, or freeze reactions triggered by common, everyday incidents. Such people easily take offense and over-react, becoming angry, frozen in terror, or filled with debilitating shame. These reactions push them out of their window of tolerance and their behavior can become erratic and dysfunctional. As Bessel van der Kolk, the medical director of the Trauma Center in Boston and a leading researcher on posttraumatic stress, describes it, "Minor irritations easily turn into catastrophes; small failures of communication are difficult to gloss over and easily turn into dramatic interpersonal conflicts."[23]

The point is this: No matter what the objective situation, subjective experiences of that situation will differ based on the interaction of a person's temperament and past experiences. No matter how extreme or normal a situation may seem to you, the other person is having a different experience. As a result, a situation or behavior that seems safe to you may be interpreted by the other as dangerous, triggering the release of stress hormones with all their physiological and psychological effects.

Conclusion

Testing our assumptions about objective events as well as our subjective interpretations of them is essential for intercultural success. One way to make our brain maps more accurate is to use universal dimensions to develop an overview of cultural differences and the underlying mind distance. Another approach is to study particular cultures in depth to get more details about the specifics of those cultures. This approach allows us to see a culture in the way an insider might. A third, more intuitive approach, is to focus on the actual lived experience of the other person.

If "test all assumptions" is a primary guideline for intercultural success, then safety first, truth second, has three distinct advantages: First, it is universal and works everywhere on the planet. Second, it gives us clear goals to aim for. If we can keep the atmosphere safe and the social engagement system activated, we can talk about almost anything. Third, it gives us a reliable way to bridge the language barrier. The body and the limbic system do not lie. Unless you are dealing with a sociopath or a trained actor, the average person is broadcasting reliable signals all the time about whether she is feeling safe or not. We only need learn how to read them. Learning to read these signals is not that difficult and the rewards will last you a lifetime.

While there is much we still do not know about the workings of the brain and the complexities of the stress response, there is no question the autonomic nervous system plays a major role in the black box of the mind. What current research makes ever clearer is that our emotions play a central role in all our thoughts, actions, and relationships. When we get emotionally hijacked, the integrity of our inner teams disintegrates, causing our behavior to become less than optimal. Promoting safety—both for ourselves and for the other—will increase the likelihood of the social motor moving in a more productive direction.

Being aware of how mind distance can make the same situation seem different to other people is a first step in creating more safety. While the mind distance between any two points of view may be large, it is not infinite and it is not random. When we can see the underlying patterns of meaning and take the other person's point of view into account, we can avoid getting emotionally hijacked and head off the reactive behaviors that could make a bad situation worse. Taking the other's point of view is a great bridge of mind distance, but it is hard to empathize when separated by moral judgments. This is a challenge for people everywhere because, as we will see in the next chapter, the social order is also a moral order.

Six

Danger and the Social Order

Morality binds and blinds. It binds us into ideological teams that fight each other as though the fate of the world depended on our side winning each battle. It blinds us to the fact that each team is composed of good people who have something important to say.

—Jonathan Haidt

Think of a person reaching into a bowl of finger food at a dinner party. Hardly a dangerous event. Or is it? Now imagine this person uses his left hand to reach for the food. In many parts of the world where people eat with their hands, India for example, a person is expected to use only his right hand when eating because the left hand is considered the "toilet hand." So you can imagine the strong visceral reactions triggered in the Indians who are present when a left-handed American uses his dominant hand to reach into the food.

From the hapless American's perspective, he has done his best to respect his Indian hosts by using his hand to eat. But because the use of the left hand is now common for most activities in the United States, he didn't notice all the Indians at the table were using only their right hands. If he had been more attentive, he might also have noticed a series of clear nonverbal signals coursing among the Indians indicating all was not well: Noses were wrinkled, eyebrows raised, and glances exchanged. Needless to say, none of the Indians partook of any more food from that bowl. What the unfortunate American may also not realize is how his behavior changed the context for the Indians. What had been a safe situation, a pleasant dinner party with an honored foreign guest, had now become an invasion by an uncouth barbarian. Our threat assessment systems evolved to protect us from physical dangers, but threats to our self-esteem can set off the alarm just as loudly. So can threats to our world views and the social orders we live in.

Social Order and Morality

Social structures are used by cultures around the world to organize the division of labor, share resources, and manage power. At the same time, the boundaries of these social structures are marked, enacted, and enforced using, among other things, notions of purity.[1] For example, in India, a large, diverse country where hundreds of languages are spoken, the relationships between different social groups is regulated by a wealth of rules and rituals. This is important to remember because the following example is not meant to be representative of India as a whole. It is just one example of how threats to our socially constructed world views can be interpreted as dangerous.

The Havik Brahmins are the dominant caste in many regions of Karnataka State in southern India. They recognize three degrees of purity:[2] The highest is necessary for worship and performing religious acts. The second is the normal level that can be expected in everyday life, while the lowest is a state of impurity. Contact with someone in a lower state will automatically cause a person to drop into that state. The only way to attain the highest state of purity is by bathing, and a daily bath is essential for a Havik Brahmin so he may worship his gods. Traditional Haviks believe three baths per day would be ideal.

Haviks also observe strict dietary rules to avoid states of impurity. For instance, they distinguish between cooked and uncooked food because cooked food can more easily contaminate their purity while uncooked food does not. As a result, an upper caste person may receive uncooked food from members of any caste without fear of pollution or defilement. This rule is most practical as it reflects the division of labor in the community where the lower castes tend to be the farmers. Similarly, fruits and nuts, as long as they are whole, do not mar one's purity, but if a coconut is broken or a plantain cut, a Havik cannot accept it from a member of a lower caste.

This is just one of the complex set of moral rules traditional Haviks use to create social order. Other Havik rules of purity relate to menstruation, birth, death, food, leather, social contacts, and bodily fluids including blood, pus, and saliva.[3] Many of these rules contain elements related to what people in the West consider hygiene, so it is easy to understand why they would be interpreted as impure or dangerous. But other rules are symbolic of the Havik's cultural history and moral order. Because they relate to maintaining a certain social structure, these rules inform a Havik's intuitive interpretation of any given context as pure or impure, safe or dangerous.

Order and Purity in the West

Modern Westerners, when they hear about such customs, often view them as superstitious and backward, failing to see how these rules are also ways of creating and maintaining a moral and social order. Missing their symbolic value, it's easy to dismiss them as irrelevant. But a good interculturalist would say, "Not so fast." Strong codes of purity and its close relative, honor, were ubiquitous in Western cultures before modern hygiene made them archaic. Today in the West such codes of purity seem to have disappeared or be dying a quick death. Or are they?

In fact, secular cultures often use a sense of purity to create social order. While individuals often think their actions are functional and rational, believing them to be based on medical science, upon closer examination we can see they are more social, moral, and symbolic in nature. Think this does not apply to you? Then try a few experiments: Next time you are getting ready for a formal social event, try wearing washed, but wrinkled garments. How do you feel among all the other guests who are wearing neatly pressed clothes? Your clothes are washed, so from both rational and functional points of view, they are as clean as everyone else's. So why do you feel so odd? And why do the others keep staring at you?

While some people may not be troubled by wearing wrinkled clothing to a social gathering, others would just as soon show up naked. This demonstrates why paying close attention to the other person's nonverbal signals is one of the best ways to determine how safe a context seems to him. Learning to read nonverbal signals is an invaluable skill for an interculturalist, and is not just limited to body language, tone of voice, and facial expressions. It also includes the way people wear their clothes and maintain their property. Learning to read these clues can give you important insights into a person's belief system.

For instance, are you the type of person whose house is so clean you could eat off the floor? Would you ever do that? What about washing your dinner dishes in the bathtub? Or how about washing your hands in that gleaming, disinfected toilet bowl? Are you feeling a little disgusted, anxious, or irritated right now? Does it seem like even asking these questions is somehow wrong or dangerous? Some people will even feel anxiety just having their pajamas scattered around their living room because of the unpleasant sense of disorder this creates, plus the worry of what others might think.

Now, run this thought experiment in the other direction: Next time you are cleaning and tidying up your house, notice if you don't get a pleasant sense of mastery and control. Do you have a subtle sense of safety, or perhaps feel you are a better person with your house now clean and ready to receive guests? Speaking of mastery and control, if you have a maid, does it make you feel better to have someone else do the dirty work? Do you feel higher in the social hierarchy, and thus a better, more valuable person? Maybe even closer to God? Where *did* the idea that cleanliness is next to godliness come from in the first place?

Not only do rituals, customs, and beliefs replicate and reflect a group's social order, the same social order is also reflected in the group's language. Consider the different ways the English word "dirty" is used in metaphorical constructions having nothing to do with actual dirt, soil, dust, grease, or grime. Unscrupulous people play dirty tricks on others and good people retaliate by giving bad people dirty looks. Crooks have piles of dirty money which they must launder. People who are indiscrete with other's secrets are said to be airing dirty laundry, and people whose hands are clean have clear consciences. If not, they may have to come clean and fess up in public, like Lance Armstrong and our other folk heroes who turn out to be less virtuous than we had hoped.

Kicking someone in the privates—the off-limits area of our bodies many people find disgusting—is fighting dirty. Perverts have dirty thoughts and people with dirty minds like to tell dirty jokes and enjoy watching dirty movies. They also tend to curse and use dirty words when talking. Prostitutes are dirty while virgins are pure and unblemished, which they signify by wearing white wedding gowns—a color that in the West signifies purity and cleanliness.

Of course white-collar workers are of higher social status than blue-collar workers, who may get their hands dirty when working. Need it be said that high-status places in our culture tend to be clean and neat, whereas impoverished and lower-status areas tend to be dirty and disorderly? Cleanliness may be next to godliness, but in the social structures we live in, cleanliness resides next to formal power and the areas where high status people live, work, and socialize. In short, symbolic dirt and cleanliness play a far more pervasive role in our society than just functional disease avoidance. They are also interwoven with issues of power, morality, and social control.

This brief exploration of purity and danger in India and the United States is just one example of how meaning and morality shape our social worlds. There are other important fields of meaning we could explore, and they are all potential entry points into understanding cultural differences. As we saw in chapter four, cultures are contexts that function like force fields to constrain and guide us. These force fields are constructed of, among other things, moral meaning, and this meaning permeates and structures our lives, just as gravity permeates and structures the very planet on which we live.

Many people are too busy just surviving to stop and reflect upon the deeper layers of meaning and morality in which they are embedded. Others are unwilling to do so for fear of the consequences it might have for their lives. While successful interculturalists must explore these fields of meaning to do their job well, anyone who wants to reduce stress when communicating with people who are different would do well to understand that social orders are also moral orders. At first glance, these fields of meaning and morality can seem arbitrary, but upon closer examination we discover a logic to their shapes and functions. As powerful as our minds and imaginations are, they are, to one degree or another, anchored in and constrained by the physical world in which we live and by the biology of our bodies. Put simply, meaning is embodied.

Purity's Humble Origin

Antonio Damasio points out that the concept of purity is derived from the emotion of disgust.[4] Disgust's biological purpose is to protect us from putting things into our mouths that might contaminate us and make us ill, such as rancid foods. But like many of nature's other good inventions, disgust was found to be so valuable, its use has been broadened through the centuries into one of our main moral emotions. Our brains use these emotions to help us know what is good or bad and right or wrong, and thus to protect the social order.

In his masterpiece, *On the Process of Civilization*, the sociologist Norbert Elias documents the evolution of manners in post-medieval Europe. He not only shows how disgust and shame were transformed into powerful social emotions, he also shows how these emotions were used to encourage more self-restraint. In short, behaviors that elicited disgust and embarrassment on the part of those with higher social status began to be avoided by the lower classes, thus reinforcing the social order.[5]

Further evidence for the role of disgust as a social emotion comes from research showing that our notions of what is considered unfair are also related to the emotion of disgust.[6] These notions influence the way a society structures itself and distributes its resources, so it is significant that the part of the brain being activated when we are confronted with something we consider unfair is the same part of the brain that lights up when we are revolted. This part of the brain, called the insula, is a part of the limbic system, a major player on our inner team.

In recent years, Jonathan Haidt and other social psychologists have been busy exploring the role social emotions play in our intuitive judgments about ourselves and others. Because disgust is a basic emotion in all humans, we should not be surprised that purity, which Haidt refers to as Sanctity/Degradation, emerged as one of the five original modules in his Moral Foundations Theory.[7]

People, places, and events considered dirty, impure, or contaminated tend to trigger disgust in people and, by extension, are felt to be bad, wrong, and even dangerous. Just as disgust encourages us not to put contaminated food into our bodies, it also encourages us to avoid and exclude people and things considered dirty and impure. In contrast, those things considered clean and pure are judged to be good, safe, and even sacred.

As Haidt shows, such social and moral intuitions guide us, letting us know how to behave by trusting our feelings.[8] Such body-based intuitions have a sense of naturalness and rightness about them that is impossible to dislodge with rational arguments alone. While these intuitions are linked with innate universal emotions—babies everywhere will spit food out that does not taste good—they are given their final form by the cultural context in which we grow up.

In other words, we humans were, and are, emotional beings first who then went on to develop language and logic, enabling us to think and behave rationally. We are not bodiless, rational beings who just happen to be plagued by the occasional emotion when someone steps on our toes. When we ignore the visceral emotionality of the other's intuitions, we are far more likely to behave in a way that denies his experience, and denying the other's experience is one of the best ways I know to trigger that person's stress response.

Denying the Other's Experience

Not only can we trigger the other's stress response by denying his experience, we are also lessening the chances he will consider, or even listen to, our message. For this reason, "safety first" is an essential guide for interculturalists. By taking care to notice if what you are doing or saying is causing the other person discomfort, you are laying the foundation for a mutually satisfying conversation. By respecting the other person's boundaries and belief system, you will be creating the safety he needs to engage with you. This allows you to begin building the trust a healthy relationship requires.

But how exactly does one respect the other? The starting place is in your mind. If your intention is to create a mutually beneficial situation—that is, to create a win-win situation—you are off to a good start. But when our own beliefs and boundaries do not accord with those of the other person, a delicate balancing act ensues. The amount of animosity in the world proves balancing the need for self-respect and respect for the other is no easy undertaking. But a useful general principle is this: Denying the other person's experience is a sure way to stop the social motor from moving towards safety. Unless you occupy a formal position of authority over the other person, any denial of his experience will tend to be perceived as a personal attack and trigger a stress response.

Safety must be created both verbally and nonverbally. If we want the other person to listen to what we are saying, we need to use words that accord with his or her experiences. For example, it is well and good to talk about how an issue like global warming is going to affect the planet and how some of the low-lying islands and coastal regions are going to be under water, causing great hardship and social turmoil for the people living there. This argument will appeal to people living in low-lying coastal areas. It will also appeal to people who have compassion towards people everywhere, but it will not be persuasive to someone who is ethnocentric and concerned only about the members of his own culture who live in a mountainous region. Developing trust with this person requires framing your words in accord with his world view and experiences.

But safety is not created by word choice alone. The fight-or-flight response is even more likely to be triggered by a harsh tone of voice or angry stare, so both your words and your body must communicate an attitude of respect and concern for the other person. This attitude of respect is a first step towards creating the safety necessary for the growth of trust.

For example, if you find yourself becoming contemptuous, a close relative to disgust, you can rest assured you are also sending nonverbal signals affecting the other person in a negative manner, slowing the movement of the social motor towards safety. Disgust and contempt are powerful, toxic emotions and hard to disguise unless you are an excellent actor. When they leak out, they can easily poison a relationship. According to John Gottman, professor emeritus of psychology and famous for his research on marital stability, "Contempt is closely related to disgust, and what disgust and contempt are about is completely rejecting and excluding someone from the community."[9]

Gottman has spent many years studying married couples and he has shown that frequent expressions of contempt are one of the best predictors of divorce. Contempt is so corrosive it can even weaken the immune system, predicting the number of colds couples will experience.[10] When we are contemptuous of others, we put ourselves above them and treat them as something disgusting. In so doing, we deny their experience and exclude them from our lives in the same way we exclude food by spitting it out. It is no surprise feelings of disgust and hatred go hand in hand.

One reason disgust and contempt have a destructive influence in our social worlds may be because the brain processes feelings of disgust in a different area from other emotions. Lasana Harris and Susan Fiske studied the brains of Americans as they viewed photos of different social groups.[11] Depending on what groups they viewed, different emotions were triggered: Pride at seeing American Olympic athletes, envy when observing rich people, and pity when viewing elderly people. All of these emotions were associated with activity in the medial prefrontal cortex (MPFC), an area active during social encounters. But when they viewed photos of drug addicts, which elicited feelings of disgust, the MPFC was not activated. Instead, the brain activation patterns were the same as when they viewed inanimate objects, such as a rock. This suggests feeling disgust towards a person or group is a form of dehumanization.

Treating people as objects devoid of feeling denies our common humanity and creates dangerous contexts, first for those who are dehumanized, and then for all involved. Denying the other's experience will almost always be perceived as a form of disrespect and will almost certainly trigger a stress response. In his disturbing and insightful book, *Violence*, James Gilligan, a former director of the Center for the Study of Violence at Harvard Medical School, shows that the perception of being disrespected is one of the strongest triggers for violence.[12] According to Gilligan, "The first lesson that tragedy teaches (and that morality plays miss) is that all violence is an attempt to achieve justice, or what the violent person perceives as justice..."[13]

When others treat us as objects, they disrespect us and we tend to feel shame and loss of honor, both of which we perceive not only as unjust, but also as dangerous. When we treat others as objects, we do the same to them. A common response to this sort of injustice is to seek revenge. Unfortunately, in our attempts to right a perceived wrong, we often overreact and use more force than necessary. Nothing gets the social motor accelerating towards the danger pole faster than excessive use of force. One of the best ways to hit the pause button and avoid overreacting is to remember trust is a verb, and to trust or not to trust is a choice.

Trust Is a Verb

If you are not successful at creating safety for the other, you will tend to trigger aloofness or polite resistance at best, and conflict at worst. One of the hallmarks of conflict the world over is that both sides blame the other for their impasse. Remember, whenever you are communicating with someone else, you are part of the context for that person. As we saw in chapter four, people tend to justify their bad behavior by blaming it on external forces. Using the social motor model, here's one common example of what that looks like:

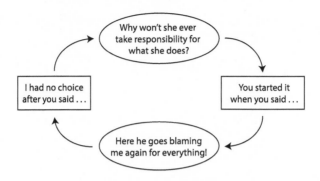

Figure 6.1 — The Blame Game

This is the archetypal blame game and we all played it as children. While this may seem childish to our adult minds, it is surprising how many times this kind of thinking is occurring behind polite exteriors in the form of passive-aggressive resistance that ends up hurting both parties. As we will see in the next chapter, the blame game gets played in ever more sophisticated forms among adults. But even among the smartest and most successful the defensive dynamics underlying the blame game are more emotional than rational. When the blame game is played with skill, neither side seems to be able to break the stalemate and so it continues, frustrating both sides and draining their emotional energy.

To trust means to assume the other's intention is good. In so doing, I encourage my inner team to view the situation as safe and to feel relaxed. This allows me to promote good will between us, which will then encourage the social motor to move towards the safety pole. Trusting the other often means giving him the benefit of the doubt when a misunderstanding causes the social motor to stall.

One leader of an international work team I was helping exemplified this approach. After a painful start in international business, he grew to realize how deep and widespread cultural differences were and how they could affect morale in both subtle and dramatic ways. After his initial learning experience, whenever there was a disconnect between members of his multicultural team, he would assume a cultural misunderstanding was occurring and seek to discover its roots. In many cases his assumption was correct and he was able to soothe the ruffled feathers of his team by clarifying their different expectations.

Of course, culture was not always the real issue and he was not a pushover. Sometimes he had to use other measures to resolve the situation, including holding people accountable for their errors and bad habits. But his initial assumption of good intent did wonders to get the team's social motors turning in the right direction. By assuming all members' intentions were good, he was able to trust them and help create an atmosphere of safety and openness. In this regard, he was different from several of his peers who were not as aware of the role of cultural differences and who did not trust their team members as much. Because of his assumption of good intent and willingness to trust, he was able to solve many challenges that were confounding his peers.

In essence, a useful principle to create safety is to start by assuming the other's intentions are good and to act in accordance with that assumption. I am not advocating naïve openness in a world where predators are lurking. But I am advocating against a fear-based, one-size-fits-all policy founded upon ignorance, prejudice, or the assumption that win-win solutions are fairy tales.

Conclusion

The eminent cultural anthropologist, Clifford Geertz, is famous for his remark that "Man is an animal suspended in webs of significance he himself has spun."[14] Geertz was right, we do spin the webs of significance in which we are suspended, but we do not spin them from thin air, nor do we spin them randomly. The foundation upon which we construct our social worlds and the meaning they have for us is embodied in our very biology. As we saw in chapter two, memory is a constructive process, but it is also a process predisposed to learn some things more easily than others. Because of our innate predispositions, it is easier to learn to fear snakes than orchids. This does not mean we can't learn to see the beauty of a snake. We can. It is, however, less common to see beauty in things we fear, which implies meaning is neither random, nor arbitrary.

Some emotions—love, empathy, contempt, disgust, shame, etc.—have evolved to become moral emotions that both guide individual behaviors and structure our societies by regulating our interactions. Of these, contempt is a strong, corrosive emotion that can increase hatred and trigger violence. When we become contemptuous towards others, it is easy to deny their humanity. When we do, we prime the social motor to move towards danger and bad things become more likely to happen.

One effective way to create more safety in a relationship is to assume the other's intentions are honorable. When a misunderstanding occurs, this assumption is even more important because it enables us to hit the pause button and remind ourselves of the immense variety of human subjectivity. When we take into account the degree of mind distance that may be separating us, we are using mindsight to avoid overreacting and making a bad situation worse.

Because we are emotional beings who are susceptible to confirmation bias and self-deception, safety first is only the first half of our mantra. We also need methods to discern whether our brain maps and our perceptions are accurate. Truth second is the remaining half of this important mantra, and it is to that half we now turn.

Seven

Truth Second

Our ineffective decisions are based on illusions we believe at the time. Our effective decisions are built on realities we recognize. That is why it is useful to ask ourselves probing questions to help us distinguish illusion from reality.

—Spencer Johnson

When I first met him, Mitch was optimistic about his new challenge.[1] He had just been hired by a large corporation to become the leader of their research and development team. This team had members located around the world, including in the United States, Germany, Slovakia, and China. He had little experience working internationally, but the multicultural makeup of his team was only part of his challenge.

Members of the department in Germany were still up in arms at the way the previous team leader, an American like Mitch, had ridden roughshod over them. In fact, they were talking openly about his unethical and, from their perspective, illegal practices. So not only did Mitch have to develop his intercultural skills fast, he also had to soothe the ire of the Germans who were upset at having another American manager.

Although Mitch had succeeded at tough assignments before, he was caught off guard by the open resistance he encountered in his first meeting with the Germans. They made it quite clear they were not happy with the situation. Luckily, he was not alone in that first meeting and the human resources representative, also a German, helped him keep the meeting on track.

When Mitch contacted me, I was impressed by his desire to learn and his sense of fairness. I agreed to deliver cross-cultural workshops to team members in the United States and Germany as well as to work one-on-one with Mitch.

Defensive Reasoning

In our first coaching sessions we explored the challenges he faced. My main goal was to help him develop the cultural awareness, mindsight, and flexibility he would need to succeed. Two challenges quickly became apparent.

First, although Mitch was sincere in wanting to be fair to all members of the team, he did not realize how ethnocentric his point of view was. To make matters worse, he found the very idea he might be biased so disturbing that when I initially pointed it out, he became defensive. My assurances that we are all biased did little to reduce his internal dissonance. Because of his reaction, I chose to back off and create more safety. I would return to the issue of his biases later.

Second, Mitch was not good at listening to people whose points of view called his own into question. Dr. Chris Argyris, a former professor at Harvard University and a pioneer in the field of organizational development, showed that it's often the smartest people who have the most difficulty in listening to constructive criticism.[2] That's because the smarter they are, the more adept they are at defensive reasoning. They can quickly think up a plausible reason why the other person's critique is not worth listening to. If what Argyris calls defensive reasoning sounds similar to the self-justification and self-deception we explored in chapter three, that's because it is.

Not all smart people are successful, but Argyris said those who are both smart and successful face a second hurdle to learning from criticism because they tend to generate much of their self-esteem from their achievements. As a result, they are often poor at managing the painful feelings, such as fear and shame, that failure can trigger. To avoid these negative feelings, they interpret even well-intended criticism as a threat to their self-esteem and use defensive reasoning to protect themselves.

At its simplest, defensive reasoning is believing our own stories while finding reasons to discount facts that contradict those stories. It's easy to see why defensive reasoning often turns into self-deception. Seen from this perspective, sincerity may be no more than our self-serving ability to believe our own stories. Because beliefs are powerful and impact our actions, it is crucial for our own well-being and for those we associate with that the stories we believe be true. Unfortunately, this is not always the case.

Brains Are Story Tellers

Like all mammals, humans eat, drink, sleep, fight, play, procreate, and so on. But only humans tell stories about what they did and why. Sitting around a fire and telling stories about the day's adventures has probably been part of the human experience for as long as we could talk. As Goethe wrote, "We must plunge into experience and then reflect on the meaning of it. All reflection and no plunging drives us mad; all plunging and no reflection, and we are brutes."[3]

Stories, then, are far more than entertaining narratives we use to while away the hours. They also help our brains organize our experiences and form our identities. By weaving knowledge, beliefs, and values into a larger whole, our personal stories help us explain and understand ourselves and the world around us. By linking cause and effect with the passing of time, stories help create more comprehensive, easy-to-remember brain maps to classify and understand our experiences. Because our personal stories incorporate memories of our actual experiences, they are laden with emotional meaning.

When groups tell stories, they are creating meaning that can be used both to develop a common identity and to create a shared world view. By telling stories and passing them from one generation to the next, this shared meaning becomes part of a group's social capital.

Because stories are so central for both individuals and groups, we need to understand how the brain uses stories if we are to develop more mindsight. To start, only part of our inner team tells stories. We now know the brain's two hemispheres, the left and right, process information differently.[4] While the idea of hemispheric differences has sometimes been over-simplified, psychologists and neuroscientists agree that the right hemisphere is specialized at processing visual and spatial information, as well as in recognizing complex perceptual patterns. In contrast, the left hemisphere is where the language-processing capabilities we use to tell our stories reside.

Dr. Michael Gazzaniga, a professor of psychology at the University of California in Santa Barbara and one of the first researchers to study split-brain patients, refers to the left hemisphere's story-telling capacity as the "interpreter."[5] The interpreter in the left hemisphere is continually receiving information from other members of the inner team responsible for processing visual, somatosensory, emotional, and cognitive information.[6] When the information the interpreter receives is complete and accurate, the stories it tells tend to be accurate. When it receives misleading or incomplete information, its stories can be quite fanciful, as illustrated by the following example.

To prevent severe epileptic seizures, split-brain patients have had their corpus callosum, the connection between the left and right brain hemispheres, surgically separated. Once the corpus callosum is severed, the two hemispheres become like two separate brains and cannot share information. In one classic experiment, a split-brain patient was shown two pictures.[7] One picture of a chicken claw was presented so only the left hemisphere saw it. The other picture of a snow scene was presented so only the right hemisphere saw it.

The patient was then asked to choose from a group of pictures placed so that both hemispheres could see them. The left hand, which is controlled by the right hemisphere, chose a shovel, which was appropriate for the snow scene. The right hand, controlled by the left hemisphere, chose a picture of a chicken, appropriate for the chicken claw.

The patient was then asked to explain why he chose those items. The right hemisphere, having no access to linguistic abilities, could not answer. But the interpreter in the left hemisphere replied, "Oh, that's simple. The chicken claw goes with the chicken." Given that the left hemisphere had seen the chicken claw, this was perfectly logical. So far, so good. The interpreter did a good job of explaining the patient's actions. But then, looking down and seeing the left hand holding the picture of the shovel, the interpreter, without missing a beat, said, "And you need a shovel to clean out the chicken shed."

Brains and Uncertainty

Thus the interpreter, without having any knowledge as to why the left hand was holding a picture of the shovel, immediately confabulated a plausible explanation. Notice that it did not state the obvious, i.e., that the interpreter did not have a clue why the left hand was holding a picture of a shovel. Uncertainty and ambiguity are challenging for some members of our inner teams, and one thing the left hemisphere rarely says is, "I don't know." Instead, it gets creative. The story-teller in the left hemisphere takes whatever information it has and improvises the rest, creating a story that makes sense according to what it already knows.

Stories told by the interpreter are only as good as the information they receive from other members of the inner team, and often these other modules in the brain send only their conclusions, not the data they used to reach those conclusions. The interpreter tries to make sense of those conclusions. Often it does a good job, but not always. Antonio Damasio puts it this way, "Perhaps the most important revelation in human split-brain research is precisely this: that the left cerebral hemisphere of humans is prone to fabricating verbal narratives that do not necessarily accord with the truth."[8] Or, as Jonathan Haidt puts it more metaphorically: "Then, when faced with a social demand for a verbal justification, one becomes a lawyer trying to build a case rather than a judge searching for the truth."[9]

This tendency of our brains to prefer internal consonance and the sense of certainty provided by a well-told story rather than recognize our fallibility is ubiquitous. Consider a classical experiment conducted by Baruch Fischhoff and Ruth Beyeth at Hebrew University in Jerusalem in the 1970s.[10] The researchers asked students if Nixon would call on Mao Zedong during his upcoming visit to China and if Nixon would view his historic trip as a success. They recorded the students' answers.

After the trip had taken place and faded from coverage in the press, the researchers asked the same students how well they predicted the events. When the predictive and postdictive responses were compared, Fischhoff and Beyeth discovered students who had made erroneous predictions had altered their memories to match reality.

Our brain's capacity to change itself, or neuroplasticity, gives us the ability to learn and adapt to a changing environment, but as this study shows, memory is not infallible and the stories we tell ourselves not always reliable. This study is only one of many that show our brains find ways to discredit information and experiences that would otherwise generate uncertainty or cognitive dissonance, a tendency that increases the older we get.[11]

The brain also has the ability to create memories from imagined events and then confuse these memories with reality. For instance, in a 2002 study done by Dr. James Ost and his colleagues at the University of Portsmouth in the United Kingdom, people were asked about the death of Princess Diana.[12] In particular, whether they had seen video footage of the fatal car crash in which Princess Diana, Dodi Fayed, and their driver all perished. Forty-four percent of those questioned claimed to have seen the footage on television, even though no such video exists.

Had I read these studies when I was in my twenties and far more arrogant than I am today, I suspect I would have dismissed them as irrelevant. Yes, I would have said, that may be true for others, but my memory has served me well and I'm convinced of its reliability. In retrospect, I see this attitude as part of a belief system I had constructed to protect me from psychological distress and dissonance. That belief system allowed me to maintain my identity and stay within my window of tolerance when ambiguity, uncertainty, or disagreements arose.

My window of tolerance was reinforced by the pleasurable sense of certainty I derived from believing my memories were accurate, but I paid a price for this pleasure. Not only did my desire to remain within my window of tolerance keep me from developing more mindsight, it also caused unnecessary disagreements with others. Recognizing that both my memory and the story-teller in my brain are not infallible has introduced more uncertainty into my life, but it has also helped me broaden my window of tolerance and see situations, events, and people from multiple perspectives. This has translated into an increased ability to listen to others with a more open mind.

Uncertainty and dissonance are unpleasant for most of us. In fact, for some people uncertainty and dissonance can activate the brain's threat assessment system, shifting a person into fight-or-flight mode. In short, we have a self-serving bias towards believing what we already believe, i.e., the confirmation bias, and we are likely to take a dismissing attitude towards new information that contradicts our beliefs or world view. This mutually reinforcing tendency of previous beliefs and stories to influence our current perceptions, and vice-versa, looks like this:

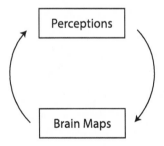

Figure 7.1 — Confirmation Bias

Examining Our Stories

Our brains are continually trying to balance two contradictory needs: On the one hand, they need to have accurate maps of their reality if they are to survive. Any early human who tried to pet a tiger probably did not survive long enough to leave a family. On the other hand, our desire for the pleasurable feelings of certainty and a coherent view of the world encourages us to discount information that causes doubt or calls our views into question. As a result, we are all prone to confirmation bias and defensive reasoning.

Knowing this, I took great pains to listen empathically to Mitch and to create safety. I concentrated first on the problems his team was having rather than on how his own views were contributing to those problems. Because he was based in Chicago, he spent most of his time talking to the other Americans on his team. Being an American himself, he intuitively sympathized with their complaints about associates at the other sites. This headquarters-periphery dynamic and his lack of experience living and working outside the United States conspired to reinforce his ethnocentric point of view. Being unable to speak any other language than English did not help matters.

Our brains' desire to maintain consistency in our beliefs is not our only bias. Humans everywhere tend to trust the views and claims of their friends, relatives, and allies while taking a more skeptical stance towards the claims of outsiders.[13] While this bias promotes social cohesion and reduces in-group conflict, it also has other consequences: We often jump to conclusions because we tend to agree with people we like.

Because of our built-in biases and limited perceptions, all stories are told from a particular point of view. Just as we cannot see all sides of a mountain at the same time, so, too, no one point of view can tell the whole truth. If we want the whole truth, we must listen to all points of view. Even biased or subjective stories have something to teach us about the human condition. Naturally, some stories are more accurate and valuable than others.

Seeking and speaking the truth is important not only because we need to avoid dangers and satisfy our needs, it is also important because few things will destroy trust faster than dishonesty. So I listened carefully to Mitch, trying to create the safety he needed to open up and begin sharing some of his deeper concerns with me. To do this, I had to suspend the automatic judgments my inner team was generating and be as open and accepting as I could of whatever he said.

For instance, I chose to believe Mitch's claim about wanting to create a fair team where the playing field was level, regardless of what country a team member came from. My trust of Mitch on this matter grew when he authorized me to begin contacting team members to hear their points of view. The goal was to have me create a report Mitch could use to create a team policy that would reduce the trans-Atlantic conflict between the Germans and Americans. As I began understanding the views of the other team members, I began feeding that knowledge into my coaching sessions with Mitch in the form of questions.

The Power of Inquiry

While recent neuroscience research provides proof of the brain's inherent biases, people everywhere seem intuitively aware of this problem. All languages have grammars that allow them to ask questions and sages from East and West have developed explicit processes of inquiry to offset our brain's inherent biases. These processes can be used to liberate us from erroneous beliefs.

For example, ancient Greek philosophers concentrated on analyzing logical fallacies. Socrates is still famous for his skill at deflating fallacious arguments with probing questions. In ancient Japan, Zen masters devised a series of quirky questions called *koans* that were used to free their minds from limiting perceptions. By reflecting upon and inquiring into mental processes, these ancient thinkers created traditions we still admire and respect.

Asking questions to improve our lives continues today. The modern scientific enterprise is, at its heart, the creation of testable questions to help us understand our world and ourselves. This method has proved so successful in helping us understand our universe while improving our lives that its use has spread around the planet.

While the questions posed in the physical and life sciences focus on external reality, other disciplines use questions to explore the nature of our minds. For example, the work of Aaron Beck, professor emeritus of psychiatry at the University of Pennsylvania, has been instrumental in examining the distortions in our thinking that lead to emotional pain and suffering.[14] By inquiring into the thought processes of people suffering from depression, anxiety, and other symptoms, Beck was able to map different types of distorted thinking in a systematic way. By showing his patients how to change their distorted thinking, he helped many of them gain relief from their suffering. Today, this method of dealing with distorted thinking is known as cognitive therapy, and it is one of the most successful approaches to treating many psychological problems.

What unites Greek philosophers, Zen masters, modern scientists, cognitive therapists, and the many others who have tapped into the power of inquiry is a simple but powerful fact: Asking questions is a way to focus our attention and focused attention enables people to improve their brain maps so they are more accurate.[15] No one knows exactly why it works, but the evidence shows that focal attention can restructure neural connections in the brain and thus retrain our inner team. In short, we can train our brains to "jump to better conclusions."

Retraining Intuition

Using inquiry and focal attention to retrain our intuition can be likened to driving to work. Most people drive to work the same way each day. Generally, this works well enough. Because we are on auto-pilot with the inner team doing the driving, we can listen to the radio, hold a conversation, or think about a pressing problem and then arrive at work with little memory of the actual trip we took to get there. This is one of the great values of our inner team: It carries out routine tasks over and over again in an almost effortless manner with little need of supervision. In the same way, our inner team follows habitual patterns when thinking and communicating. That is, we use the same time-tested ways of communicating because they work well and use fewer precious resources.

But imagine you are on your way to work and an unexpected traffic jam occurs. You could wait it out and follow your normal route to work. Or, you could focus your attention, reflect upon other possible routes, and decide to take an alternative path. To navigate the new route you will need to concentrate. This requires attention on your part, but it helps you avoid the traffic jam.

In the same way, using inquiry to focus our attention and examine our usual ways of thinking isn't necessary if things are going fine. If things aren't broke, why fix them? But if we are encountering problems in our lives, using inquiry to examine our thinking is a powerful way to get things back on the right track. Inquiry gives us the power to retrain our intuitions so our lives can become more satisfying.

Now imagine a further development. After the traffic jam caused you to get off auto-pilot and change your normal way to work, you discover that this alternative route has less traffic and you get to work quicker than usual. Or maybe it is more scenic, or has some other advantage you didn't know about. So you decide to take this new route to work every day. At first you have to concentrate to make sure you are on the right road. But then, lo and behold, after using your new route for a few days, your inner team will have internalized it and you will again find yourself driving to work as effortlessly as you had before the traffic accident. This is the power of inquiry. It allows us to change old ways of thinking so we can develop better habits.

The power of inquiry to focus our attention can be used in almost any field of human endeavor. Take, for instance, athletic performance. If a tennis player is consistently hitting her forehand into the net, an astute observer might notice it is because the player is turning her wrist too much as she swings. This observer might be tempted to begin telling the player what to do: Don't turn your wrist so much as you swing. This might help, but a more effective tactic is to ask the player specific questions to direct her attention to the problematic movement: When you hit your forehand, how are you turning your wrist?

Such skillful questions direct the brain's inner team to not only notice the problematic behavior, but also to connect that behavior with its results, in this case, where the ball lands. This sets up an internal feedback loop and, as the player directs her awareness more attentively on the problematic movement, an amazing thing starts to happen. She hits the ball into the net less often.

Neuroscientists now believe learning can take place at any point in life. By consciously intending to improve and then focusing our attention on our feelings, thoughts, and behaviors, we speed up this natural process. It does not happen overnight. But if we practice on a regular basis, we will notice our inner team responding to challenges more effectively and efficiently. Continuity is essential. Speaking metaphorically, you must use the new route to work every day until the inner team has fully internalized it. Only then will you get the effortless flow of behavior we all seek.

The Power of Belief

Our brains are continually generating thoughts over the course of a day and we tend to act on those thoughts we believe. When we believe things that are not true, we suffer. For instance, beliefs in sorcery are common to many cultures and are used to explain why illness, death, and bad events occur. Such beliefs are common throughout the world, and Papua New Guinea is no exception. Citing media reports, Amnesty International states that fifty people accused of witchcraft in Papua New Guinea were murdered there in 2008. Some of them were burned alive.[16]

The consequences of beliefs about sorcery in Papua New Guinea may be extreme, but all beliefs exert an influence on the social realties we live in. This was true for Mitch and the rest of his team. What he needed to learn was not to believe every thought his culturally conditioned mind was generating. When we uncritically believe our thoughts, we run the risk of confusing our brain maps with reality. Many times our maps and reality are similar enough and our lives go smoothly. But when our maps and reality differ, we run into problems.

As we will see in later chapters, groups use stories to promote cooperation among group members. Among these stories are those about the group's history and its positive qualities that children internalize during the process of enculturation. Often these stories are ethnocentric in perspective, portraying the group's way of life as more positive and valuable than that of other groups.

Because of his lack of experience outside the United States, Mitch's ethnocentric beliefs were influencing his attitudes towards the Europeans on his team. He needed to better understand their points of view if he was going to communicate with them more effectively. I began presenting their beliefs and perceptions in the form of questions so Mitch could reflect upon them.

I started by asking him why he thought the Germans were so unrelenting in their resistance towards him. He attributed their resistance to the abusive behavior of the previous leader. That was true enough and we didn't spend much time on it. I asked if he thought there might be any other reasons. He guessed some of the Europeans were envious of the American lifestyle and were reacting emotionally because they wanted what the Americans had. Since that might have also been true, I didn't dwell on it, but drilled deeper. Was there anything else he could think of to explain the resistance?

When he couldn't think of anything, I asked if the Germans might see some of the Americans on the team as opportunists who conformed with the boss to promote their own careers. Mitch was caught off guard. He couldn't see how anyone would view Americans as other than the conscientious, freedom-loving individualists he had grown up believing in. What also caught Mitch off guard was the detailed knowledge the Germans possessed about the United States. Their fact-based approach made their critiques of America's way of life harder to discount, but facts alone rarely carry the day against ingrained beliefs.

For instance, Mitch believed the United States was the freest country in the world and he downplayed the number of Americans who were incarcerated—as compared to the smaller percentage in European countries—choosing to see this as an irrelevant anomaly. This was part of his defensive reasoning. As a result, he found it challenging to listen to the Europeans who saw America from a different perspective.

Mitch was also convinced the United States had the highest standard of living in the world and was dismayed to discover most of the Europeans on the team did not believe this. In fact, he got annoyed when I asked him why he was so sure the United States had the highest standard. He had never questioned this belief and it turned out he had little real evidence to support it. This left him feeling vulnerable and triggered more defensive reasoning. Asking people how they know what they know is a powerful question, but it can also trigger strong emotional reactions if they realize they don't have much real evidence for their beliefs.

But it was the question about the qualifications of his team's members that caught his attention. There was no doubt in his mind that the Europeans on the team were as qualified as the Americans, and in some cases more so. Mitch wanted to know more about the German educational system and how it was able to produce so many qualified employees. He was surprised to discover there were no elite German universities towering over the rest, but rather a uniform system of universities, all with rigorous educational standards. As Mitch put it, there were no superstars among them, but everyone on the team could make the starting lineup and this impressed him.

As Mitch learned more about German education, it led him to reflect upon the country's economic system as a whole. He began to see that while both countries utilized a form of capitalism, those forms differed. Each country's economic system had advantages and disadvantages, and as Mitch began to understand what the Germans meant when they talked about "capitalism with a conscience," he found it easier to listen to their points of view.

Mitch had found an entry point that allowed him to bridge the mind-distance separating him from the Germans on the team. As he continued to learn how they thought and felt, he was able to broaden that bridge and more social motors on the team slowly started turning in the right direction.

Age and Our Beliefs

When we are young, our brains are like sponges, soaking up experience and incorporating countless assumptions and beliefs about all aspects of reality. While brains remain able to learn until the day we die, the degree of neuroplasticity is more limited in adults. By the time we are around twenty-five years old, our brains have fully developed and we have internalized a generalized belief system and world view that won't change much without intentional effort. Instead of changing their maps to match reality as the brain of a child does, adult brains try to make reality conform to their internal maps.[17]

Bruce Wexler, a professor of psychiatry at the Yale Medical School, has studied how attempts by adults to reduce their dissonance by changing the world is the source of much suffering, misunderstanding, and conflict.[18] From Wexler's perspective, much cross-cultural misunderstanding results from our brains' decreasing neuroplasticity and our inherent tendency to use force on the world around us to make it match our brain maps, rather than vice-versa. This is a provocative way to understand the conflicts that litter the path of human history, but growing evidence supports such a view. For example, consider the quick and defensive reaction people show when their beliefs are called into question.

A team of researchers led by Dutch psychologist Jos J.S. van Berkum of Amsterdam's Max Planck Institute monitored the brains of men who were presented with a hundred and fifty-eight statements about controversial issues such as homosexuality, women's liberation, and euthanasia. Based on their findings, van Berkum's team concluded that our brains react defensively within a mere quarter of a second to statements that contradict our ethical beliefs. What this means in practice is that we almost instantly stop listening and start arguing, if not verbally, then at least mentally.[19]

Trust Grows in Steps

Mitch had a number of skillful habits that stood him in good stead as he took over the leadership role on this conflicted team. Not least of these was his assumption that a person was trustworthy until proven otherwise. His initial willingness to trust me allowed us to get off to a good start. Trust is complex, but in general there are two prerequisites that must be met.

One of these is competence, the other is good intention. If either is missing, we are unlikely to trust someone. For example, if you need major surgery, you may be convinced of a friend's good intentions for your health and well-being, but unless he is an accomplished surgeon, you will probably not be willing to let him operate on you. On the other hand, if you know a surgeon whose technical competence is beyond question, but whose ethics seem shady, you will probably not trust him either.

In addition to Mitch's general willingness to give people the benefit of the doubt, he probably trusted me because of my track record at his company. By listening empathically, I deepened his trust in my good intentions. As the trust grew, I began asking more challenging questions and providing him with facts he had not been aware of before. In effect, we were slowly revising his brain maps and enlarging his ethnocentric view of the world.

Safety and trust go hand in hand. When we feel safe with people, we are more likely to assume their intentions are good and more willing to open up and engage with them in a mutually satisfactory manner. Trust is not an all or nothing affair, it is a matter of degree and develops over time. As we engage with one another, our threat assessment systems are always on the lookout for danger. If we feel safe, we open up a bit and expect the other to do the same.

Building trust requires us to risk some vulnerability in the hope it will be reciprocated. If we open up and the other does not take advantage of our vulnerability but instead shows some vulnerability of her own, we feel safer. At the same time, we are looking to see if the other's actions match her words. When they do, we are also more likely to feel safe and willing to open up further, moving another step up the ladder of trust. While simple in theory, climbing the ladder of trust can be difficult in practice.

Giving up cherished beliefs and ways of seeing the world can be distressing. My questions were not always easy for Mitch, but when he handled them well, he got a direct payoff. Having a larger viewpoint allowed him to better understand and work with the Europeans on his team. As his point of view expanded, he was better able to listen to opinions that would have previously set off his threat assessment system. The more he was able to see the world through their eyes, the more safety he was creating on the team. It took time, but gradually safety and trust were being built, allowing members from Europe and the United States to reduce their mind distance.

Expecting Instead of Accepting

Mitch's willingness to broaden his viewpoint went a long way to reducing team conflict, but it did not work with everyone. Some of the team refused to trust him. One of those who never got over their mistrust was Anders, a Swedish engineer working in Germany. Anders was smart, successful, and every bit as good as Mitch when it came to defensive reasoning. In addition to Swedish, he spoke fluent English and German and he seemed to love the give and take of a good argument. Not only was he not afraid to speak his mind to Mitch, he seemed to relish it.

This was part of the problem. Anders did not behave the way Mitch expected an employee to behave. In the "hire and fire" cultures of the American companies in which Mitch had developed his leadership skills, managers had a great deal of discretionary power. Mitch was used to employees acting as if their job was to ask "how high?" when he said "jump." Even those American employees who were resistant to authority tended to express their displeasure in a less direct, more passive-aggressive manner. As a result, Mitch was not used to being challenged, especially not in front of other team members. What's more, while American workers are well aware of hierarchical differences, it is common for American managers to downplay these differences by couching their orders in the form of requests or suggestions. But when Mitch would suggest Anders do something, Anders responded with "why?" instead of "how high?"

Mitch hadn't yet learned the differences in the ways power is managed in other cultures. He didn't realize to what degree his perceptions of Anders's behavior were influenced by his own cultural background. His inner team expected Anders to behave the way American employees behaved. When Anders didn't, Mitch got upset and began making assumptions about Anders's motivations. Unfortunately, Mitch seemed unwilling to test these assumptions.

Anders did more or less the same thing, but in reverse. He expected Mitch to behave like a Swede in a leadership position. From his experiences growing up in Sweden, a country that placed a high value on equality, Anders assumed it was appropriate to question a leader's statements and he did so whenever he thought it necessary. In his experience, managers were used to such questions and expected them. As long as the questions were rational and could help the team accomplish its mission, such questions were accepted. Only a poor manager would take them personally. Unfortunately, that's exactly what Mitch did. Rather than see Anders's behavior as influenced by Swedish culture, Mitch concluded Anders was trying to make him look bad.

Because their implicit assumptions about the roles of manager and employee were not being tested, their expectations distorted their perceptions of the other's behavior. Mitch saw Anders as selfish, immature, and rebellious, the sort of person who enjoyed causing trouble for anyone in a leadership position. For his part, Anders saw Mitch as part of an arrogant cultural imperialism that was trying to impose the American way of doing business on the older, more humane cultures of Europe. He saw himself as a freedom fighter who was standing up and speaking truth. For him, Mitch was another self-serving American who was out for his own good and did not care for the well-being of the team, the company, or the larger community.

Of course Anders never said as much to Mitch. A key
characteristic of defensive reasoning is that we keep our assumptions
private so they cannot be investigated and found wanting. But with
colleagues he trusted and was close to, Anders was more open about
his assumptions. Among this small group, Anders's resistance to Mitch
was viewed not only as necessary to protect Anders's security, but also
as part of a noble effort to protect the general well-being of the
Europeans from the crassness of American capitalism.

Untested Assumptions

I was not able to help these two understand how their untested
assumptions were distorting their perceptions and driving their
interactions in a direction that was hurting both them and the larger
team. They expected each other to behave in ways that did not accord
with their cultural conditioning. When these expectations were not
met, they blamed each other for the problems occurring between them.
Rather than question their own assumptions and take responsibility for
their own role, they each attributed questionable motivations and poor
character traits to the other—the fundamental attribution error—and
the blame game continued to spiral downwards. As a result, whatever
good will and trust might have been there at one time got eroded. In
essence, it looked like this:

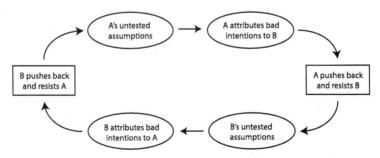

Figure 7.2 — Consequences of Untested Assumptions

Mitch had more problems to manage in his challenging role than just his relationship with Anders. His team was spread around the world and they needed to achieve the goals the CEO demanded of them. This provided Mitch with the perfect excuse to marginalize the problem with Anders and focus his time, energy, and attention elsewhere. As a result, for the several years I worked with Mitch and his team, he and Anders never managed to bridge their differences.

Their inability, or unwillingness, to question their assumptions made it impossible for these two intelligent, well-intentioned men to develop a good working relationship. To his credit, Mitch did not let the problem with Anders derail his desire to create a level playing field for the entire team. Internal surveys indicated the team's morale improved over the course of several years.

Working with Mitch was not always easy for me, but in the end it was a rewarding experience. As is common in good coaching relationships, I learned as much from Mitch as he learned from me. By slowly building safety before challenging his views, I was able to help him test assumptions he had never thought about before. Maybe it was his background as an engineer, or maybe the result of growing up in a pragmatic culture focused on performance, or maybe just his innate intelligence, but his willingness to think about my questions helped him become less ethnocentric. This helped him become a more effective manager and both the morale and performance on his team improved. His growing success made him more willing to question his stories and beliefs. Today he is a successful executive who has a deeper understanding of the role cultural differences play in our perceptions.

As we developed more trust, we both began looking forward to our phone sessions. Many was the time I hung up the phone, satisfied with what we had accomplished. This was certainly the case after one of our last sessions when he thanked me for helping him learn to listen more empathically. Not only had it helped him as a manager, he said his wife also appreciated it.

Conclusion

While it is crucial that we bring truth to the table if we want to have a satisfying conversation, before we can do that we must be truthful with ourselves and not fall prey to self-deception. Mitch and Anders are not unique. We all use defensive reasoning to avoid testing the deep assumptions and expectations we have of ourselves, other people, and reality. When we believe the stories we are telling ourselves and refuse, for whatever reason, to test those stories, our assumptions can negatively influence both our perceptions and our behaviors.

Our brains are natural story tellers and when our stories are accurate, they enable us to understand both ourselves and reality. But when our stories are inaccurate or misleading, they create problems. Because our brains are biased, all stories are told from a particular point of view and no story contains the entire truth. But truth is essential for our well-being and nothing is more corrosive to trust than dishonesty.

By inquiring into the beliefs and stories we tell about our problematic relationships, we can make our brain maps more accurate. Inquiry also teaches us to distinguish between map and territory, between internal state and external reality. When we do so, we liberate ourselves from the cultural conditioning that causes problems when we interact with people who are different. Not only can we use inquiry to become better communicators, we can also use it to become happier and healthier individuals. Cognitive dissonance and other forms of internal conflict are like friction in a motor and lead to indecision, reduced performance, and distress. By bringing inaccurate beliefs into conscious awareness, we have the opportunity to revise them while at the same time training our inner team to make better intuitive decisions. When we do this we can better live according to our deepest values.

Asking the right question is the key to using inquiry. One of the most important questions an interculturalist can ask is about the nature of cultures: Why are they so different? That is the topic of the next section.

Part Three

Culture and Communication

It is clear that each party to this dispute—as to all that persist through long periods of time—is partly right and partly wrong. Social cohesion is a necessity, and mankind has never yet succeeded in enforcing cohesion by merely rational arguments. Every community is exposed to two opposite dangers: ossification through too much discipline and reverence for tradition, on the one hand; on the other hand, dissolution, or subjection to foreign conquest, through the growth of an individualism and independence that makes cooperation impossible.

—Bertrand Russell

Eight

Answering Yali's Question

Two roads diverged in a wood, and I –
I took the one less traveled by,
And that has made all the difference.

—Robert Frost

Professor Jared Diamond and his Foré companions were returning to their base camp in the jungles of New Guinea when their journey was stopped.[1] The mountainous jungles of New Guinea are steep, rugged, and fractured by precipitous cliffs and deep valleys. Heavy rains and constant humidity give rise to dense jungle vegetation with limited visibility. Even established trails quickly become overgrown, and on a good day Diamond only expects to travel an average of three miles.[2] But these jungles are home to an amazing variety of exotic birds and Diamond, a passionate birdwatcher since he was seven years old, made his first trip to New Guinea as a young biologist studying bird evolution. That was over forty years ago and he has been coming back ever since to continue his research.

Diamond is a tall, slender man whose gray, Amish-style beard gives him the appearance of a modern Abe Lincoln dressed in the jungle garb favored by Western explorers.[3] The contrast between him and his Foré friends could hardly be more striking. They are shorter and have the lean, muscular bodies that befits their lifestyle. They are slash-and-burn horticulturalists who complement their diet with food hunted or gathered in the jungles. Wearing only old, ragged pants or shorts and carrying bows and arrows, they seem as at home in the dense greenery as you and I would be strolling through the local supermarket.

Diamond views the people of New Guinea as his friends and admires them for their ingenuity. That says a lot coming from a polymath who first graduated from Harvard and then earned his Ph.D. in physiology and membrane biophysics from the University of Cambridge at twenty-four. He went on to become a Professor of Geography at UCLA, as well as a world-renowned expert on New Guinean birds. So when a man like this says he thinks the tribal peoples of New Guinea are every bit as intelligent as modern Americans, we would be wise to take note.

New Guinea is the world's second largest island and its steep cliffs, isolated valleys, and sheer impassibility kept its many tribes separated. The result is a great deal of cultural diversity in a small geographic area. That there are approximately a thousand different languages spoken on this island gives us a hint of the many differences among New Guinea's tribes.[4] Not all of the tribes are as peaceful as the Foré and as Diamond reports in his master work, *Guns, Germs, and Steel*, violence is common. When men encounter strangers, it is their practice to begin talking about their relatives and extended clans to find some common connection and preempt violence.[5] And right now, the trail back to the supply camp that Diamond and his friends wanted to reach was blocked by strangers from another tribe. So Diamond and his companions were waiting for the strangers to clear out so they could make their way home without any trouble. The problem was, Diamond and his companions were starving.

So when he saw one of the Foré return from foraging carrying a sack filled with mushrooms, his first thoughts were of a tasty dinner. But as the man began roasting the mushrooms over an open fire, he had an unsettling thought. What if the mushrooms were poisonous? After all, even mushroom experts in the United States have died from mistaking a poisonous mushroom for an edible one. As hungry as he was, he began to explain to his friends that the risk was too high and they should not take a chance on being poisoned.

Whereupon the Foré became irate with their American visitor.[6] They berated him for his ignorance. Only an American could be so stupid as to eat a poisonous mushroom and get sick or die. Hadn't he been coming here for years and quizzing them about the plants and wildlife in their environments? Hadn't they always given him intelligent answers? Did he really think they could survive in such a challenging environment if they were so stupid as to go around eating poisonous mushrooms? Then they lectured him on the twenty-nine species of edible mushrooms, where they grew, how they could be recognized, and the name for each in the Foré language. This particular mushroom was a *tanti*. It grew on trees and was both delicious and completely safe. Diamond knew better than not to believe them. Without them he would have been helpless and dead many times over during his research trips into these jungles. The ability of the Foré to penetrate the thick jungle and then create a group shelter in just a few hours of concentrated work had impressed him from the first. He took the roasted mushroom they offered him.

Yali's Question

In July, 1972, Diamond was walking along a beach on the New Guinea coastline when he met a prominent local politician named Yali.[7] Diamond was impressed by Yali's charisma and energy. While both Diamond and Yali were aware of the tensions existing between the indigenous peoples and their European colonizers, their conversation remained friendly. Yali's curiosity was insatiable and he listened intently as Diamond answered his questions about evolution, world history, and life outside New Guinea. And then Yali posed a question which would change the course of Diamond's life: "Why is it that you white people developed so much cargo and brought it to New Guinea, but we black people had little cargo of our own?"[8]

When Europeans reached New Guinea two hundred years ago, one difference was obvious. They possessed a wealth of material goods and advanced technologies that the New Guineans did not. At that time, the New Guineans had not developed metal working and were still using stone tools.[9] During World War Two, when Europeans began penetrating into the interior of New Guinea, the tribal peoples were amazed by the airplanes, phonographs, radios, tools, weapons, and even the canned foods the Europeans brought. The tribal people referred to these material goods as "cargo," for which they had an almost religious reverence. They assumed cargo was indicative of some magical power. The Europeans saw it differently. They attributed their more advanced technologies to their genetic and cultural superiority. This technological inequality and the different interpretations of its origins led to the Europeans doing what they have done to tribal people everywhere. They subjugated them.

Diamond was startled by Yali's question. The question was clear enough and he felt like it should have an obvious answer but he didn't know what to say. The more he thought about it, the more he realized how complex that question was. For him, the interpretation that Europeans were genetically superior to the New Guineans was absurd.[10] His many years of experience convinced him that the average New Guinean was as ingenious and smart as the average American or European. After all, they were able to survive and adapt to one of the most challenging environments in the world. So why was it the Europeans and not the New Guineans who developed metalworking and other technologies?

Diamond could also not accept the notion that it was Europe's cultural superiority that explained the stark inequalities that exist in the world today. To him, cultural differences were more of an effect than a cause. As he pondered Yali's question, he was fascinated by its complexity and he set out to find an answer. Little did he know he would spend the next thirty years working on it.

To answer Yali's question, Diamond had to bring all his intellectual and scientific training to bear. He had no training as a historian, but he knew understanding humanity's history was essential for explaining today's inequality. What he discovered in thirty years of research is captured in the breadth and depth of his fascinating book, *Guns, Germs, and Steel*. Why did history unfold and cultures develop differently in different parts of the world? Diamond's answer to this question can be summed up in one word: Geography!

To understand why geography played such a key role in the European conquest of the world, we need to understand how it shapes cultures. There are numerous useful definitions of the word culture, but at its simplest, we can say a culture is the way of life of a particular group of people. That way of life develops as a group adapts to the particular natural environment—the context—in which the group exists.

Cultures have developed over millennia by mastering fundamental challenges all human groups face. Two of those challenges are physical survival and social cohesion. It's obvious that if its members become extinct, a culture will not survive. Just as many of the world's languages disappeared when the speakers of those languages died, so, too, do cultures disappear when their members die without leaving offspring or records.

In the same way, for a group to maintain its way of life, it needs to create forces of social cohesion that will allow it to remain together despite the internal conflicts all groups experience. Social cohesion is just as essential as sheer physical survival, but it is more complex. So let's begin our investigation by exploring the ways cultures support physical survival and what this has to do with Yali's question.

Survival and Decision-Making

From one point of view, modern cultures can be thought of as vast extended families. This should come as no surprise, since the roots of today's cultures can be traced back to a time when all humans lived in small bands of closely related individuals. These hunter-gatherer bands were often comprised of a single nuclear or extended family.[11] Others formed larger groups of multiple families by using language to create terms for different kinds of relatives, thus creating a sense of being members of a single family or clan.

Just as the parents of a family must provide food, clothing, shelter, and so on for their children, a culture must provide essential physical resources to its members. And just as parents must teach their children how to acquire and use these resources to live, cultures must teach the skills and knowledge its members need for survival.

Life is a precarious affair and death is inevitable. We all know this and our urge to live and postpone our demise for as long as possible is a fundamental aspect of human nature.[12] This knowledge is part of the context in which we must make the decisions that shape our lives. Each of us is, as Robert Frost's "The Road Less Traveled" suggests, continually reaching junctures where we must choose our direction.

Just as our current personal situation is a consequence of the decisions we made in the past, current cultures have been shaped by our ancestors' decisions. In the long course of human history, our forebears were continually making decisions that had serious consequences: Is that mushroom poisonous or can I satisfy my hunger? Should we leave this oasis and look for one with better water or should we stay here? Should we plant now even though the rains have not come, or should we wait? The history of humanity can be viewed as a long series of decisions, some big and some small, all with consequences, some of them fatal.

Because all our decisions are made in the context of an uncertain future, it's easy to become paralyzed by doubt when we must make decisions that might have grave consequences. Nonetheless, we cannot avoid these decisions because not to decide is also a decision. If I reach a crossroads and stay rather than going left or right, I have decided to stop rather than move on.

While many of our decisions are complex, others are simpler and often amount to no more than, "Should I do this, yes or no?" But even deceptively simple choices can have unintended, longer-term consequences—sometimes good, sometimes bad. That's because one decision and the resulting action leads to another, and with each action, we tend to engage, if we think about it at all, in self-justification about our previous decisions and actions.

What would you do, for example, if a distinguished-looking scientist in a white lab coat offered you twenty dollars to participate in an important science experiment? What if he further told you this experiment was designed to test the effects of punishment on learning and you would be required to administer painful, perhaps life-threatening shocks to a person if they got the answer wrong? If you are like most people, you would say no.

But what if this same distinguished-looking man took a more gradual approach, offering you the same amount of money, but saying the experiment was about learning, and you would have to administer a mild, hardly perceptible shock of ten volts. To show you how innocuous the electrical shock is, he lets you test the ten volt shock yourself and you can barely feel it. If at this point you say yes, you have begun to descend what Carol Tavris and Elliot Aronson call the "pyramid of choice."[13]

Next the scientist encourages you to increase the shock you are administering to the person in the other room by another ten volts. Well, you say to yourself, ten volts doesn't hurt and I am doing this to help science learn something important, so you go ahead and increase the voltage to twenty. The process continues, each time the scientist asking you to up the voltage and each step of the way you engage in further self-justification so your actions accord with your beliefs. At some point, you do become aware the increased voltage is painful for the other person, but it becomes harder and harder to know where to draw the line and stop. The further down the pyramid of choice we travel, the more difficult it becomes to acknowledge that we are on the wrong road.

It was this process of gradual, external pressure combined with internal self-justification that allowed so many otherwise decent Americans to end up administering what they believed were intensely painful, life threatening shocks to people they did not know. While the Milgram experiments were designed to test obedience to authority, they also provide evidence for the way we justify our decisions to reduce internal dissonance.

Tavris and Aronson use the pyramid of choice metaphor to show not only how self-justification is used to reduce cognitive dissonance, but also how it leads to the creation of greater mind distance. They do this by citing a classic social science experiment about cheating.[14]

Imagine two boys at the top of the pyramid of choice. Both have more or less the same attitude towards cheating: It's not a good thing to do and should be avoided if possible. Now imagine these two boys in a competitive situation for a desirable prize. It is almost impossible to win the prize without cheating and the experiment is set up so that cheating without getting caught seems easy. One boy cheats and the other does not—they have each chosen to walk down different sides of the pyramid of choice. By the time they get to the bottom, one boy has won the prize but lost his integrity. The other has maintained his integrity but lost the prize.

This scenario of two boys and cheating is drawn from an experiment conducted by Judson Mills over fifty years ago and cited by Tavris and Aronson to show how our brains work to reduce dissonance. After the experiment, children who had cheated to win had a more tolerant attitude towards cheating whereas those who had resisted the temptation to cheat now had harsher attitudes towards cheating and cheaters. While the children's attitudes towards cheating at the top of the pyramid were similar, by the time they got to the bottom, their attitudes had diverged and more mind distance had been created between them. Needless to say, had these children tried to reach consensus on the morality of cheating, they would have had much more difficulty after the experiment was over than before.

But that's not all. The children's memories had changed after the experiment as well, leading them to think they had always felt strongly, one way or the other, about cheating. As we saw in previous chapters, memory is far less a reliable narrator than we might wish, and it shows amazing creativity in shaping itself to accord with what it believes it should remember. As Tavris and Aronson put it,

> "...between the conscious lie to fool others and the unconscious self-justification to fool ourselves lies a fascinating gray area patrolled by that unreliable, self-serving historian—memory. Memories are often pruned and shaped by an ego-enhancing bias that blurs the edges of past events, softens culpability, and distorts what really happened."[15]

Our decisions and actions have both internal and external consequences. Internally they influence the way we construct our identities, while externally they have consequences for the social worlds we live in. Because some of these consequences can be very serious indeed, making decisions in the context of an uncertain future is an existential dilemma all individuals and groups face. The higher the stakes and the more uncertainty at play, the more challenging a decision can be. This is confirmed by lab experiments showing that the ability to predict the future is an important factor in reducing the levels of stress hormones coursing through our bodies.[16] So it is no surprise our ancestors did their utmost to gather reliable knowledge to make better decisions and thus ensure their survival.

Cultures Are Learned

We see such accumulated knowledge and decision-making skills in the Foré knowing, among countless other things, how to construct bows and arrows, how to build a shelter of local materials, and where to find edible mushrooms. Diamond says whenever his New Guinean companions visited other areas, one of their chief topics of conversation was about the local flora and fauna.[17] Hunter-gatherers were storehouses of knowledge about local plants and animals and their languages were filled with words to help them catalog and remember this knowledge, which was accumulated over thousands of years and passed down from generation to generation.

To be useful, this knowledge needs to relate to the group's geographic environment. Knowing which tropical mushrooms were edible was valuable knowledge for the Foré, but hardly essential for the Sami people of northern Scandinavia whose traditional way of life revolved around herding reindeer. For the Sami, knowing how to make warm clothes, shelters, and snow shoes was crucial for survival.[18] Similarly, knowledge about reindeers or tropical mushrooms would have been wasted on the San people of the Kalahari. For them, knowing how to find water and food in a barren desert meant the difference between life and death. But what the Foré, Sami, and San cultures have in common is that they used their accumulated knowledge, or collective intelligence, to help them develop viable ways of living in some of the most challenging environments on the planet. In short, groups had to adapt to the local conditions if they were to survive. The interaction between human brains and different environments spawned not only different ways of life, it also created more mind distance, making communication between members of different cultures more difficult. So one part of the answer to Yali's question about cultural differences and technological development relates to the challenges and opportunities different environments presented.

To best answer Yali's question, Diamond needed to find a time when all cultures on the planet were more or less equal in terms of technological development. There is a lively debate these days about what life was like for our ancient ancestors. It is seductive to engage in sweeping generalizations that paint all of them with the same brush. Whether we envision their lives as a romantic golden age of naturalness before the stress of modern life, or as the Hobbesian vision of nasty, brutish, and short, our generalizations say as much about our own world view as they do about ancient cultures. Given what we now know about confirmation bias and the selective nature of memory, such divergent beliefs about humanity's past is exactly what we would expect. It is also another example of the mind distance that makes successful dialogue so challenging.

As we saw in the previous chapter, a brain will use the evidence at hand to concoct the best story it can, but the evidence it attributes the most importance to and the story it considers best are those in line with its biases. In other words, we not only need reliable evidence, we also need methods to use that evidence accurately or we end up with distorted stories. As we also saw, using inquiry to distinguish between evidence and interpretation is a powerful method for updating our brain maps. What, then, is the evidence we have about the lifestyles of the countless bands of hunter-gatherers who lived in the tens of thousands of years of prehistory?

The evidence can be described in a single word: scant.[19] Because our earliest ancestors left no written records, we don't know much about their social interactions or their brain maps. We are well advised to temper any sweeping generalizations by distinguishing between evidence, which is scarce, and speculation, which abounds.

If we take this advice to heart, what seems beyond doubt to most serious researchers is that until about thirteen thousand years ago humans were foragers using stone tools and living some sort of nomadic lifestyle.[20] While there is much we do not know about these foragers' different ways of life, all evidence points to their being on equal technological footing. This universal equality changed radically with the development of agriculture.

Cultures Are Systems

The development of agriculture marks a turning point in human history. Farming was a fundamental technological breakthrough that changed our ancestors' ways of life in two ways. First, it encouraged foragers to give up their nomadic lifestyles for the more sedentary life in a settlement. Second, it generated surplus food that allowed for the growth of larger populations. No foraging cultures were able to accumulate enough surplus food to support large, complex cultures.[21] In fact, as Diamond soon discovered, all the earliest civilizations—Sumerian, Chinese, Egyptian, Mayan, Aztec, Persian, Greek, Indian, Roman—emerged only when conditions were suitable for the development of farming.

Agriculture was thus the launch pad from which the rocket of technological development took off. This rocket's flight was determined by the synergies that agriculture provided for the first farmers. Having gotten a technological head start, some agriculturalists increased it by developing other, more advanced technologies. For instance, when sedentary farmers captured wild animals and domesticated them to increase their supply of protein, they also discovered that animal dung could be used to fertilize their fields, which in turn increased food production. Increased food production meant it was possible to feed even more people, which allowed some people to do things other than farm, i.e., to become specialists.[22] One of the things these specialists did was develop metallurgy, which in turn allowed for the development of the metal plow, which further increased food production. This in turn allowed for further population increases leading to more social complexity. So we see that different technologies complemented and expanded each other, and these synergies accelerated cultural development.

Writing was another technology that increased the sharing and accumulation of knowledge through time.[23] No longer would the management of knowledge rely only on word of mouth and people with outstanding memories. No longer did the death of the most knowledgeable people in the group signify the loss of crucial knowledge. Now humans could accumulate, store, and share knowledge with people across time and space. The development of these four fundamental technologies—farming, animal domestication, metal working, and writing—created synergies that form the basis of the modern cultures we live in today. As cultures grew, they became more socially complex. New social structures—economic, religious, political, military, and more—began to develop and with them came new occupations and the social roles to fill them.

In other words, cultures are complex systems that are more than the sum of their parts. The positive feedback loops between the different technologies, as well as continual external pressure from the environment, encouraged people to keep developing newer and more powerful technologies. Today we are able to put a man on the moon, perform open heart surgery, communicate with the other side of the world, and, yes, murder millions of people with a single bomb. None of this would be imaginable had our foraging ancestors not developed farming.

Cultures Are Dynamic

The last part of Diamond's quest to understand today's inequalities was to understand why some parts of the world developed agriculture and its attendant technologies sooner rather than later. Why was it Europeans who dominated the rest of the world and not some other group? Once more the astounding answer seems to be geography.

The first known examples of agriculture, animal domestication, metal working, and writing are all found in the small area of the Near East known as the Fertile Crescent. Its native plants—wild wheat and barley—were both easily domesticated and provided sufficient nutritional value for the growth of larger populations.[24] They could also be stored for longer periods of time than other food stuffs. Also native to this region were easily domesticated animals—pigs, cows, sheep, and goats—and horses were not far away. By a fortuitous coincidence both the wild plants and the wild animals that are the basis for the development of complex societies were found in the same location.

Other places in the world were less lucky. No large animals suitable for domestication lived in New Guinea, nor in many other parts of the world, thus restricting the use of the plow. And while many places in the world have domesticated local plants and developed a form of agriculture, these food stuffs are rarely as protein rich and amenable to human use as the wheat and barley found in the Near East. One major exception to this was wild rice, which was originally cultivated in East Asia. And just as wheat and barley served to jumpstart cultural development in the Near East, rice was a major building block in the development of ancient Chinese civilization. Today the wheat and barley first domesticated in the Fertile Crescent have been transplanted to Europe, the Americas, and diverse areas of the world to feed the large populations and industrialized cultures that have developed there.

But if these technologies all developed first in the Fertile Crescent, why was it Europe and not the Near East that subjugated the rest of the world? The short answer is that environments are always changing and for a culture to survive it must adapt to these changes. Agriculture and other technologies gradually spread East and West from the Fertile Crescent to India, Egypt, Greece, Rome, and ultimately into Europe, providing Europe with many of the tools it would use to conquer the world.

But while it was the birthplace of these technologies, the Fertile Crescent's fragile ecology and arid climate proved to be its downfall. When agriculture was first developed, the region was wetter and greener than it is today. Today the forests that once grew there have been decimated, and much of the original fertile land has been eroded. Europe, in contrast, has a physical ecology that is wetter, more robust, and more able to sustain intensive agriculture.

If we survey the course of world history, one thing becomes obvious: Civilizations rise and fall. Change is the only constant. Europe was one of the least developed areas of the world until around 1500 A.D. During the Dark Ages in Europe, the Chinese and Islamic cultures were far more advanced. They also possessed knowledge and technology, such as how to make gunpowder, that Europeans would acquire and use to further their own development.[25]

Population Pressures and War

The development of technology, then, was not without its shadow side. It did allow population growth, but increasing populations led to the need for more land to farm. As population pressures increased, formerly separate groups came into contact with one another and conflicts over resources became more common. One consequence of increasing population density is the innumerable wars that have marked history for at least the last two thousand years. As metallurgy and other technologies were developed and refined, they were used in warfare and another, more terrible, synergy began operating. War allowed the victors to increase both the size of their territory and the number of people in their empires. At the same time, more territory, more wealth, and more resources allowed these cultures to further develop more advanced technologies that would make them even more formidable. The numerous wars fought on European soil led to the highly developed military technologies that Europe would use against other peoples around the world.

We need to be aware that some of the most sophisticated technologies that characterize today's information economy, such as the Internet, were originally developed for military purposes. Seen in this light, technology has always been a double-edged sword. Even today, population growth combined with weapons of mass destruction makes physical survival seem almost as precarious as it was thirteen thousand years ago.

It is useful and valuable to understand how today's current technological and social complexity developed for several reasons. First, understanding the role that geography played in our development makes us less susceptible to fallacious arguments about the technological disparity that currently exists in the world. Knowing more about our history serves as an antidote for outdated stories and distorted thinking. As we will see in later chapters, erroneous reasoning and distorted, ethnocentric stories are often used to fan the flames of fear and animosity between different groups.

Second, when you know the facts, you can teach them to others and thus promote more understanding. When people understand how and why other groups developed differently than they themselves, they tend to become less judgmental and more tolerant. We saw this dynamic in the previous chapter. As Mitch became more aware of how the German education system functioned, he became more open to the Germans on his team. More understanding and acceptance allowed them to communicate and cooperate more effectively.

Third, if the past is any predictor of the future, we can expect further population growth, along with increased competition for land, water, and other precious resources, to lead to more conflict between groups. If that's the case, the world will need informed interculturalists more than ever.

Conclusion

Why do cultures vary so much in terms of size and social complexity? And why did some cultures develop advanced technologies while others did not? These questions have been at the heart of intense debates for years. Today there is a general consensus among researchers that our foraging ancestors lived a life of approximately equal social and technological complexity. The development of agriculture was the game changer, creating synergies that led to the development of ever more advanced technologies and complex societies.

While not all people are in complete agreement with Diamond's argument that geography played the leading role in the development of social inequity—some think the idea too simplistic, others find it overly deterministic—no expert denies the importance of geography in our development. Diamond's argument provides both a clear and compelling explanation that unifies most of the current scientific and historical evidence.

Cultures are socially constructed by humans, but they are not constructed out of thin air, nor do they exist independently of their environment. They emerge and evolve as the result of decisions by individuals and groups in response to the challenges posed by their natural environment. Ways of life that different groups developed as they adapted to their particular environment form the social context in which individuals live.

As we saw in chapter four, the power of context to influence our behavior is indisputable, but so is our power to choose, creating an existential tension we all must manage if we hope to survive and thrive. By making decisions to change the social contexts in which we live, we can hope for a better future. For example, some people say the high birthrates and young ages at which many girls marry is part of African culture, implying it is some fixed and permanent characteristic that will never change. But two hundred years ago it was just as common for girls in the United States to marry at such a young age. Contexts change and our choices influence the direction those changes will take.

Diamond's inquiry into the source of today's material inequality was spurred by Yali's question, providing us with another example of the power of questions to focus our awareness and harness our intellectual capacities. By proceeding like a good detective who asks the right questions, we can untangle the enormous complexity of our social realities and better understand the human condition. Understanding geography's role in cultural development helps us better understand today's world, but we must also understand how groups create social cohesion if we want to more fully understand the nature of cultural differences.

Nine

Dilemmas of a Story-Telling Animal

The movies did not describe or explain America. They invented it, dreamed up an America all their own and persuaded us to share the dream. We shared it happily, because the dream was true in its fashion—true to a variety of American desires—and because there weren't all that many other dreams around.

—Michael Wood

Scott should have been happy. He had been promoted when his company announced a major reorganization to manage the challenges of the global market. He was now in charge of a large engineering team and was pleased with his increased responsibilities.[1]

As a hard worker who put in long hours, he liked to get things organized quickly. But right now he was facing a cultural roadblock. Although members of his diverse team were located around the world, many of them were in Sweden and it was now August. In August, Sweden, like other countries in Europe, grinds to a halt. "Gone to their cabins in the woods," a fellow American had complained. Scott was chomping at the bit to get things moving and thirty percent of his team was absent.

He was not only a smart, accomplished engineer, he was also a successful manager who knew morale was a make-or-break factor in a team's success. Having worked in different countries before, he was also aware what a huge impact cultural differences could have on a team's morale. This was especially true on a remote team like this one, which included engineers, technicians, and assistants in Korea, India, Sweden, Belgium, and the United States.

Other Americans started complaining that it was hard to contact the Swedes even when they were not on vacation. Like Scott, his compatriots tended to work long hours when the situation demanded it, but the Swedes arrived punctually every morning and then left just as punctually every evening. By five o'clock Swedish time only a few of the managers were still there. Almost everyone else was gone. Most Swedes were putting in the required forty hours but rarely more, and talk among the Americans characterized them as slackers who showed little loyalty to the company.

When he began talking with the Swedes to get their perspective, he was surprised. In contrast, they saw themselves as more loyal than the Americans, but they didn't measure their loyalty by hours worked. Instead they saw themselves as the true team players because they were *duktig*, i.e., because they stayed focused, prioritized wisely, did their job well, and took responsibility when things went wrong. Furthermore, they viewed loyalty as remaining with the company and working hard whether they got a bonus or not. Scott was even more surprised when he heard they thought of the Americans as poorly trained, inefficient workers who could not prioritize well. What else accounted for the Americans' inability to get their job done in the standard eight hours? According to the Swedes, if the Americans would spend less time walking around with coffee cups in hand talking to their co-workers, they'd be able to go home on time, too.

They also had doubts about the Americans' core values. When the Swedes left work, they looked forward to spending time with their friends and family. For them a good work-life balance was central to their well-being and few were prepared to sacrifice their personal life for monetary gain or a higher position in the company. To them, it seemed personal ambition, if not outright greed, was the basic motivation for many of the American associates' attempts to climb the corporate ladder. As they said this, Scott sensed a vague disdain in their voices for the very idea of a hierarchy.

Scott began to realize that what at first glance seemed like a simple issue—the Swedes taking longer vacations—was the logical consequence of deep, complex cultural values and social structures. In his mission to build a strong international work team, Scott was faced with the way different cultures create social cohesion. Just as in a modern work team, all groups, whether ancient bands of foragers, clans, empires, or modern nation states, must get many things right if the group is to stay together and function well. These include, but are not limited to:

- Ethics, laws, and behavioral norms as well as social roles and structures must be established so members can coordinate their efforts and cooperate effectively.
- Limited resources must be distributed so that basic needs get met. These resources include food, tools, and knowledge, as well as social resources such as status and decision-making power.
- Good decisions must be made so the group's survival and success is assured while keeping group members reasonably satisfied. This means finding ways to handle conflicts and disagreements to avoid infighting.

If even one of these conditions is not met, a group's morale and performance suffer. These challenges become increasingly difficult the larger the group gets. One reason bands of foragers during the Paleolithic period remained small was because they often split apart to avoid violence when difficult disagreements arose. Robert Carneiro, an eminent anthropologist, assumes this splitting caused humans to spread over the planet during the Paleolithic era as they sought resources and food.[2]

Great Civilizations Revisited

Let's examine how the challenges of social cohesion our ancestors faced are similar to those of corporate teams today. As bands of nomadic foragers evolved into farmers and herders, foundations were being laid for the growth of modern, complex civilizations. Two important commonalties shared by even the earliest civilizations include large, socially stratified populations with centralized governments and well-organized work forces.[3]

In short, the earliest civilizations found ways to create social cohesion that allowed them to grow in size and diversity in ways that more egalitarian foraging bands couldn't. Because these civilizations had a tendency towards autocratic rulers, rigid class systems, and the use of coercion to encourage compliance, they may seem unacceptable to modern sensibilities, but they did find ways to manage the challenge of social cohesion all groups face.

In doing so they provided their members—or at least some of their members—with several advantages. Having a centralized decision-making structure was one way to regulate power and manage conflict. For example, a standing army allowed a ruler to maintain order while it also protected the group from outside invaders. Having an army also allowed one group to invade and subjugate other groups while taking over their lands. In turn, a larger population allowed a group to develop economies of scale, new technologies, and new occupations to produce not only material goods and food stuffs, but also arts and sciences.

Organizing humans turns out to be a challenging undertaking because the larger and more complex the group, the more things there are that can go wrong. In particular, every group faces fundamental dilemmas and they must be managed skillfully if the group is to function well. One fundamental dilemma all groups face can be called the "Who should I take care of?" dilemma.

Who Should I Take Care of?

The wide variety of frogs, salamanders, lizards, snakes, crocodiles and tortoises have some common features in terms of motivation that are important for understanding the "Who should I take care of dilemma?" First, they avoid pain and dangers such as large predators and toxic plants. Second, they approach rewards and opportunities such as food or a potential mate.[4] In addition, they generally reproduce by laying eggs and leaving their offspring to fend for themselves. Their relatively simple nervous system with its basic approach-avoid motivation has worked well enough for these creatures to have survived an often dangerous, constantly changing environment for hundreds of millions of years. This "sticks and carrots" motivational system gave these creatures clear guidance about how to take care of themselves and ensure their own survival. Reptiles and amphibians were, without even knowing it, the original masters of the "look out for number one" and "do your own thing" philosophies of life.

Because this approach-avoid motivational system worked so well, nature hung onto it when mammals began to evolve. Just as nature chose to conserve implicit memory when it later evolved explicit memory, so, too, nature conserved the more primitive sticks and carrots system of motivation when it added a new emotional system to make mammalian behavior more complex and adaptable. Squirrels, horses, dogs, and other mammals also avoid things they fear and approach those that provide them with pleasure. But mammals evolved an additional motivational system known as the attachment or affiliate system.[5] This system appears on the evolutionary scene with the expansion of the mammalian or limbic brain, also referred to as the emotional brain. It sits atop of and envelopes the older brain stem, which resembles the simpler brains found in reptiles and amphibians. These are the first two levels of the triune brain structure we explored in chapter five.

With the expansion of the limbic brain, we see new behaviors appearing in mammals that we don't see in lizards and amphibians. First, they often enter into pair bonds. Second, they care for and nurture their young after they are born. In other words, in addition to the more primitive "take care of yourself" urges, we see a new motivation whose dictate is "take care of your family." So while amphibians and reptiles mate, lay eggs, and wander away, male and female mammals often pair up to nurture their offspring.

This tendency for parents and young to become attached to one another ensures that helpless young mammals are protected until they have matured enough to take care of themselves. Mammals' more complex brains, plus the extended period of development, allowed them to thrive, proving the value of the "take care of family" motivational system. This system also works in conjunction with the more advanced social circuitry that emerged in primates. The affiliate motivational system did not go away with the development of primates' more advanced brains and larger social groups, rather it grew to include a more general "take care of your group" system.

Human beings are ultra-social. Not occasionally or by chance, but by nature's design and our ultra-social ways are built into the structure of our brains. As group size grows, so too does social complexity. Making sense of social behavior in large groups is staggeringly complex, requiring great social intelligence. Various theorists suggest that one reason for the increase in human brain size is this need for increased social intelligence.[6]

The brain size/body weight ratio in humans is radically higher than in all other primates.[7] Humans also live in the largest, most complex social groups. Furthermore, humans have the most extended developmental period between conception and adulthood. This extended developmental period, combined with the experience-dependent plasticity of our brains, has allowed us not only to adapt and survive in just about every part of the planet, it has also allowed us to develop diverse cultures.

Creating social cohesion is a universal challenge all cultures everywhere, large or small, must master. To do this, groups and individuals must find ways to manage the inherent tensions created between the "take care of yourself" and the "take care of your family/group" motivational systems.

This tension between individuals who want to satisfy their own personal needs and the often opposing needs of other family/group members must be managed skillfully. While the interactions of these forces may not be visible to the untrained eye, they create tensions in all groups. Knowing all groups must manage this tension gives you a powerful tool for locating and understanding cultural differences. By zeroing in on how this dynamic is managed in any given culture, you can both deepen and broaden your intuitive understanding of a particular situation.

One way to do this is to become more aware of the ways you manage this tension in your own life. For instance, when you are at a party and the other guests are leaving, notice whether you leave or hang around to help the host clean up. If you leave because you are tired, you are taking care of yourself. If you stick around and help with the cleaning up, you are taking care of the other. Another example from daily life: Do you take the time to recycle your trash (part of belonging is doing things for the good of our shared environment) or are you so stressed by your own busy life that you can only take care of yourself?

If you reflect upon the decisions you make in the course of your life, you will discover the "who do I take care of?" question has played a central role in you becoming who you are today. While each of these decisions starts at the top of the pyramid of choice, by the time you have reached the bottom, you will have engaged in the self-justifications we all use to affirm our beliefs and avoid internal dissonance.

The essence of the self-group dilemma can be summarized with the following questions: What rights and privileges does an individual have, and how much may she pursue her own interests rather than working for the common good? Or, asked another way, what duties and obligations does the individual have towards the group and how much can she be expected to sacrifice to promote the common good? These rights, privileges, duties, and obligations can be written or unwritten, conscious or unconscious, but they are a major social force in every culture. Understanding how members of a particular culture manage this dilemma allows the astute observer to communicate more skillfully.

Lagom är bäst!

This Swedish proverb can be translated as "the right amount is best." Scott discovered that something the Swedes called *lagom* undergirded the views they had towards their obligations to the company. There is no exact English equivalent for *lagom*. Depending on the context, it can mean enough, sufficient, appropriate, adequate, just right, fair, balanced, or moderation. *Lagom* is a central value of utmost importance to Swedish culture and implies things are finely tuned, balanced, and just right.[8] As Scott began to grasp the wide-ranging applications of *lagom* in Swedish culture, his views of the Swedes began to change. While they were clearly hard workers, they also believed they needed time with friends and family to avoid burn out.

Lagom also influences the way Swedes manage the self-group dilemma. In the Swedish view, a person should work hard, but not too hard; should earn enough money, but not too much money; and should be self-sufficient, but not too self-sufficient. To promote social cohesion and avoid conflict, a person should get a big enough slice of the pie to satisfy her needs, but not take so much that others have to go without. A well-known Swedish legend tells how Vikings met in assemblies to make decisions. After the assembly, a bowl of mead was passed from man to man for each to drink. The trick was to drink just enough so that even the last man got his fair share. Of course everyone was tempted to take a big drink as the bowl went *laget om*, i.e., "around the group," but that would not have been fair. According to the legend, *laget om* got shortened to *lagom* and explains why this value is so important to Swedes today.[9]

Cross-cultural research consistently points to the cultures of the United States, Britain, Germany, Switzerland, Scandinavia, the Netherlands, Canada, New Zealand, and Australia as more individualistic or self-oriented than the rest of the world.[10] That is to say, they tend to emphasize the rights and autonomy of the individual over obligations and duties towards the group. In these cultures, the core unit of social identity is the individual person with self-reliance and personal freedom being idealized. But even within cultures that emphasize the individualism end of the continuum, there are many differences in the way they manage the self-group dilemma. This is amply illustrated in the way Swedes and Americans, both individualist cultures, view loyalty and obligations.

In those cultures of the world that are more sociocentric, or group oriented—which includes most cultures in Asia, Africa, Latin

America, and the Near East—values and world views tend to place more emphasis on family and group identities. In these cultures, the group is the basic social unit and relationships are of paramount importance. In sociocentric cultures conformity, loyalty, and obligations to the group as well as the overall well-being of the group tend to take precedence over individual desires.[11] As a result, members of such cultures tend to have a diffuse sense of self that is more enmeshed with others in the group, as compared to the stronger sense of being a separate self typical in individualist cultures. Members of sociocentric cultures also place more emphasis on in-group/out-group distinctions than do members of individualist cultures.

To call a culture either individualistic or sociocentric is to engage in black and white thinking. While some cultures lean more towards one end of the spectrum or the other, if we zoom in we find all cultures are a mixture of both self- and group-oriented behaviors. This is because the self-group polarity must be managed by all cultures. These opposing motivations must somehow be balanced if a group is to maintain social cohesion.

Visualizing a Polarity

The metaphor of a balance beam is useful for understanding dilemmas created by a polarity. A polarity is different from a problem which can be permanently solved.[12] Polarities can't—they can only be managed, more or less skillfully. Breathing is a basic polarity—a whole consisting of two opposing processes. We need to inhale oxygen to satisfy our energy needs, but we also need to exhale carbon dioxide to avoid suffocation. To neglect either of these two processes leads to illness or even death. It makes no sense to say, "I will inhale continually to ensure that I will always have enough oxygen." Nor can I simply exhale all the carbon dioxide in my lungs and think, "Good, now I am cleaned out of those nasty waste products once and for all." Instead, I must continually balance these two essential needs and coordinate my breathing in a dynamic process of exhaling followed by inhaling followed by exhaling, etc.

The self-group polarity creates a similar dynamic in all individuals and groups. We must continually balance our individual needs with the needs of those we are in relationship with. When we must make tough decisions, we are pulled in different directions and this internal dissonance is often difficult to manage. It is like trying to find the balance point on a very sensitive scale upon which two opposing tendencies keep moving. If we represent these two opposing tendencies that exist in all of us as two cartoon characters, it might look like this:

Figure 9.1 — Who should I take care of?

Whenever person A moves, it will affect the center of gravity and thus force a response from person B if they hope to maintain balance and not crash to the ground. Managing a dilemma is thus about balancing two dynamic tendencies in a way that allows them to co-exist in a harmonious manner. We can make this dilemma a little more detailed and precise by remembering Aristotle's advice that any virtue, when taken to an extreme, becomes a vice. Visually that would look more like this:

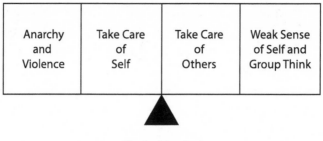

Anarchy and Violence	Take Care of Self	Take Care of Others	Weak Sense of Self and Group Think

Physical Survival

Figure 9.2 — Self-Group Dilemma

Notice that the two boxes in the center of the beam contain the two halves or virtues of the polarity we need to manage. If we remember that these are two halves of a single whole, a dilemma that we need to manage, we can avoid mistaking half the dilemma for a problem. Notice, too, that the balance beam rests upon the pyramid of choice. When we move too far in one direction, we start going down the pyramid and will tend to justify our behaviors in a way that leads us to see a problem rather than a dilemma.

The outer boxes represent the extremes, the vices we fall prey to if we see only half of a polarity and think it is a problem we can solve. If, on the one hand, people are only concerned about their own needs and desires and ignore the needs of the others in the group, social trust will be damaged and the group will become chaotic and violent. Just as reptiles are known to eat their own young, humans who are only concerned about their own needs turn into social predators, destroying the peace in a community.

If, on the other hand, individuals ignore their own needs and conform to the group, the group may fall prey to bland mediocrity and groupthink. To avoid either of these two extremes, cultures must find ways to manage these opposing tendencies in a balanced manner. As we will soon see, the self-group polarity is not the only dilemma groups and individuals must manage. There are others, and when they are not managed well, they lead to suffering.

A key skill for managing polarities well is "both/and" thinking, which allows us to transcend the limits of "either/or" thinking and see the larger system created by the opposing forces.[13] People who are only good at either/or thinking are less adept at managing the internal tension that conflicting viewpoints generate in them. To reduce dissonance and stay within their window of tolerance, they view one side of a polarity as right and the other as wrong. Unable to see both sides, they polarize with other either/or thinkers who view the other half of the polarity as right. When people polarize like this, the effect is to create more mind distance, which makes the situation even more difficult.

Both/and thinking helps us offset this tendency to see only one side of an issue. We can improve our ability to see other perspectives by remembering we all see the world subjectively and we all engage in self-justification. Both/and thinking also helps us hit the pause button to stay within our window of tolerance. As we increase our ability to see the other person's point of view, we also increase the odds that our interaction will be both satisfying and transformative. As Henry Ford, the great industrialist, put it, "If there is any one secret of success it lies in the ability to get the other person's point of view and see things from their angle as well as your own."[14]

Luckily for Scott, he was adept at both/and thinking as well as hitting the pause button, and this helped him quickly see both sides of his team's cultural impasse. To create a successful team, Scott needed to manage the tension between members who thought working long hours was the mark of the good team player and those who thought a good team player was one who worked hard, but balanced this hard work by maintaining strong relationships with friends and family.

As Scott was educating himself about Swedish culture and the social structures Swedes had constructed, he realized there was another core dilemma that Sweden and the United States managed differently: The dilemma of inequality. If "Who should I take care of?" captures the essence of the self-group dilemma, the question at the heart of the equality-hierarchy dilemma is, "Who decides?"

Who Decides?

Social inequality is a complex, controversial topic debated by experts and lay people alike. I am not an expert in this field, but the fact that this topic has generated such a vast literature as well as so much controversy affirms its importance for managing cultural differences. Because the issues of power and equality are so central to the human condition, we all intuitively understand their importance in our daily lives. One pragmatic approach to dealing with cultural differences as regards power, rank, and status is to notice that at the center of most inequality issues is an equality-hierarchy polarity that all groups must manage.

Groups everywhere, no matter how egalitarian, are composed of individuals who exhibit different traits and qualities. In one of the most famous historical discourses on social inequality, the eighteenth-century philosopher Jean-Jacques Rousseau pointed out the central role played by natural inequality: "The one who sang or danced the best, the handsomest, the strongest, the most adroit, or the most eloquent became the most highly considered; and that was the first step toward inequality..."[15]

Regardless of which characteristic we choose to measure—physical strength, mathematical ability, courage, eloquence, social skills, musical ability, running speed, physical beauty, defensive skills, age, and so on— we find that individuals differ. As a result, some individuals gain more favor and influence within a group and tend to function as leaders, whereas others occupy the roles, either happily or unhappily, of followers. Such behavior is not limited to humans, as we see in troupes of chimpanzees, wolves, and other social animals whose groups are organized hierarchically. With the possible exception of foragers, we see some form of hierarchical social structures in cultures all around the world. Rank and status are ubiquitous and knowing how any given culture views these can help us better communicate with members of that culture.

Despite our inherent inequality, everyone has needs that must be met if the individual is to develop into a healthy human being. These include not only the basics for safety and physical survival, but also love, belonging, and respect from others as well as the opportunity for self-expression. The desire to satisfy our needs is inborn and we see this in the loud cries of a baby when it is hungry or cold. Even the most helpless among us have a natural urge to satisfy their needs and to remain within the window of tolerance.

Thus the inherent inequality of individuals and everyone's innate desire to have their needs met creates another fundamental tension that groups everywhere must manage. Every group must organize itself to keep this polarity from generating violence or social malaise. At the heart of this dilemma is the issue of decision-making power, i.e., who has the power to make decisions for whom? Who decides whose needs are to be satisfied and whose are to be sacrificed for the good of the group? Who decides how resources should be distributed? Who decides who has the right to punish and what sorts of punishments are appropriate? Who decides how conflicts should be resolved?

Making the issue of inequality more complicated is the matter of attitudes towards rank and status. How should one view people who are higher or lower in the social hierarchy? Are leaders and other high-status individuals just other people who happen, for whatever reason, to occupy higher social roles, but who are essentially the same as those lower in the hierarchy? Or are those who are higher special beings to be admired and revered from afar, much like the ancient Egyptians viewed their pharaohs as minor deities? Or are those in the higher ranks part of a corrupt dynasty exploiting the lower ranks? In other words, is social inequality part of the natural order of things and thus to be accepted, or is it another social construction that we can modify?

And what of the consequences of inequality? Are more egalitarian countries, such as Sweden, healthier and happier than those countries, such as the United States, that exhibit greater disparity between the highest and lowest members of society? Managing attitudes towards the distribution of decision-making power, resources, and status is another fundamental challenge facing cultures around the world.

In short, the natural diversity of individuals creates another dilemma that groups must manage. How a group balances each individual's uniqueness and innate inequality with every individual's desire for respect and well-being is another dimension on which cultures differ. We can again use the balance beam to illustrate this dilemma.

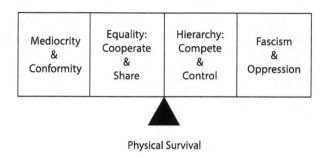

Figure 9.3 — Equality-Hierarchy Dilemma

Equality in Sweden

Scott realized one reason the Swedes talked so positively about equality and fairness for all was because they were proud of the way their culture managed this dilemma. As he got to know them better, he realized it was also part of the reason Swedish business meetings were different from American business meetings. When Americans met, those with lower-rank tended to defer to the higher-ranked individuals. Not so with the Swedes. They strove for consensus. Even the lowest ranking among them was willing to offer up her opinion and even publicly contradict the group's leader. This not only made for longer meetings when the Swedes were present, it upset the Americans and others on the team who came from more hierarchical cultures.

Those team members with no conceptual framework to understand these differences were more easily pushed out of their window of tolerance when meetings did not run as they expected. Had they understood the underlying dilemmas all groups face, they might have been better able to hit their pause buttons.

Finding the right conceptual framework is a challenge for the beginning interculturalist, not least because of the wide variety of labels experts use to refer to the same thing. For example, in Moral Foundations Theory, the equality-hierarchy dilemma is referred to by Haidt as the Hierarchy Foundation, whereas in Hofstede's system, it is referred to as the power distance index. While both systems are based on solid empirical evidence and seem to be measuring the same underlying dilemma, the different labels creates a Tower of Babel situation for the practical interculturalist. Understanding cultural differences as expressions of fundamental dilemmas provides us with great explanatory power, but we need to remember that not everyone will understand or explain behavior in terms of such dilemmas.[16]

To make matters more difficult, these dilemmas do not exist independently of each other, but are entangled in complex webs of social meaning. Take, for instance, the notion of private property. Most bands of foragers organize in an egalitarian manner with members owning little private property. As societies grow larger and become more complex, we see the appearance of more and more private property and laws to protect it. According to Rousseau, the creation of private property was a primary step on the road to creating hierarchical structures and social inequality. In this regard, what is considered public property and what is considered private illustrates the entanglement of these two dilemmas and it is informative to study actual examples to see how particular cultures manage them.

For instance, Swedes visiting the United States often find it striking how many signs there are in rural areas warning of the consequences, sometimes dire, for trespassing on private property. In Sweden everyone is allowed to wander freely around the countryside, including across private property.[17] This ancient rule of *allemansrätten*, or everyman's right, allows anyone to cross anyone else's land as long as they respect the rights of the owners. *Allemansrätten* is a perfect illustration of how the self-group and equality-hierarchy dilemmas are interwoven in Sweden. It also illustrates not only how the skillful management of a polarity can create social cohesion, but also how such balancing acts can seem paradoxical at times.

Swedes use the notion of "freedom though obedience" to manage what at times can be a vexing dilemma.[18] By obeying the rules of *allemansrätten*, Swedes recognize their obligations as members of a larger community to care for other's property, and, at the same time, their right as individuals to hike where they choose.

Dilemmas are more than theoretical constructs, they also have real consequences for individuals and cultures when not managed well. In the case of the equality-hierarchy dilemma consequences can be severe. For instance, if we use socioeconomic status (SES) to measure hierarchy, we discover that levels of stress are generally higher with lower SES.[19] As medical research is now proving, degenerative diseases are one of the consequences of the elevated stress levels found in modern cultures. As Robert Sapolsky, one of the world's leading neurobiologists, writes,

> The health risk of poverty turns out to be a huge effect, the biggest risk factor there is in all of behavioral medicine—in other words, if you have a bunch of people of the same gender, age, ethnicity and you want to make predictions about who is going to live how long, the single most useful fact to know is each person's SES. If you want to increase the odds of living a long and healthy life, don't be poor.[20]

There are other unavoidable dilemmas cultures must manage and this brief look at two core dilemmas facing all groups is neither comprehensive nor exhaustive.[21] But by understanding how core dilemmas influence both individual behaviors and group dynamics, we acquire a powerful tool for noticing and interpreting a wide range of diverse behaviors. By remembering these dilemmas are composed of two opposing but interdependent forces, we gain a broader understanding of the challenges we all face as we go about managing the web of social tensions we live in.

If we return to our balance beam drawing and think of the interlocking nature of these core dilemmas, we can see that keeping them in balance to provide social cohesion while simultaneously ensuring our physical survival is an ongoing challenge for any group.

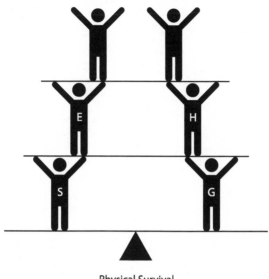

Physical Survival

Figure 9.4 — Challenges of Physical Survival and Social Cohesion

The Importance of Shared Meaning

Scott's position as manager of a global team was not easy. In addition to all the work a regular manager has, he also had to serve as the cultural facilitator for the different values, world views, and behavioral expectations of his team members. In his attempts to bridge cultural differences, he discovered the importance of stories to create shared meaning.

My job was to assist Scott and his team by creating enough safety for cultural differences to be talked about openly. We used a series of structured questions to guide the participants as they discussed what are sometimes difficult topics. As they talked, I served as a catalyst, helping the team create more shared meaning. I have been surprised and gratified again and again by how grateful people are to have the opportunity to tell their stories.

We humans are meaning-making creatures. Meaning nourishes us, gives us purpose, and promotes our well-being just as much as food. A life without meaning creates psychological pain, and, if Viktor Frankl is right, leads to addictions, despair, and even suicide.[22] Similarly, groups use shared meaning to manage dilemmas and the tensions they create. In essence, shared meaning promotes social cohesion by functioning as a group's collective memory that then guides individual decisions. By carving out time from the team's busy schedule to discuss and understand their different expectations, Scott discovered that misunderstandings and complaining decreased. And as they did, performance increased.

According to another Swedish legend, a troop of marauding Vikings was approaching Paris and the prince of the Franks sent an envoy to negotiate with them.[23] The envoy came back and reported that he had failed. He explained he could not find the chief of the Vikings. Whenever he had asked to be taken to the chief, each Viking claimed he was the leader. How could one negotiate with a tribe in which everyone was the chief?

Modern Swedes like to retell this legend to show they have always been big believers in equality. In the same way, telling the story of the shared drinking bowl at Viking assemblies helps explain why they value *lagom*. Like cultures everywhere, Swedes tell stories to explain who they are and how they came to be. By harnessing our universal tendency to tell stories, groups create shared meaning and social cohesion.

Cultures use stories—myths, legends, folk and fairytales—in many ways to create shared meaning. For instance, some stories explain how the world began and how people and other forms of life were created. Other stories provide explanations of natural phenomena, such as fire or the behavior of animals. For example, in ancient Greece, the myth of Prometheus explains how he stole fire from the gods and gave it to humans. In North America, most tribes had a myth of how fire came to the people. In the Choctaw version, Opossum, Buzzard, and Crow all tried to steal fire and failed. In failing, they were burned by the fire, which explains why today's crows are black, opossums have no hair on their tails, and buzzards have no feathers on their heads. In the end, it was Grandmother Spider who succeeded in stealing fire and bringing it to humans. Such stories are often considered sacred truths by the cultures that tell them.

The explanatory power of stories helps us understand our lives, our minds, and the universe. In this sense, our stories correspond to the brain maps we create to help us navigate through time and space. Just like a good map, a good story should be accurate. If we have stories that tell us rattlesnakes make good playmates or that love is a weakness, we are not going to be around long to keep telling those stories.

Creation stories not only serve to explain who we are and why, they also allow us to express our awe and wonder at the mystery of existence. While many adults have lost this sense of wonder, as children we were all amazed by the glow of the moon or the fleet arc of a flying bird. Our stories allow us to recapture a glimpse of this lost sense of wonder.

Justifying a Way of Life

Just as individuals use self-justification as they descend the pyramid of choice, so, too, groups use stories to justify their way of life. For example, at gatherings and holiday reunions families tell funny, embarrassing, and memorable stories about their past. Such stories both affirm who we are and help make sense of our lives. Similarly, organizations tell stories about how they were founded to explain their existence and justify their way of doing business.

The story of fierce Viking warriors sitting in assembly and sharing mead from the same drinking vessel is a powerful story. Even a small child hearing it for the first time can imagine the last Viking becoming irate if there were no mead left. Having such a vivid, concrete story not only explains why *lagom* is good, it implicitly supports the way modern Swedes organize their educational and social welfare systems so no one is left out. Understanding this simple story even helps to understand the Swedish tax code, which redistributes wealth in the hope that every Swede gets his or her fair share of the mead.

While the story of sharing mead from a common drinking vessel teaches the importance of sharing limited resources, the tale of young George Washington chopping down his father's cherry tree teaches American children the importance of honesty. In the same way, when American teachers tell their pupils the story of the Boston Tea Party, it instills the value of freedom and teaches the need to fight against tyranny. From tales told around a campfire to those told in classrooms, cultures use stories to inspire their members to think, feel, and act in accord with other members.

For example, movies, books, and popular songs about our heroes and past wars persuade us to remain vigilant and stand united to defend our way of life. Similarly, songs, books, and movies about love and romance encourage us to find a mate who will help us live "happily ever after." Romantic stories also help us understand and manage our feelings of jealousy and sadness when a relationship goes wrong.

As growing children learn the language of a group, they also learn the stories of the group and these stories become brain maps. As we saw in chapter two, it is this growth of brain maps that underlies the enculturation process we all went through as children. At these early stages in development, children are not able to think critically and tend to believe all the stories they are told. For the young child, these stories and the characters they portray are as real as sunshine and birdsong.

While the story of sharing mead teaches Swedish children to share their toys and behave so everyone has enough, the converse is also true: When Swedes behave in the ways their stories encourage them to do, they are reinforcing those behaviors, beliefs, and stories in their own minds and in the minds of their fellow Swedes. This is the other half of the cycle of enculturation.

The meaning shared by members of a group shapes their world view and the consensus reality in which they live. Some members of a culture may view their consensus reality as so incontrovertible, or even sacred, they will fight to protect it. This is another reason safety first, truth second is an essential maxim for successful communication.

Shared Identity and Purpose

Stories central to a culture's world view are often enacted as rituals to promote a sense of community among members. For example, in the United States, the Fourth of July is a national holiday with parades, fireworks, baseball games, family picnics, concerts, and more. On this day the United States celebrates its Declaration of Independence, which emphasizes individual freedoms and human dignity, values central to the world view of most Americans.

In the same way, Christians celebrate and retell the story of Christ's crucifixion and resurrection at Easter, Jews celebrate Passover to commemorate the Exodus from bondage in Egypt, and Great Plains Indians celebrate the Sun Dance to honor the Great Mystery and the Web of Life. By re-enacting these stories in the form of ceremonies, a group affirms its common identity and counteracts disagreements which might otherwise fracture a group. Our ability to use stories to extend our identities beyond that of just our individual selves or our biological families is an essential enabler for the growth of a culture.

There can be no higher testimony to the centrality of stories in our lives than the very fact that people have shown, time and again, their willingness to sacrifice and even die for them. Given the centrality of stories in our lives, one of the most effective ways to reduce mind distance and promote understanding is to learn the stories of other individuals and groups and to reflect upon their meaning.

As Scott and his team told their stories, the natural power of empathy, coupled with their desire to succeed, helped them listen attentively. As they explained what important qualities, such as respect and trust, meant in their different cultures, they were often surprised by how differently they saw the world and how much mind distance existed between them. Each session they spent talking together helped them better understand why they did things differently. As they saw the good intentions behind the actions that might otherwise have upset them, they were able to develop ways of interacting that were mutually satisfactory, and this in turn fostered more trust.

Because our stories implicitly incorporate both our world views and our identities, they are central to who we think we are. Many of us find it difficult to listen to people tell a story that contradicts our own. At the same time, there is hardly a more powerful tool for bridging differences than the ability to listen with an open mind and heart as the other tells her story. People who have learned how to do this are the best leaders, the best at building relationships, and the best at bridging cultural differences.

Conclusion

At the heart of the challenges facing all cultures—physical survival and social cohesion—are a number of universal dilemmas. One of these revolves around the question, "Who should I take care of?" Another core dilemma relates to hierarchy and equality. All groups must develop ways to manage these and other dilemmas if they hope to survive and prosper. Recognizing the fundamental difference between dilemmas and problems encourages us to add both/and thinking to our mental repertoires.

While it is useful to view the challenges of physical survival and social cohesion as separate, in daily life they are interwoven. The same is true of the core dilemmas. Thinking about self-group and equality-hierarchy as separate dilemmas is a useful "divide and conquer" strategy, but it can cause us to lose sight of the forest as we get fascinated with the trees.

One useful technique to understand how different cultures maintain social cohesion is to study their stories. All groups tell stories to create shared meaning that helps us understand our minds and bodies, our identities and social roles, and the workings of the universe. Because stories are always created in a particular context, they inform us about how the men and women of a particular era or region view the complexities of human existence. Seen from this perspective, stories and other forms of shared meaning serve as both a group's collective memory and as the mental software that guides its members' behaviors.

It is the nature of our minds to infuse all that we perceive with meaning. While stories are central in the lives of both groups and individuals, much shared meaning gets created in everyday conversations. Because different cultures have developed different speech styles for sharing meaning, we need to understand how to read "between the lines" of our everyday conversations. As we will see in the next chapter, these different communication styles act like traps, waiting to catch the unprepared.

Ten

Reading Between the Lines

It is frequently the most obvious and taken-for-granted and therefore the least studied aspects of culture that influence behavior in the deepest and most subtle ways.

—Edward T. Hall

Heinz Willebrand is of medium height with a solid build. He exudes warmth, vitality, and enthusiasm. When people meet him it's this energy they notice first. Right now he was having trouble keeping all that energy from exploding. Did Lightpointe's CEO just say what he thought he did? Heinz admired the CEO for many qualities, but he couldn't understand why Jim didn't see what was going on.

"Jim, there is nothing we can do to keep them from taking their vacation," Heinz said as he did his best to stay calm even though everything he worked for was starting to unravel. "German law is completely on their side and there is no way we can force them to come back to work now."

"Well, let's just pay them to come back. Give them a bonus. Do whatever it takes," said Jim. Heinz could hear the tension in Jim's voice and he knew how much pressure the venture capitalists were putting on him. This was just one of the many times he was glad he had chosen to concentrate on running the technical side of the company and passed on being CEO. He wanted to help, but he wasn't sure how as Jim continued talking, "We need them to train the Americans who are coming over if we are going to meet that new order. It's huge! You know what will happen if we drop the ball now."

Heinz tried to explain to Jim that there was no way the Germans would come back. They felt betrayed and were not about to train Americans to take over their jobs. But Jim was having trouble digesting this bad news as he searched for a way out of their predicament.

"Well, what about Thomas? Couldn't we get him to move to San Diego?" Jim pleaded. "If he's there to supervise the assembly, we could still meet our deadline."

What upset Heinz most was that this crisis was unnecessary. Lightpointe was a pioneer in free-space optics providing high-speed, high-frequency information transfer using laser technology. They had a great product with a lot of potential, but were under pressure from their investors to make money soon. A few days before this phone call Jim had sent Heinz a spreadsheet containing a new timeline for the company. That timeline included closing the manufacturing site in Dresden and moving it to the United States. After studying the spreadsheet, Heinz asked Jim what his plan was. The CEO replied confidently, "That's it, that timeline is the new strategy. We close the site in Dresden, move manufacturing to our San Diego site, and save time and money as well as gain economies of scale. That increases our profits and the investors will relax. Once we get these venture capitalists off our backs, Lightpointe will really take off."

Freedom from asking the investors for more money was an appealing idea. But he sensed it was not going to go down as Jim envisioned. Even worse, the idea of firing the German associates hurt. Heinz knew and liked most of them. They had done a good job and he had been working with many of them for five years. His sense of loyalty made him feel guilty. It felt heartless to let them go. But when Heinz tried to talk to him about this, Jim changed the subject. Since that talk, business had been crazy and Heinz had not found the right time to reopen the topic.

The Turning Point

So here they were. It was March, 2005, and Jim had flown from San Diego to Dresden on Thursday. On Friday morning he spent a few hours at the plant. During a brief meeting, he announced the plant would be closed in four weeks, at which time everyone except the sales force would be let go. Equipment and inventory would be shipped to San Diego. He closed the hour-long meeting by announcing that he had to return to the States immediately. Then he got up and left. Forty jobs vanished in a region with already high unemployment.

Heinz and a crew of Americans arrived in Dresden on Monday to mop up the mess and prepare for the equipment transfer. When Heinz arrived, hardly any of the Germans were there. After Jim left the plant on Friday, the Germans continued the meeting to discuss their options. Seeing none, most of them decided to go on vacation right then.

Now Heinz was on the phone trying to explain the situation to his boss. "Jim, there is no way that Thomas will move to the U.S. He just lost a child in a car accident and his wife is pregnant. And you know what he thinks about the health care and educational systems in the U.S, he'd just as soon go to Somalia. Besides, his family has lived here for centuries and all his friends are here. He won't even consider moving."

"Well, find out what his price is," Jim snapped back, "Whatever it is we'll pay him. Just get him, Heinz. Get him or we're sunk."

This was not the first time Heinz found himself caught between the American executives headquartered in San Diego and the German manufacturing employees in Dresden. There had been cultural issues since the Americans first bought the company in 2000. That surprised Heinz. He had expected differences with the folks in Dubai, Hyderabad, Singapore, and Hong Kong. But the problems between the Americans and Germans caught him off guard. They looked and talked so much alike. And the English and German languages were so similar. It was this trap of similarity which had blindsided him several times to the subtle but significant differences between Germans and Americans.

In fact, Heinz had been surprised by the trap of similarity soon after he arrived in the United States in 1994. Then he was a newly minted physicist with a Ph.D in applied physics from the University of Münster. He got a post-grad position in the physics department of the University of Colorado in Boulder and was exploring the field of free-space optics and laser technology. He was good at what he did and he knew it. But one thing kept annoying him.

Confusing Compliments

The first time he noticed this annoying issue was when John, his American supervisor, congratulated him on the work he did writing a grant proposal. Heinz knew he had done a good job, but was surprised to be praised for it. After all, he was getting paid to do his job. And his work hadn't been that brilliant. So why did his boss bother to mention it? He wouldn't have paid much attention to it, but it kept happening. And not just with his boss. It happened with colleagues and friends as well. The Americans just kept complimenting him for the silliest things. Heinz was confused.

When we are in the midst of it, adjustment to a new culture has a way of distorting our perceptions so that what used to be a solid, predictable reality suddenly seems to move and wobble. As his brain maps went through the process of adjusting to a new social environment, he felt disoriented and wondered what was going on. Could the Americans be mocking him? Was it some sort of joke?

To understand the confusion Heinz was experiencing, we need to understand the nature of human communication. While billions of people talk to each other every day and think nothing of it, holding a good conversation turns out to be far more complicated than most people ever notice. What are we actually doing when we communicate with one another? Communication is the process of creating, sharing, and managing meaning. Or, as W. Barnett Pearce, an authority on human communication, would say, it is the "coordinated management of meaning."[1]

But wait, you might say, what about the times we talk with someone and we don't succeed in sharing meaning? What about the times people fight and walk away with different ideas about what just happened? Isn't that also communication? Of course it is. But not all conversations are equally successful. Sometimes very little meaning gets shared. But regardless of how much meaning is shared, meaning is being created and reinforced whenever we communicate. For instance, imagine a couple talking. Let's call them Kasha and Nathan. After Kasha and Nathan have a blow up, Kasha walks away with hurt feelings, muttering to herself, "What a jerk he is. I can't believe he just said that to me. Who does he think he is!"

Meanwhile, Nathan is left behind, regretting having lost his temper but also thinking, "We were having such a great time until she started talking about Ted. Why couldn't she just leave well enough alone? I don't want to blow up like this but sometimes it seems like she goes out of her way to provoke me."

While both Kasha and Nathan would agree they just had a fight, they would probably also tell very different stories about the nature of that fight. In other words, what just happened meant very different things to each of them and very little shared meaning was created. Another way of saying this is that rather than reducing mind distance, this interaction increased it. When mind distance increases, we tend to diverge and in the worst cases to polarize and flip into conflict. Represented visually, this lack of shared meaning might look like this:

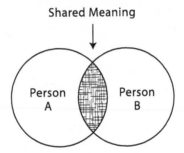

Figure 10.1 — Decreased Shared Meaning = Increased Mind Distance

But now imagine Kasha and Nathan have just spent a wonderful evening together. They laughed and joked as they prepared dinner together. While they were eating Nathan told Kasha about his childhood and how he had always had trouble controlling his temper. That really interested Kasha because she had never been good at expressing her anger. In fact, when someone got angry it terrified her. Nathan hadn't even considered that as a possibility. As they both learned more and more about one another, the mind distance between them shrank. By the end of the evening they felt even closer to one another than before. In this case, both would have been more likely to tell the same story about what they had experienced. Represented visually, this increased shared meaning might look something like this:

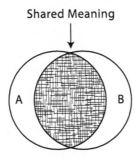

Figure 10.2 — Increased Shared Meaning = Decreased Mind Distance

Creating more shared meaning not only decreases mind distance, it also has other benefits. For one, as people share their meaning it allows them to assess how accurate that meaning is. More accurate shared meaning can be compared to the collective intelligence that allows people to make better decisions.[2] Second, shared meaning also enables people to coordinate their actions more effectively, thus promoting improved cooperation.[3]

Four Dimensions of Meaning

While the above imagined scenarios may make creating and sharing meaning seem simple, it's a complex undertaking that can go wrong in many different ways. According to Friedemann Schulz von Thun, a German communication psychologist, every time we talk we are sharing meaning on four dimensions:[4]

- Content
- Intention
- Identity
- Relationship

The **content** dimension is what a conversation is about and answers the questions, "What are we talking about?" and "What are we focused on?" In Heinz's case with John, the content was his advisor's reference to the grant Heinz had written.

The **intention** dimension of a message answers questions such as, "Why is this person saying what he is saying? What does he want from me? What is his goal?" The common saying about people who don't "walk their talk" implies that walking and talking are very different things. In fact, talking is an action and, like every other action we carry out, it always has a purpose. We may not always be conscious of our purpose for saying what we say, but if we are willing to explore our minds a bit, we will discover we always have a goal, making talk an action. And if you are one of those who believe talk is cheap, watch out where you say "I do" because divorces can be expensive. In short, to understand the meaning of a conversation, it is crucial to understand what it is we are intending. The intention dimension is so important for successful communication that it is the main topic of the next chapter.

The **identity** dimension of the message provides information about the speaker and who the speaker thinks he is. It answers questions like, "Who is the speaker? How is he feeling? How does he see the world? What does he think his social role is?" No matter what else you may be talking about, every time you say something, you are also sharing information about yourself. This information can be shared intentionally or unintentionally.

When you intentionally share information about yourself, it is often called self-disclosure. Information communicated unintentionally is often referred to as leakage.[5] We are all concerned about how and what we communicate so as to create an image of ourselves that we like and believe to be socially appropriate. This is often called face work or impression management.[6] Because we are often unaware of all the signals we are sharing, we are sometimes saying more about ourselves than about the content, i.e., we are telling about our world view, values, and who we are by the position we take towards the content at hand.

The **relationship** dimension tells who the speaker thinks the other person is and what kind of relationship they have. Are they equals or does one have more power and status than the other? Are they both members of the same group (insiders) or do they belong to different groups (outsiders)? What are their social roles? Are they husband and wife? Friends or enemies? Teacher and student, or any of the many other types of relationships that humans establish among themselves?

Each person in a conversation must interpret—consciously or unconsciously—each of these four dimensions accurately to understand what the other person means. If four messages are being communicated simultaneously, there is a lot that can go wrong, even among people who know each other well. If we complicate the situation by having people from different cultures who use different communication styles, you can see how much potential misunderstanding there is.

Schulz von Thun uses drawings of people with four ears or four mouths to drive home the point that whether we are listening or speaking, meaning is always being shared on these four different dimensions and they will always play a role whenever we communicate. If we transpose the four dimensions of meaning onto our social motor, it would look like this.

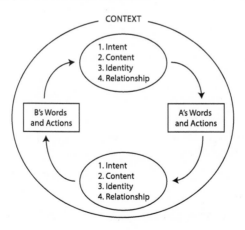

Figure 10.3 — Listening with "Four Ears"

Because of the complexity of human communication, cultures work out conventions—often unwritten and learned implicitly—about what sort of meaning should be communicated on each dimension and how this should be done. Creating conventions to share meaning in our face-to-face encounters is a major way that cultures promote social cohesion.

Let's summarize: Communication is about creating and sharing meaning and meaning gets shared on at least four different dimensions. Not occasionally, but every time we communicate. Communicating well, an essential skill for reducing mind distance, has much to do with our ability to manage these four dimensions of meaning skillfully. This is not always easy. For example, it will do you little good if you are right on the content dimension, but alienate the other person on the relationship dimension. To promote both safety and truth, it is crucial to remember that the listener can choose to pay attention to any of the four dimensions. For example, it can be a difficult conversation if the listener places his attention on the identity and relationship dimensions, taking everything personally, when you insist on getting the facts straight on the content dimension.

Transatlantic Compliments

To understand these different dimensions better, let's look at what was happening with Heinz when John complimented him on a job well done. The situation was clear enough. Heinz had done a good job at writing a grant proposal. After cursorily skimming Heinz's proposal, John said, "Heinz, great job!"

There is no misunderstanding on the content dimension. Both men believe Heinz did a good job and this is what John said, if somewhat hyperbolically. But the deeper question in Heinz's mind was about John's intention. "Why is he telling me this? Of course I did a good job. That's what I am supposed to do. That's what I get paid for. So why is he telling me something we both know?" So what this first meant to Heinz was that John was saying something obvious and thus a waste of time and energy. If it had only happened once, Heinz would have forgotten about it like the million other details we forget as we go about our lives. But the pattern kept repeating itself and not just with John. That's what got to Heinz. Why were the Americans always making such a big fuss about something that was so normal? To understand that, we need to examine where things went awry on the intention dimension.

From Heinz's perspective, it was both unnecessary and unusual to compliment someone for a job well done. This attitude is quite common in Heinz's home country of Germany, and the phrase *nicht geschimpft ist schon Lob genug*, heard regularly in areas of Germany, is quite typical. Translated literally it means, "If you weren't criticized, that's praise enough." In other words, no news is good news. If you don't hear anything from your boss, it means you are doing a good job and he is satisfied with your work. If you do hear something, you are probably in for some criticism. But you are not likely to hear compliments for a job done well.

In the United States, the situation is different. Employees expect regular feedback from their managers. Naturally enough, they prefer compliments and praise. For a number of reasons, American managers have gotten into the habit of praising people. Why the Americans and Germans differ in respect to making compliments is a complex question that merits a separate book.[7] But for our purposes, we can say Heinz's confusion was caused because the two cultures have different conventions with regard to compliments. And this affected his interpretation of the Americans' intentions. At that point, he had only been in the United States for a short time and hadn't yet noticed that many educated, middle-class Americans spend a lot of time complimenting each other. In trying to understand the Americans' unexpected behavior, he even considered that they were mocking him.

But for the life of him, he could not understand why they would want to do that. Heinz knew he was an accomplished physicist who was competent in solving tough computational problems as well as an articulate person who could write and speak well. This was his job, so on the identity dimension there was no conflict between what John had said and what Heinz believed.

And there was no problem on the relationship level. Heinz knew he was the employee and that John was his supervisor. He accepted the supervisor-employee relationship as did John so there was no misunderstanding there.

It was only on the intention dimension that a misunderstanding had occurred. And it occurred because different cultures have different unwritten rules about what kinds of meaning should be shared on what dimension, as well as how this meaning should be interpreted. As we will see again and again, these different dimensions of meaning cause unexpected problems when people from different cultures try to cooperate with one another.

I understand why Heinz felt confused. In fact, such confusion is a common experience among expatriates as they are going through the process of adjusting to life in a new country.[8] When I first moved to Germany and was just becoming fluent in German, I was at a local bar with some friends. It happened to be my birthday and when I mentioned this, my friends declared that I had to pay for the drinks. We were a raucous band of young guys so I knew they were pulling my leg and trying to get free drinks. And I was determined to not be taken for a fool. So I adamantly resisted their insistent demands. Again and again they tried to make me believe it was indeed the custom in Germany for the "birthday child" to buy the drinks. You can imagine how embarrassed I was the next day when I asked my German girlfriend and she assured me that it is indeed traditional in Germany for the person with the birthday to buy the drinks.

Since you now know that we always have an intention when we communicate, you may be wondering what my purpose is in disclosing a story that might make me look like a cheapskate. The answer is simple: Developing mindsight requires us to take risks and make mistakes as we learn new skills. In this regard, living overseas or trying to learn a new language are useful learning opportunities and you inevitably make mistakes. Good interculturalists have developed the ability to laugh at themselves and they have lots of funny stories to tell about the embarrassing mistakes they made and what they learned from them. In the end, experience is a more powerful teacher than theory.

Share All Relevant Meaning

Because meaning is always being communicated on four dimensions, and because we are often consciously aware of only one or two dimensions at any given time, there are three corollaries to the principle of safety first, truth second that are wise to remember.

Number one: Never assume you are aware of all the meaning you are communicating to someone else. In other words, never assume you know exactly what your words and actions mean to the other person.

Number two: At signs of danger, switching from the content to relationship and identity dimensions is one way to restore safety and create trust. For instance, if I notice a frown flicker across the other's face, I might stop pushing my agenda and ask if I said something he found upsetting. If my previous remark upset him so much that he can no longer listen to me because alarm signals are going off in his head, clarifying his reaction will save time in the long term.

Number three: To increase the odds your communication is successful, make sure all relevant meaning gets into the pool of shared meaning. If I cannot express what I consider relevant when we talk, I am not going to be satisfied with our conversation. And the same is true for you. But what constitutes relevant meaning?

That will depend on many factors, both objective and subjective, and will always be influenced by the context. It will also depend upon what your culture considers relevant and this has a great influence on the different communication styles used by different groups. As we will see in the next chapter, diversity in communication styles is a major source of misunderstanding. In essence, if you leave a conversation feeling satisfied and energized, chances are relevant meaning was communicated. If you leave dissatisfied, there may have been too much or too little meaning shared.

Let's examine another example from Heinz's experiences at Lightpointe to understand what constitutes relevant meaning. By the time he founded Lightpointe in 1998, Heinz had been in the United States for four years. In those four years he had adjusted—sometimes consciously and sometimes unconsciously—to the basic differences between America and his home country. But in 2000 Lightpointe acquired the free-space optics division of a German company and Heinz was confronted with cultural differences in a much more demanding way. Not only was he now the middleman between the Germans in Dresden and the Americans in San Diego, he was also confronted with the cultural differences between East and West Germans. The next six years were to be a true test of his intercultural skills.

Lightpointe renamed the new acquisition Lightpointe Europe and American executives began showing up regularly at the plant in Dresden. That's when the cultural frictions began. No one could fault the Americans for not being friendly. They insisted the Germans call them by their first names and they did their best to let the Germans know they saw a bright future for the newly expanded company. But to the Americans' dismay, working with the Germans turned out to be a lot tougher than they expected. Meetings began to drive them crazy. Whereas the Americans wanted to get the big picture and move on, the Germans wanted to understand the reasoning behind every decision. Meetings seemed to drag on forever and the Germans didn't seem much concerned when the American bosses tried to speed things up.

In this instance, the Germans needed more information to feel satisfied and the Americans needed less. They had different ideas about what constituted "all relevant meaning" and this led to stress for both sides. Heinz was caught in the middle, the unofficial cultural ombudsman everyone turned to when the going got tough. He felt like he was caught in a cross-fire as he tried to explain to both sides what needed to be done. But sometimes he didn't know himself. Many times cultural rules are so far below the waterline of awareness they seem invisible. Take for instance the matter of titles.

Heinz or Herr Doktor Willebrand?

Heinz knew that by German standards he should be addressed as Herr Doktor Willebrand, not Heinz. In Germany, expertise is accorded great respect and it is common for people in business and politics to have a

Ph.D degree. On the relationship level, calling an expert Herr or Frau Doktor is the expected way of showing respect.

Using the person's last name also indicates that this is a professional setting and the communication is going to be more formal and *sachlich*, i.e., people are going to take care to be rational and matter-of-fact.[9] To be *sachlich* also implies they will focus their attention almost entirely on the content dimension and do their best to create clarity about the topic being discussed. This means German discussions tend to be both comprehensive and detail oriented. This German desire for clarity is one reason why the meetings with the Germans tended to last longer than the Americans expected. But this was only part of the problem.

To be *sachlich* also implies Germans will do their best to restrain their emotions and remain task oriented to accomplish the job in an efficient manner. This is one common convention Germans use to manage the self-group dilemma. On the identity and relationship levels the meaning being communicated is, "We are a team and I am controlling myself in order to be a good team player." All this is obvious to the Germans when they are at work. In fact, it is so obvious no one would even think to explain it to anyone else or even to talk about it.

If Heinz had been able to identify himself as Herr Doktor Willebrand, he would have had more authority and been able to direct the Germans to be more succinct. But Heinz was not able to use his title to gain respect as he would have liked. That was because when the Americans first arrived, they were all smiles as they introduced themselves using their first names.

From the American perspective, the messages they were sending on the identity and relationship level went something like this, "Hey, I'm a regular guy. Just because I'm the manager doesn't mean I need to act like some stuck-up jerk. Let's be friendly with one another and it will be easier to get the job done." In other words, the American managers were behaving pretty much the way they would have behaved at the American office. In the U.S. this first-name approach serves as a social lubricant to help people develop good working relationships.

Creating a Transatlantic Identity

So while Heinz would have liked to be Herr Dr. Willebrand with the Germans, to do so would have made him stick out from all the other Americans. This raises a deeper question, was Heinz a German or an American at this point? That was also part of the problem. Heinz wasn't sure himself. He had come over with the Americans and they treated him as one of them. And he was a partial owner of Lightpointe, which was an American company. And he liked living in the U.S and intended to stay. He had adjusted well and was no longer the same person who had left Germany six years earlier. Somehow he was both German and American, or some strange hybrid. In any case, he didn't feel comfortable demanding that the Germans address him as Herr Dr. Willebrand. At the same time, he sensed he was giving up both credibility and authority in their eyes.

This was because, like most European languages, German has a grammatical system that forces a speaker to choose between a formal or informal system of address. These two systems use different pronouns for the word "you"—*sie* is formal, *du* is informal—as well as different verb forms to make it clear whether the formal or informal system is being used. *Sie* is used with a person's last name whereas *du* is used with a person's first name. Associated with this grammatical distinction are many behaviors that Germans use automatically. That's why Heinz would have preferred to be addressed as Herr Dr. Willebrand. It would have activated the formal system and he would have had more authority.

The Americans didn't speak German, so all meetings had to be conducted in English. Unfortunately for the Americans, English no longer uses such obvious grammatical markings.[10] So the Americans didn't realize that by introducing themselves with their first names, they were implicitly telling the Germans to act as if they were using the German informal system of address. This is, of course, a message about the relationship level of meaning. What it meant for the Germans was, "We are now on more of an equal footing, more like that among friends, not as that between boss and employee and we should behave accordingly." And so they did. They voiced their criticism to ideas they didn't agree with and took other liberties the Americans were not expecting. All of which caused the meetings to run even longer.

Much to the Germans surprise, the Americans pulled back. They didn't act like they were really equals or wanted to be friends. Instead they acted like impatient bosses who just happened to smile a lot and use first names. This confused the Germans. So while the Americans got impatient with the Germans for talking so long in meetings, the Germans began to think of the Americans as closed-minded and arrogant. This was one of the more disruptive cultural differences occurring on a regular basis and Heinz was kept busy trying to smooth over disconnects.

The Devil's in the Hidden Rules

Little things, like whether office doors were open or closed, took on surprising significance. The American executives instigated an open-door policy to show they were approachable. The Germans found this irritating. In Germany, as everyone knew, doors are meant to be closed. Closed doors keep noise levels down, save heating costs, and send signals that this is an orderly place where privacy is respected. As simple things took on increased significance, the level of tension in the group went up, which affected everyone.

We have already defined culture as a group's way of life. From the above examples, we can see that a group's way of life is undergirded by countless behavioral norms. Some of these norms are explicit and visible. Consider something as simple as the following sentence: *This sentence follows the rules of English grammar.* Now let's use the same words but ignore some rules: *Rules follows this sentence the English of grammar.* The first sentence makes sense. The second sentence uses the same words but results in meaningless nonsense. The norms for building proper English sentences are formal, explicit rules American children learn in the course of growing up. Of course not everyone speaks grammatically correct English in the United States, but it is the normative ideal as modeled by people in positions of power.

But now consider a radically different sentence: *Frozen rules fell down loudly as the happy trees danced and shook with laughter.* Even though this sentence does follow the rules of formal English grammar and syntax, it is not meaningful, except perhaps as avant-garde poetry. That's because it contradicts the assumptions about reality upon which the American world view is constructed. These assumptions are the informal and unwritten rules that exist below the waterline of awareness, yet we all seem to know them. In this sense, our shared assumptions act as invisible rules for how we should understand the world.

The point is this, cultures are held together by both explicit and implicit rules and the shared meanings associated with them. The explicit rules are taught openly and are easy to ascertain. The implicit rules are hidden, talked about only indirectly, and difficult to put into words. But whether formal and explicit or informal and implicit, these rules structure our lives and provide more of the shared meaning that holds a culture together. Knowing these hidden rules and meanings is essential for members of a culture to coordinate their actions.

Of course, it is the invisible, implicit rules that give us the most trouble. Imagine you are newly immigrated to the United States and are hoping to live the American dream. Which of the following behaviors would help you succeed in the United States?

- You are middle-aged and walking down the street on a cold winter day. You notice a teenage mother carrying her baby who is not warmly dressed. You stop the mother and berate her, telling her she should clothe her child more warmly and be a better mother.
- Your boss has invited you to his house with some other employees for a barbeque. It's a weekday evening and all the other employees show up at or shortly after 6:00 p.m. You show up after 7:00 p.m. and neither excuse yourself, nor explain why you are late. But to show your respect and good intentions you stay, talking animatedly, until 10:30 p.m.

- You are scheduled to meet a potential new client. Your boss has told you it is critical to get this new account. To make a good impression you present the potential client with a handsome leather briefcase worth several hundred dollars.

All of the above examples would be perfectly acceptable behaviors in different parts of the world. But they wouldn't have much chance of succeeding in the United States because they violate rules Americans follow to coordinate their actions and promote social cohesion. In this sense, the rules and the shared meaning they convey in a particular culture can be likened to the rules in a game. Just as different games have different rules as to how people should play them, so, too, our perceptions, thoughts, feelings, and behaviors follow the cultural rules we have grown up with.

Thinking of cultures as a game with rules is a powerful metaphor, and when we begin to understand the rules of different cultures, we gain in mindsight. In addition, we have the opportunity to increase our behavioral flexibility. This is one reason why people who have lived overseas for any length of time often say they feel as if their lives are richer, freer, and less constrained than before.

Technology of Communication

Unfortunately, few of the Germans and Americans at Lightpointe were taking the time to learn the unwritten rules of each other's culture. If Heinz had more time, he might have been able to keep repairing the growing misunderstandings before they poisoned the relationship between Dresden and San Diego. But immediately after the acquisition, demand skyrocketed. Within a few years they had offices in Dubai, Hyderabad, Hong Kong, and London. At its peak, Lightpointe was a global organization and Heinz was continually on the road. As Lightpointe's chief technical officer, he was flying over a hundred thousand miles a year and kept his suitcase packed by the bed because he could be called away at any instant.

Heinz became adept at calling in from wherever he was in the world to take part in virtual meetings. He also found himself using technology to stay connected with his wife and kids. As he became more and more skillful at using these new technologies, he became painfully aware that they could not replace face-to-face communication, especially with his family. And at work it seemed the more emails and teleconferences there were, the more the misunderstandings increased. On the surface there was lots of information flowing, but it didn't always translate to more shared meaning among the Lightpointe associates.

Modern communication technologies are changing the face of the planet by creating an interdependent virtual world. These technologies are fantastic in their ability to help us stay connected but each one—email, telephone, video conference, social media, and so on—strips away portions of the nonverbal signals and thus the meaning that normally gets shared in face-to-face communication. In general, this leads to more misunderstandings, not fewer. For example, email only allows us to share written words and it's easy to overemphasize the content level of communication. This is especially problematic when people from cultures that place more importance on explicit verbal communication use email to communicate with people from more relationship- and context-oriented cultures, because it's often the nonverbal signals that communicate intention, relationship, and identity messages. As these signals go missing, misunderstandings become more common and feelings get hurt.

Worse, because nonverbal signals encourage our inner teams to tone down dissent, they help us avoid conflicts when we meet face-to-face. Because these signals are missing when we communicate online, arguments, insults, name-calling, and other hostilities are found more frequently on the web.

Primacy of Nonverbal

In short, our brains need the nonverbal signals from the other person to understand what he means. This is not surprising, since our brains evolved in social groups where face-to-face interactions were a continual part of life. While our oldest hominid ancestors did not have a spoken language, they did use facial expressions, gestures, and sounds to communicate emotions, intentions, and relationship issues to each other. In the history of our species, nonverbal communication came first and today much nonverbal communication occurs below the level of conscious awareness. This is another example of the brain's dual process strategy to free up conscious awareness for challenges that require more reflection.

The discovery of mirror neurons by Italian neuroscientists in the nineties was one of the most exciting developments in our understanding of the social nature of the brain.[11] These neurons were first discovered in the brains of chimpanzees and called mirror neurons because they activated when a chimpanzee was about to carry out a particular movement, or when that chimp saw another chimp carry out the same movement. In other words, they acted as mirrors for the actions of other chimps. It seems mirror neurons in humans are involved in much social cognition. They help us learn new behaviors that we first observe in others and then imitate. This explains the important role of mimicry and imitation for babies as they naturally begin behaving like the people around them. Mirror neurons also help us intuit the emotional states and intentions of others and thus play an important role in face-to-face communication as well as provide a mechanism to explain the contagious nature of emotions.

Large, complex brains outfitted with various social circuits and mirror neurons help explain why humans can be such exquisite communicators. This ability to communicate so subtly and precisely— both verbally and nonverbally—allows us to pass onto our offspring our group's way of life, including its ways of communicating. That's because our brains are predisposed to internalize the language, knowledge, attitudes, emotional strategies, and behaviors of our parents.[12] At the same time, the baby's brain is also taking in direct sensory input about the environment. By combining the experiences it has with its parents and the inputs it gets from the environment, the baby's brain begins creating the brain maps—including models of how to communicate—that it will use to navigate its way through life.

Attuned Communication

This learning process starts immediately after birth when the attachment systems of the mother, or other caretaker, and infant predispose them to bond and begin communicating nonverbally. This is another reason why nonverbal communication is so powerful. It is not only our species' first language, it is also the first communication medium we learn as infants. These first experiences—the perceptions, feelings, and related behaviors—are etched into our implicit memories.

Regardless of the particular family or culture a baby is born into, one general pattern lies at the heart of satisfying communication everywhere: The tendency to attune with and mirror those we feel safe with and want to be close to. In other words, we adjust our verbal and nonverbal behaviors to minimize differences when communicating with people we like. [13] Conversely, we tend to emphasize our differences with individuals we do not like or feel safe with. Emphasizing differences is a fundamental way to indicate we are separate from one another and to maintain mind distance. This tendency to converge with those we like and to diverge from those we dislike influences the boundaries we use to structure our relationships.

Attuning and minimizing differences can be done in a wide variety of ways. Consider some typical differences in nonverbal communication between Germans and Americans. If everything else is equal, German men tend to look a little bit longer and more directly into each other's eyes when speaking than do American men. As already noted, German men tend to smile less than Americans, especially in business situations and public spaces. German men who feel comfortable with one another tend to stand a bit closer to one another when talking than do American men. Because they are standing closer, they need to talk less loudly. German men also tend to stand with their legs slightly closer together and their bodies drawn in more than do American men, who tend to take a broader stance. These are just a few of the general nonverbal differences between German and American men.

So what happens when a German and American male speak together face-to-face? If they like one another and feel safe, they will tend to downplay these differences. For instance, the American might stand slightly closer than usual—slightly in this case can be as small as an inch or two and probably not more than six inches—or the German might feel comfortable standing further apart and talking slightly louder than he is used to. Similarly, the American might find himself looking slightly longer and more directly into the other's eyes than he is used to, or the German might react less negatively than usual to reduced eye contact.

On the other hand, if these two men don't like one another or feel safe in the other's presence, their behavior will tend to diverge. In that case, the American might continue to stand further apart, or even talk more loudly than he usually does. Or the German may open up even less and tighten his body even more while keeping his voice lower and more controlled than usual as he looks directly into the eyes of the American. If asked for his impression after such an encounter, the German might say the American seemed too loud, childish, or even aggressive and threatening. And the American might say the German was stiff, hard to get to know, or even arrogant and domineering.

But if you ask Americans and Germans after an encounter during which they felt safe and where their nonverbal behaviors tended to converge and attune, you will hear different interpretations. Then the Germans will often say they found the American to be friendly and outgoing, open and spontaneous. And the Americans will tend to find the Germans direct, honest, reliable, and easy to connect with.

Verbally, this universal pattern can also be found in accent, choice of vocabulary, correctness of grammar, degree of formality, etc. Whether done verbally or nonverbally—usually we do both at the same time—we are doing much the same thing as when we dance with someone. If we accept the invitation to dance, we must find a way to coordinate our movements with those of our partner so we can move smoothly as a unit around the floor. In the same way, the give and take of a good conversation is a series of coordinated actions that enable the two partners to attune and minimize differences.

Windows of Tolerance

An infant develops a secure attachment with its caretaker via attuned communication. Unfortunately, the attachment process does not always go well and people who are avoidantly attached often develop communication patterns that make it harder for them to attune with others.[14] The feelings of attuning and converging with another person can be emotionally intense and they can even trigger fear or anger in some people. Any experience that is too intense can potentially push us beyond our window of tolerance, making it harder for us to respond appropriately. As we will see later, communication styles are also associated with norms of emotional expression, and different degrees of emotionality can challenge our attempts to attune with one another.

For this reason attuned communication is about finding the right balance between converging and diverging, between closeness and distance, so that both partners feel safe. It's about maintaining healthy boundaries so both individuals feel at ease with the interpersonal distance between them. Maintaining healthy boundaries sends important messages on the identity and relationship dimensions and the bottom line is this: When we maintain mutually satisfying boundaries, it is much easier to share the relevant meaning that is necessary to develop trusting relationships.

As we will see, people can use any of the four primary dimensions of meaning to create boundaries and this can be done both verbally and nonverbally. These different ways of maintaining boundaries to regulate the basic process of attuning and converging are often done by our inner team without much conscious awareness. Developing more self-awareness of our nonverbal signals is one way to improve our ability to attune while maintaining healthy boundaries.

The events after the plant closure in Dresden are complicated, but the short version is this: Lightpointe lost its largest customer. The venture capitalists pulled the plug and Lightpointe was auctioned off. Jim, the CEO, left for another position. Heinz tried to save the company he had founded, but a larger bid was made that he couldn't match. He was heartbroken. He felt like a boxer who had just fought the fight of his life only to be knocked out by a fluke punch in the last round. But Heinz has the emotional resilience and stamina typical of the best interculturalists. He got back up off the mat and founded a new company, Rayawave.

In 2008 the new owner of Lightpointe discovered that his replacement CEO did not have what it took to keep the company afloat. Heinz was contacted by the new owner of Lightpointe. Rayawave and Lightpointe merged and Heinz, wiser and more mature, became CEO and president. Since then he has worked hard to make up for the good will that had been lost. Lightpointe is now regaining both its old customers and market share.

It is also what it has always been, an organization with a global vision. When Heinz founded the company in 1998, he made his personal vision part of the company culture. Growing up in Germany forced Heinz to confront the horrors of Germany's National Socialist period. Like so many Germans of his generation, Heinz found it difficult to come to terms with what had happened in Germany during the thirties and forties. As a teenager, he began an intense study of modern history to understand how his own people had fallen into the trap of extreme nationalism and rampant militarism. As a young scientist he began traveling to Russia to meet physicists working on the same material he was. His experiences in different countries led to a clear conclusion: Most people everywhere are basically good, but sometimes they get led astray by fear, laziness, hatred, and bad leaders.

The answer for Heinz was to become a citizen of the world and develop good relationships with anyone who showed good will. It is this willingness to overlook superficial differences and see the deeper commonalities in others that has helped Heinz make friends around the world and build a customer base that is helping Lightpointe succeed in the wireless market. It is also this attitude that defines Lightpointe's diverse workforce, which is currently made up of Asians, Europeans, and Americans.

Like many of the best interculturalists, Heinz assumes people do the best they can with the resources at their disposal. Heinz's intention to be a citizen of the world informs much of what he does and accounts for much of his success. While Heinz is very talented technically, he is also very much a people person. He focuses just as much on relationships as he does on the technical end, and this explains why he is still a welcome guest whenever he returns to Dresden.

Conclusion

While some cultures seem very different, others seem quite alike and this very similarity can become a trap, as it does when Germans and Americans try to cooperate. Much of culture is invisible and one of the best ways to understand a different culture is to examine their communication practices. Even subtle differences, such as the way compliments are made or not made, can create irritation and confusion. They can also disrupt the smooth functioning of the social motor and its ability to pump meaning into the shared pool.

Communication is the creation and sharing of meaning, and this meaning gets shared on at least four dimensions: Content, intention, identity, and relationship. Communicating well requires us to manage all four domains of meaning in a skillful manner. If the signals of even one of these domains is misinterpreted, it can lead to awkward disconnects.

To promote social cohesion, cultures use rules—both explicit and implicit—to help their members coordinate the sharing of meaning. When we don't understand these rules, misunderstandings are inevitable. Cultures can be likened to games and the smart interculturalist will invest time and effort in learning the rules of the communication games that different cultures play. By learning the unwritten rules, we can revise our expectations and increase the likelihood of being able to connect well with the other.

While content is usually communicated verbally, meaning from the other three domains is often signaled nonverbally. Nonverbal signals are so important because humans first learned—both as a species and as individuals—to communicate nonverbally. The relationship and identity levels of communication are about boundaries and by maintaining mutually acceptable boundaries, we increase our chances for creating trusting relationships.

Because it is difficult to track all four dimensions of meaning when we are speaking, it is easy to assume the other person has interpreted our meaning the way it was intended. This is the sort of assumption that can start wars. To implement the principle of safety first, truth second, it is essential to learn to listen with all four ears. If you notice disconnects occurring and you or your partner are feeling uncomfortable, switching to the identity and relationship levels is one way to restore safety.

When people meet, they tend to either converge and exchange meaning in a way that reduces mind distance, or they diverge, which creates more mind distance. In this regard, communication is like a dance and learning the universal dance of attuned communication is one of the most valuable skills a human can develop. As we will see in the next chapter, having the intention to communicate in an attuned manner is a key to personal, professional, and intercultural success.

Eleven

The Centrality of Intention

Don't aim at success—the more you make it a target, the more you will miss it. Dedicate yourself to something greater than yourself.

—Viktor Frankl

When Shawn Camden approached him about teaching English to immigrants, Lee Shainis got excited. Back in 2000 Shawn was working in a thrift store and Lee had a day job at the local elementary school. Lee had graduated from college and moved to Colorado the year before and was looking for something to do with his life. The idea of helping poor immigrants who were struggling to learn English and adjust to life in the United States appealed to him. Lee's motivation was not completely altruistic: Learning Spanish and getting to know a different community of people was enticing.

So in the evenings after work, Shawn and Lee began teaching English to immigrant families and helping them understand the basics of life in the United States. Shawn was already helping a family from Colombia and Lee began working with a family from Mexico. They had no training and made mistake after mistake. But they had a passion to help and a willingness to learn.

They bought English grammar books at Barnes & Noble and spent countless hours researching teaching methods. In time, they became adept at teaching the immigrants, many who were barely literate, to speak English and survive in the United States.

Lee had a head start in dealing with different kinds of people. As a high-school student he had begun volunteering at a homeless shelter in southeast Washington, D.C. Then, as a student at the University of Michigan, he volunteered at a local prison where many of the inmates were young African-American men from the roughest neighborhoods of Detroit. For a young, white man from an affluent suburb, working in the prison was like entering another world.

Lee has real skills in communicating with different people. You notice it in the enthusiasm with which he greets you the first time. And you notice it later when he remembers your name with a smile that lights up his face. You sense he is sincerely happy to meet you, that this is more than just glad-handing and that he cares deeply about others. All of this makes people feel at ease with him. By helping others feel safe, he creates the atmosphere needed to connect with them.

Those prisoners in Detroit had grown up in poverty and violence and many believed no one cared about them. Lee was able to convey that he did care and his caring created safety, reduced mind distance, and built emotional bridges. For some it may have been the first time in their lives anyone showed true warmth and affection and the experience was powerful, both for them and for Lee. Connecting with others whose lives were filled with suffering gave him deep satisfaction.

This ability to care for others and make them feel safe was one of the major skills that helped Lee and Shawn grow their informal volunteer work into a significant non-profit organization in the Boulder-Denver area. Shortly after they began, it occurred to the two young men that this might become more than just working one-on-one with immigrants. Within a few months, they began recruiting other volunteers to help.[1] They taught the volunteers how to teach English and connected them with immigrants who needed help. Within six months of starting, they applied for and received a grant to grow their tiny organization. They called their undertaking Intercambio because they were excited by the idea of the exchange that would take place between volunteers and students.

Intercambio Uniting Communities has now grown into a vibrant organization that helps immigrants improve their English skills and their ability to live, work, and care for their children in the United States. Since 2001, the non-profit has enlisted well over four thousand volunteer teachers who have helped approximately ten thousand students and it now has an annual budget of one million dollars with fifteen employees. In addition, Intercambio's teaching materials and training methods are now being used in forty-eight other states.[2]

The Power of Intention

When they first started working with immigrants in Boulder County, Lee and Shawn had no idea their initiative would grow so rapidly. Their original intent was to support people who were struggling to improve their lives. Today, if you ask Lee how important his and Shawn's intentions were in the formation of Intercambio, he will tell you they were huge. Their success suggests it is difficult to overestimate the power of intention.

Setting smart goals and having a clear vision of the intended outcomes are the starting points for achievement in all areas of human performance. Coaches and sports psychologists have used the power of goal setting for years. To help athletes improve, their coaches work hard at helping them clarify their intentions. As John Whitmore makes clear in his best-selling book, *Coaching For Performance*, setting smart goals as a way to harness the power of intention is much more than just wishful thinking.[3] Whitmore should know, he began his own career as a winning professional race car driver before becoming a sports psychologist and running successful consulting companies in the United Kingdom, Switzerland, and the United States.

In *Flow – The Psychology Of Optimal Experience*, Mihaly Csikszentmihalyi shows how setting clear goals to focus our attention helps us achieve those flow states most humans aspire to.[4] Like asking questions, setting goals creates internal order in our minds that allows us to enjoy the actual experience of working towards our goals. Some people may think setting goals is something that happens only in particular contexts or in achievement-oriented cultures, but that is too narrow an understanding of what goals are. People everywhere use goals to guide their behavior and no realm of human endeavor is devoid of goal setting.

When we set healthy goals and organize our actions to achieve them, we not only create order in our minds, we also increase the odds of our success. Clear goals give us a standard by which to measure our progress and this sense of moving towards our goal is a key component to positive experiences. It can even reduce the effects of stress on the body.[5] Achieving healthy goals not only satisfies our needs, it also helps grow our confidence. Our confidence is further augmented if our achievements are recognized and lauded by those whom we respect. Lee is one of the most energetic and profoundly happy people I know. I suspect this is not only because he is so often in flow states, but also because his achievements have received such positive recognition from people around the country.

Stephen Covey also recognized the power of intention in *The 7 Habits of Highly Effective People* and he reminds us that "all things are created twice," first in our heads and then in real life.[6] He said the ideas, visions, and intentions in our minds are the blueprints for our actions. Having clear intentions means having blueprints that are easy to understand and ready to use whenever we decide to act.

Having clear intentions and smart goals also helps us develop the emotional resiliency to keep going when things get tough. Plus, having a purpose in life gives us the drive we need to get back up when we fall down. For these reasons, Covey suggests developing a mission statement for our lives. This harnesses the power of intention to create the life we want.

In addition to promoting health and resilience, clarifying our intentions encourages coherence. Because our brains and minds are so complex, it's easy for different members of our inner teams to be pursuing different ends at the same time, which creates internal dissonance, reduces satisfaction, and impedes progress. When we become aware of dissonance in our minds and bodies, we can reduce it by clarifying our needs and intentions. Then we can use goal setting to meet those needs and increase the odds of reaching a state of flow.

When we ignore internal dissonance, it often slips out of awareness only to get expressed in subtle nonverbal signals. Internal dissonance not only reduces our ability to achieve flow states, it can also affect our relationships in the form of "double messages" and "incongruent actions."[7] For all these reasons, clarifying our intentions is a powerful step in communicating more effectively.

Intention and Mindsight

To make sense of the other person's words and actions, we need to know what the other person is intending. To accomplish this task our brains try to "read" the internal states of our conversational partner to understand what her verbal and nonverbal signals might mean. Understanding each of the four dimensions of meaning in a message—content, intention, relationship, and identity—is essential for knowing what a person means, but the intention dimension is special in several ways.

As we saw, the content dimension answers questions like, "What is it we are focused on here?" and, "What are we paying attention to?" In contrast, the intention level answers questions like, "What is she trying to do here?" and "What are her goals?" Obviously, if two people have different goals in a conversation, it is going to be difficult for them to communicate successfully. As we saw in the previous chapter, it was the intentions that were often at odds between the Germans and Americans working at Lightpointe. In contrast, having their intentions so clearly aligned allowed Lee and Shawn to cooperate so successfully.

For social beings like ourselves, understanding the intention of others is crucial for survival and for social cohesion. Without understanding the other's intention, communicating effectively would be virtually impossible. For this purpose, nature has equipped our brains with amazing intention detectors to continually assess—either consciously or unconsciously—the intentions of those around us. As we saw earlier, mirror neurons in the motor cortex fire when we are about to initiate an action, and they also fire when we see someone else perform the same action.

When a person's mirror neurons are activated by observing an external action, that person experiences the emotional and bodily sensations associated with performing the action, not just witnessing it. This somatic information is fed back into the higher-level circuitry of the frontal cortex, specifically the area associated with conscious experience, i.e., the inner team's leader. This feedback loop helps explain why we often feel an urge to imitate another person. For example, why we get thirsty and have an urge to lift our own glass when we see someone drinking from their glass. Or why we begin to yawn when we see someone else yawning. Or why people have an urge to dance in the streets after watching an old Fred Astaire and Ginger Rogers movie.

This complex feedback loop allows us to interpret the myriad nonverbal signals of our partner and translate them into feelings so we can feel something similar to what she is feeling. This is the physiological basis for empathy.[8] We are literally feeling sensations similar to those of someone else. This allows us to intuit the other's internal state and provides important information about her intentions.

Of course, we can only empathize with the internal states of others to the degree that we are aware of our own internal states. Without accurate mindsight into the internal states of my own mind and body, I will not be able to assess the internal states of others. Mindsight, empathy, and the ability to assess the other's intentions are thus essential for satisfying conversations and successful cooperation. But what happens when a person's expectations, based on her past experiences, leads her to misinterpret the intentions of the other person?

Doing Things with Words

Think about all the things we do with words: We greet, promise, apologize, threaten, forgive, suggest, disagree, command, etc. In any given language you'll find dozens of what linguists refer to as speech acts.[9] Speech acts are the actions we engage in with words and they are one of the basic building blocks of the conversations we use to promote our survival, build social cohesion, and generate the shared meaning we need to lead healthy lives.

When we link letters together to form words and words together to form sentences, we follow rules. By following these rules we create and share meaning in mutually understandable ways. The same is true for speech acts. What constitutes a good apology, a socially acceptable greeting, a believable promise, an untoward quarrel, an appropriate command, and so on, will be determined by the rules and conventions shared by a particular community.

Because conversations in general, and speech acts in particular, are governed by rules, some researchers point out the ritualistic nature of communication. For example, Deborah Tannen, a professor of communication studies, writes that, "Conversation is fundamentally ritual in the sense that we speak in ways our culture has conventionalized and expect certain types of response."[10] Note that in likening conversation to ritual, Tannen also emphasizes the clear expectations we have of the way the other will respond, not only in terms of content but also in the way the response is enacted.

In a ritual, spoken words are formulaic and rarely carry new information on the content level. But rituals are meaningful because of the way they are done and by the fact they are being enacted. This is true of much daily communication. If we were to focus only on the content level of communication, conversational rituals would appear to be a waste of time and energy. But when we consider that meaning is also being shared on three other dimensions, the ritualistic nature of communication begins to make more sense. By doing a speech act appropriately, we indicate our membership in a particular speech community. Following the rules not only shows we are good team players, it also allows us to synchronize our verbal and nonverbal actions with the actions of the other person, thus affirming we are part of something larger than our individual selves.

Think, for example, of the ritualistic nature of how you greet people. If you meet someone for the first time (relationship) in a more formal situation (context) and you are an older, well-educated, white male from the East Coast (identity) you might say "How do you do?" Whereas if you meet that same person in a more casual setting, you might greet her with, "Hi, how ya' doin'?" Whether or not you feel friendly towards this person and look forward to getting to know her (intention) will be signaled via your tone of voice, facial expressions, and so on.

On the content level, both of these formulations are essentially the same, that is, an inquiry into the other's state of well-being. But in terms of relationship, identity, and intention, which of these two greetings you choose will tell much about who you think you are, how you perceive the other, what you think your relationship is, and what your assessment of the context is.

Who would have thought a simple greeting could be so complex or convey so much meaning? If you take the time to reflect on the common speech acts you use in daily conversations, you will discover that the rules and conventions you use turn out to be quite complex. The reason we rarely notice this complexity is because they are done on auto-pilot. Once more we need to thank our inner team for making so many decisions autonomously that we can pay attention to other things. Much of the correct way of executing a speech act was learned by imitating those around us, while other aspects result from actively learning them in the past. Either way, they have now become habitual and function below conscious awareness.

While this degree of complexity can seem daunting, it becomes even more challenging when we remember that different speech communities teach their members to do conversational rituals differently. As a result, members of different cultures have different expectations about what constitutes a socially appropriate speech act executed in a competent manner. As noted before, when our expectations and reality do not match up, problems ensue.

Here's why: Imagine you meet someone for the first time and their first words are, "Where are you going?" Depending on their tone of voice, this may not seem like a greeting at all, but rather an intrusive question that disrespects your personal boundaries. Your internal reaction might be something like, "Who does he think he is (identity) to talk to me (relationship) like this? That's none of his business. Is he trying to disrespect me (intention)?" But in some parts of the world, "Where are you going?" is a ritualized greeting, just as "How are you doing?" is in the United States.[11] And just as an American does not really want to hear about your health problems or the messy divorce you are going through, so, too, the Filipino who asks, "Where are you going?" does not expect you to tell him. Instead, he expects the ritualized answer, "Over there," just as the typical American expects to hear "Fine," or something similar.

People always have an intention when they are communicating. Our problem is knowing which speech act to use in which setting, and how to say it. Developing conventionalized speech styles for their members to use is one method cultures use to promote social cohesion and help members coordinate their actions. Speech styles are composed of numerous elements, e.g., how direct or indirect one is expected to be, what topics are acceptable in which contexts, how fast or slow one should talk, the way turn-taking is organized, when silence is appropriate, how much self-expression and authenticity is expected, how emotions should be expressed, what constitutes an interruption, and many, many more. Creating conventional styles for communication within a group allows people to share meaning in an attuned manner as they coordinate their actions, both essential abilities for the long-term success of any group. Because attuned communication is pleasurable and creates a sense of commonality, it also promotes social cohesion.

Assuming different cultures are using the same rules to do the same speech acts with the same intentions is a path to misunderstanding. If we want to increase the odds of having satisfying conversations, we would do well to study the other culture's use of speech acts. For example, what rules are Japanese following that has them apologizing so frequently? What conventions are Spaniards expecting that cause them to feel talked down to when a German explains a procedure in a way she considers clear? What rituals are Americans enacting when they repeatedly say "thank you" for many things other cultures take for granted? By remembering that different cultures do different things with words and in different ways, we can remember to pause and reflect before assuming we know what the other person's intentions are. Or, as Deborah Tannen puts it, "You can't assume that the other person means what you would mean, if you said the same thing in the same way."[12]

Acting Out

Who has not had the experience of starting a conversation with the good intention of resolving a misunderstanding only to end up in an argument with both sides doing their best to prove the other wrong? The capacity to assess intention is built into our brains, but our assessments are not always accurate. And when we are in a state of dissonance, we may not even be aware of the intentions of some members of our own inner teams.

Clarifying our intentions before going into an important conversation increases the odds of a satisfying outcome. If I, as the leader of my inner team, intend to have a safe, mutually satisfying conversation, I need to make sure all team members are in accord with me. Otherwise I run the risk of some members sending subtle, nonverbal signals that contradict my main message. Congruence between verbal and nonverbal signals is perceived as both more sincere and more charismatic, while messages with mixed signals can confuse our partner, weaken the impact of our message, or even trigger the perception that we are being deceptive.

One effective way of making our messages more congruent is to clarify in advance both what we do and do not want.[13] For instance, do I just want to connect and enjoy the pleasure of an attuned conversation? Or do I want to get critical feedback about my unskillful behavior from the day before? Maybe I'm feeling nervous and want to talk to fill the silence? We speak for many reasons and knowing our intention is crucial because it affects how and what we share on the other three dimensions of meaning.

Knowing what I do not want is equally important before an important conversation. For example, I don't want this conversation to spiral out of control and turn into an argument. Or, I don't want to let my fears keep me from asking the tough questions. Or, I don't want the other person to believe I've disrespected her boundaries, and I don't want my own boundaries trampled on, either.

Once I know both what I do and do not want, I can make my intentions clear at the start of the conversation: "I'm sorry about last week and I really don't want to get into another argument with you, but I need to clarify that misunderstanding so I can feel more comfortable around you. Would that be alright?" By asking for the other's permission to proceed, I am saying this is a request—a speech act that respects the other's autonomy and creates safety—and not a demand—a speech act that implies an asymmetrical relationship in which I have the one-up position of power.

Of course, the way my partner will really know if this is a request and not a demand is the way I respond should she choose not to fulfill my request. If I get angry or sulk, she can assume I was covertly making a demand and not truly requesting her participation in a conversation. As this hypothetical example makes clear, the speech acts we choose not only shape our conversations, they also affect the way trust and other forms of social capital get created.

Do Unto Others…

Cultures can generate social cohesion in various ways, but these ways are not infinite and a few methods are so successful they are found in most cultures and traditions: Empathy, kindness, and honesty are stressed by all major religions as is reciprocity. According to the eminent political scientist, Robert Putnam, "The norm of generalized reciprocity is so fundamental to civilized life that all prominent moral codes contain some equivalent of the Golden Rule."[14] The golden rule is not only an efficacious way to manage the self-group dilemma, it is also at the heart of most successful communication practices.

Communication is about sharing and exchanging meaning. This can take many forms such as the exchange of knowledge, attention, time, kindness, trust, etc. Regardless of the form of meaning, we are always engaging in some sort of exchange when we communicate. The golden rule encourages us to exchange that which we would like to receive: Either to treat others as we would like to be treated or, conversely, not to treat others in a way we would not like to be treated. Such considerations of reciprocity influence the speech acts we choose to use, but we cannot assume the other person wants what we want.

For example, Deborah Tannen notes that exchanging compliments is a common conversational ritual, but that American women tend to use it more than American men, a difference that can lead to hurt feelings.[15] She tells the following story to show how this can happen. Susan, a human resources manager, and Bill, her colleague, were flying home after a national conference. They had both made presentations and Susan complimented Bill on his, telling him she thought it was a "great talk." Bill thanked her, but did not mention her talk so she asked him what he thought of hers, expecting a compliment. Instead he launched into a detailed critique of her presentation that left her feeling like a novice in an uncomfortable one-down position.

Did Bill think Susan was literally asking for feedback, or did he use the opportunity to enjoy the pleasure of being in a one-up position? This example shows another way our expectations influence our conversations. In other words, it's not only what you say that is important, it's also important what the other person expects to hear. In terms of intentions, it's not what you intended that counts as much as what the other person thinks you intended. And by now, the litany should be obvious: The chances of your intentions being misunderstood are increased if your partner belongs to a culture that has different expectations.

This misunderstanding between Bill and Susan contains three important lessons for the wise interculturalist. First, while reciprocity is used everywhere, we shouldn't assume everyone expects the same thing we do. Second, gender differences and conversational styles are correlated, and third, cultures develop speech acts that ritualize reciprocity and promote social cohesion. The first lesson should be obvious, so let's go to gender differences.

The roles of males and females and the ideas people have about what is considered natural or normal behavior for a man or woman vary within and between cultures. Gender roles are a sensitive, complicated, and nuanced topic and I only want to note that the many discussions about male and female roles are part of another dilemma all cultures must manage: The physical survival and social cohesion of any culture depends upon males and females relating well to one another. This means working together to promote the common good and individual well-being. Which social roles and behaviors become expected from a male and which from a female are part of this dilemma. As we will see in the next chapter, the behavioral expectations for males and females vary significantly between cultures, and these variations are often most noticeable in the ways men and women communicate.

Tannen makes this point clearly: "In every community known to linguists, the patterns that constitute linguistic style are relatively different for men and women. What's 'natural' for men speaking a given language is, in some cases, different from what's 'natural' for most women. That is because we learn ways of speaking as children growing up, especially from peers, and children tend to play with other children of the same sex."[16]

While I may choose to maintain my own communication style with all its attendant values and moral implications and not conform to the expectations of another person or culture, I am better off at least knowing what those expectations are. This knowledge not only gives me more options for the way I choose to communicate, it also allows me to reflect upon those differences and increase my mindsight. This, in turn, helps me remain more accepting and less judgmental.

In Tannen's popular books, *That's Not What I Meant* and *You Just Don't Understand*, she shows we don't need to go to an exotic culture to encounter mind distance and misunderstandings caused by different communication styles. We can find many subtle, almost invisible misunderstandings between men and women here at home. We need the same skills to bridge those differences as we need when communicating with someone from a foreign culture.

The third point is that ritualized speech acts can help cultures to promote reciprocity. Reciprocity helps people share meaning more efficiently and supports social cohesion. But speech acts only work when both sides are following the same rules. Because speech styles vary so much between cultures and among individuals, one of the best ways to understand the other's intentions is to listen better.

Seek First to Understand

Listening with the intent to understand the other's needs is one of the best ways to start building trust. Many good communicators turn out to be great listeners. So powerful is listening empathically that Stephen Covey discovered it to be one of the seven habits of highly-effective people. "Seek First to Understand, Then to Be Understood" is how he titled the chapter about listening empathically.[17]

Listening empathically means listening to the needs of the other person, a move that sends a powerful message on the relationship level. Listening empathically also creates the safe atmosphere people need to communicate more authentically.

Empathic listening requires more than just using our ears to hear the other person's words. It is a full-bodied undertaking that can make us feel vulnerable. If your mindsight skills are well developed, you can prove this to yourself the next time you're talking with someone you dislike or who is not saying what you want to hear. If you pay careful attention and empathize with your partner as she expresses her views, you will not only notice reactive thoughts and judgments being triggered in your mind, you will also notice tensions and unpleasant emotional sensations in your body.

Empathic listening can be difficult because it may require us to expand our point of view. Expanding our own viewpoint beyond its usual limits can be both frightening and challenging. It requires not only imagination and courage, but also effort. If the other person's views are too different from our own, it can seem dangerous to members of our inner team who trigger the stress response. But if we are able to face these difficult emotions with equanimity, listening empathically allows us to understand the other's point of view and reduce the mind distance separating us. When we listen empathically, we sometimes connect so deeply with the other person that we ourselves are changed in ways we might not have predicted. Not knowing what is going to happen and how we might be changed can be scary, but it can also bring more meaning and satisfaction to our lives.

For instance, Lee Shainis remembers when he was five years old and saw another child crying because he had spilled his soda. Young children are naturally empathic to the emotional states of others and the boy's crying moved Lee. He had fifty cents his mother had given him for his own use, but he chose to give this money to the boy so he could buy another soda. This basic ability to empathize with another person's plight is a first step in developing the ability to take the other person's point of view. When we connect emotionally like this, we are utilizing the basics of attuned communication and also growing our own identity.

What Lee remembers most about this incident was how good it felt to help the other child. He realized helping other people feels good and he felt more gratified than if he had had a soda of his own. In fact, helping others felt so good he wanted more of this elevated pleasure. As I mentioned earlier, while still in high school he began volunteering at a local homeless shelter. By the time he was in college, he felt his life purpose taking shape. At first it was just a vague feeling, but years of continual reflection helped refine and clarify it. Today it is his personal motto: To inspire human elevation.

The Joy of Caring

Many people have come to believe nature is "red in tooth and claw" and evolution driven by "selfish genes" and "survival of the fittest."

But scientists are showing human nature to be more than just selfish competition. Today, the theory of evolution is being refined and expanded in surprising ways. For instance, scientists now use the concept of reciprocal altruism to understand cooperation and ultra-social behaviors that can't be accounted for by notions of competition alone.[18] What is becoming ever clearer is that nature has programmed us both to cooperate and compete. If we reflect on this notion, we can see how competition and cooperation are underlying forces in the self-group dilemma I introduced in chapter nine. Our dilemma is to balance this polarity.

One of the ways nature has programmed us to cooperate is to make helping another person pleasurable.[19] Acts of kindness light up the brain's reward centers, a phenomenon neuroscientists have dubbed the "warm glow effect."[20] In addition, the growing field of positive psychology suggests that being involved in something larger than just our own limited sense of self is essential for our well-being and happiness.[21] For example, studies have documented improved health in those doing volunteer work.[22] And, in a recent scientific study, researchers have shown exactly what Lee discovered when he was five years old: When people spend money on others, they feel more pleasure than when they spend money on themselves.[23]

In other words, the golden rule is anchored in our very biology. That helps explain why reciprocity is found in cultures everywhere. But neither listening empathically nor giving generously are panaceas and the ethic of reciprocity, while found everywhere, varies from culture to culture and from individual to individual. We all know people who are terrible listeners such that no matter how empathically we attend to them, they do not return the favor.

Reciprocity can also be a double-edged sword because not all gifts are given with good intent. Because reciprocity is so powerful a force in our lives, con men use it to fleece innocent victims and salespeople are quick to offer "free" samples to potential customers, knowing people will then feel more obligated to buy something.[24] In the same way, organizations that send you a free gift, such as personalized address labels, also know many people will feel they owe something in return.

This calculated use of reciprocity is part and parcel of the trading and negotiating that form an economy as well as a nation's political system. While *quid pro quo* may differ in intent from the innocent joy of giving we all felt as young children, both forms help build relationships and reinforce social cohesion. In the same way, altruistic reciprocity towards strangers and acquaintances not only lets the giver feel good, it also promotes an atmosphere of public trust within a society.

Other forms of reciprocity also promote the social good. For example, giving one's peer the first turn at talking and listening empathically may not always be reciprocated, but it usually contributes to a civil atmosphere. Similarly, giving the other person the benefit of the doubt and trying to understand her point of view can build trust, avoid the blame game, and create long-term synergies for all involved. It can also help us better manage the dilemmas of daily life. For example, safety first, truth second implies the need to balance respect and honesty in our conversations.

We all want to be respected as worthwhile, valuable people. When treated with respect, we feel safer. We also know what it feels like to be disrespected and the emotional reactions it can trigger. At the same time, we all have a deep desire to express our truths in an honest manner that accords with our core values and beliefs. But, as we also know, too much truth and authenticity can often come across as disrespectful. Because we need both honesty and respect if we want to have a mutually satisfying conversation, we are dealing with another dilemma.

Not surprisingly, there are cultural variations in expectations regarding respect and honesty and these are noticeable in the conversational styles different cultures encourage their members to use. As noted before, unconscious expectations work fine until we meet people who do not share them. For instance, a common challenge when Europeans and Asians communicate is the matter of directness, especially around rank. As the following example demonstrates, the core dilemmas are often interdependent, making managing them all the more difficult.

Consider a team of Korean engineers and their recently appointed Swedish manager. In many of the more communal Asian cultures that emphasize obligations to the group, such as Korea, it is common to find a preference for speaking more indirectly as a way to respect the sensibilities of the other person. This is especially so if the other person is one's manager. In such situations, people are sometimes reticent about raising problems for fear it might cause their boss to lose face.

In contrast, in more individualistic European cultures such as Sweden, honesty and self-expression are idealized and people tend to be more direct in expressing their opinions, even to their managers, and even if the news is bad.

Imagine, then, that an important deadline has been missed because the Korean engineers hadn't told their Swedish manager about problems delaying the project. After getting over his initial anger, the manager called a meeting to discuss the issue. Because the manager had heard that directness was a cultural issue, he asked for an experienced facilitator. The Korean engineers were shocked when they learned that their Swedish manager viewed their behavior as less than honest. It hadn't even occurred to them that their actions might be construed as lying. From their perspective, they were doing what any sensible person would do in such a delicate situation. In essence, they were trying to create safety for their manager and protect his "face" by shielding him from unpleasant news.

As this example shows, if we only focus on creating safety, we can actually make the situation unsafe. We also run a variety of risks, from boring, inauthentic conversations to groupthink and mindless conformism. But if we just focus on telling our truths and being honest, we run the risk of making the situation so unsafe for the other that she shuts down and is unable to listen to us. As T.S. Elliot once remarked, "humankind cannot bear very much reality," and when our truths get too loud, people often ignore us. If we hope to communicate satisfactorily, we need to find a way to manage these two seemingly opposite forces of respect and honesty.

Unfortunately, we often assume our own viewpoint and way of speaking is in the middle of any given polarity, i.e., "I'm doing a great job of balancing the need for both respect and honesty." But whenever we assume we are on the balance point, then anyone who does not agree with us automatically becomes the radical who is creating danger by upsetting the natural order of things. Thus, we tend to see the other person's point of view not as an example of a particular value, but as an example of the vice that value becomes when taken to an extreme. Speaking metaphorically, instead of seeing the other person, we see her shadow.

This was certainly the case with our Swedish manager and the Korean engineers. The manager thought his position clear and sensible. He expected his associates to tell him whenever something was going wrong. He saw his candor as a way of showing respect for their competence and maturity. In his eyes, he was the reasonable one standing in the middle of the respect-honesty dilemma. It was the engineers who were tipping the balance by not telling him what was going on. Rather than see their attempts to protect his feelings as a sign of respect, which is clearly a virtue, he saw them as a lack of trustworthiness, which is a vice. Visually it looked like this to the Swede:

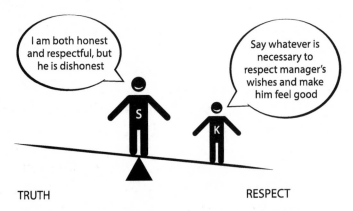

Figure 11.1 — The Swedish manager's point of view

For their part, the Korean engineers also believed they were in the middle of the balance board and doing a great job of managing the respect-honesty dilemma. They saw the manager's often direct manner not as a sign of honesty, a virtue, but rather as a lack of respect and even, at times, as a sign of his lack of social skills. From their perspective the situation looked like this:

TRUTH   RESPECT

Figure 11.2 — The Korean engineer's point of view

In this particular case, the meeting facilitator was able to help both sides see the other's point of view and resolve the tension. A key lesson in this example is that individuals and cultures have different ideas of what constitutes a lie. That is, lies, honesty, and politeness are social constructions. The two major criteria we use to determine if a lie is really a lie are the person's intention and the truth value of her words. Was she trying to manipulate me or was she trying to help me? Because people apply these criteria differently, one person's lie is another person's diplomacy. This distinction has a strong influence on conversational styles.

Realizing the range of people's interpretations of abstract social constructions such as honesty and respect reinforces the importance of listening. We will never solve the black box problem and the mind distance it creates unless more of us learn to listen with the sincere intention of trying to understand the other person's point of view.

You may not be able, or even want, to start an organization or dedicate your life to helping others like Lee has done, but you can certainly give others the benefit of the doubt and assume, until proven otherwise, that they are good people with good intentions who just happen to see the world differently. If you use your power of intention to make understanding the other person's point of view and conversational style your goal, you will discover your conversations becoming more vibrant and fulfilling as differences of opinion become less distressing.

Conclusion

Clarifying our intentions and setting clear goals are essential steps for communicating well. They are also essential for achieving the satisfaction and synergies that good relationships provide. When we align our intentions with those of others to create a mutual purpose, synergies become more than just a buzzword, they become reality.

To balance our needs for both autonomy and belonging as well as manage other social dilemmas, speech communities have developed conventionalized speech acts and communication styles to help their members share meaning. When members of a culture share the same expectations, speech styles promote social cohesion. But when people with different expectations meet one another, mind distance can cause them to misinterpret intentions and drive the social motor in the wrong direction.

Without mindsight, empathy, and the intention to develop a mutually beneficial relationship, all of the insights in this book become no more than short-term, unsustainable practices. While much has been made of the competitive aspects of human nature, more and more scientists are coming to realize that empathy, altruism, and the desire to cooperate are just as natural. Caring for others feels good, and when we transform these feelings into conscious intentions, they help us develop the healthy relationships and communities we need.

Relationships are systems of exchange. The golden rule, sometimes referred to as reciprocal altruism, is used intuitively to regulate these exchanges. While reciprocity is part of the ethical systems used in all cultures, exactly what form this reciprocity takes and what is expected varies from culture to culture and individual to individual. In our conversations these exchanges take place on different levels and can involve sharing knowledge, respect, trust, loyalty, love, and more.

Talk is as much an action as playing tennis or driving a car. Becoming more aware of the speech acts we use—and expect others to use—creates more satisfying conversations. Understanding the nuanced ways speech acts are enacted is also effective for developing the mindsight necessary to interpret the intentions of the other. When we misinterpret another person's intentions and assume them to be bad, we judge the person harshly and act accordingly, often creating a self-fulfilling prophecy. For this reason, one of the most powerful speech acts of all is empathic listening. Listening with the intention to understand the other creates a safe atmosphere and helps meaning flow more smoothly.

The joy of caring is about following your heart. Setting smart goals is about using your head. One without the other leaves us less than fully human. When our hearts and minds are aligned, we prosper.

Twelve

Sitting in the Fire

All sentient beings developed through natural selection in such a way that pleasant sensations serve as their guide, and especially the pleasure derived from sociability and from loving our families.

—Charles Darwin

I met Banu Golesorkhi when we were working at a company that prepared American executives for overseas assignments. That was over twenty years ago and since then we had pursued individual paths as professional interculturalists. We hadn't met for over ten years, but maintained sporadic contact so I knew she had been grieving and going through a rough patch. She and her husband, Robert, had been inseparable and it seemed as if her entire world collapsed when he died.

As I walked into the restaurant and caught a glimpse of her, I was relieved. I remembered her as a sophisticated, highly educated woman whose professional skills, hard work, and passionate defense of the company's reputation were known throughout our workplace. What I found was the same vibrant woman whose warm smile glowed as she rose to greet me. I was amazed by how little her grief and the stress of running her own company affected her. Her luxurious black hair, as thick as ever, was stylishly short and she retained her trim, athletic figure. I was delighted to see how healthy she looked and was searching my memory for our previous meeting—was it possible she looked even younger than the last time we met?

As we talked about our lives, I realized Banu's innate intelligence and youthful energy had been tempered and transformed into wisdom and soulfulness. She was assessing where she was in life. She had been grieving for years while wrestling with survivor's guilt. Why had death taken her beloved Robert and not her? Why had cancer also taken both her parents at such a young age? Why was she left alone by the people she had loved and needed?

She had no answers for those questions, but she'd made a decision. She was tired of suffering and determined to regain her love of life that had carried her through many challenges. She'd been forced to flee her native country when she was still a child. Then the cancer killed first her father, then her mother, and finally her cherished husband. And now her best friend was struggling with the disease and Banu was flying back and forth between Europe and the United States whenever she could to help nurse her. Some people get hard and bitter when fate strikes, while others find ways to become more caring and compassionate. Banu was one of the latter and I could not help wondering how I would have reacted to so much loss and suffering.

First Steps on the Journey

Banu remembers her childhood in Tehran as a happy time. Her family lived at the foot of the Alborz Mountains, near the banks of a roaring river. For her first twelve years she had been ensconced in the warm, protective cocoon of a large and loving family. Many members of her extended family lived nearby and Banu had companionship from morning to night. Friday afternoons were devoted to gatherings of the extended family at her grandparent's home to socialize, play backgammon and cards, and then eat the evening meal together. Often as many as seventy people were present and the house was filled with laughter and good-natured hollering.

Banu treasures the memories of her childhood when she would play with her brother, sister, and their many cousins who viewed the family neighborhood as their magical kingdom. The only time Banu ever remembers being alone was when she was doing her homework.

Other than that, life was lived in gregarious groups of relatives and friends. Hearing about her childhood helped me understand how she became such a poised, socially intelligent woman who is at ease in large groups.

People who can tolerate wider ranges of arousal while maintaining their capacity for reflective self-awareness have a great advantage in stressful situations.[1] Just why this is true is the topic of important research. But most researchers agree an individual's sensitivity to stressors is the result of some combination of genetic pre-disposition and experience-based learning. It is also agreed that babies everywhere are born helpless and cannot maintain their window of tolerance without the help of their caretakers.

The fields of attachment research and child development have made clear that children learn to regulate their internal states—physiological, emotional, and mental—in conjunction with their caretakers. As Siegel puts it:

> Children need to be able to regulate their bodily and mental states. They respond directly to their parents' neural activation patterns through the process of emotional communication and the alignment of states of mind. A child's response to a parent's patterns can be described as the child's "internalization" of the parent. From a basic biological perspective, the child's neuronal system—the structure and function of the developing brain—is shaped by the parent's more mature brain...The attunement of emotional states provides the joining that is essential for the developing brain to acquire the capacity to organize itself more autonomously as the child matures.[2]

For example, when a child cries, signaling something is not in order, a caring parent responds by first determining why the child is crying—is the child hungry, cold, sick, wet, or something else? In essence, parents are using mindsight to determine how the child is feeling. When the parent then responds contingently, that is, does what is necessary to relieve the child's discomfort, the child is learning what it can expect from future encounters. If the child cries and is comforted, it learns to feel loved, cared for, and safe. These feelings are being encoded in brain maps that will lead the child to expect others to listen empathically and respond contingently in the future. The child is also learning distress can be relieved and need not be permanent, as well as how to self-activate these memories to calm itself down. In other words, the attachment patterns created between children and their caretakers are stored as implicit memories that play a large role in a person's response to future experiences. Half a century of research shows that the relationship between child and parent is a key factor in how a person learns to self-regulate emotional responses.[3]

Attachment research also shows that when child and caretaker develop a healthy bond, what is known as a secure attachment, the child has an increased probability for developing well in the cognitive, emotional, and social realms.[4] In other words, a secure attachment with a primary caretaker predicts a child will learn to emotionally self-regulate, will realize its intellectual potential, and will develop healthy relationships.

In addition to patterns of emotional self-regulation, parents are also sharing other brain maps with their children. For this reason, studying differences in child-rearing practices can provide a wealth of insight for an interculturalist.[5] For example, whether a baby is allowed to sleep in the same bed with the parents, or is put in a separate room at an early age, offers us insights about how a culture manages the self-group dilemma. But no matter what the general child-raising patterns in a culture may be, differences between individual families of a culture may be great and stereotypical generalizations that ignore an individual's personal history are risky at best. That said, a secure attachment and loving family does give a child a head start in life.

In Banu's case, that head start includes a healthy sense of self-esteem and the profound conviction she is part of something larger and worthwhile, as well as the ability to manage her emotional states. These beliefs and abilities serve as an internal compass she can depend upon no matter how different the cultural context, enabling her to adapt to different situations while at the same time remaining true to herself.

Having a secure attachment to both her parents and growing up in a warm, loving family provided Banu with many skills, but if your own childhood was less than optimal, this does not mean you can't develop these skills and a healthy sense of self. But to communicate well, it's important to note that ideas about what constitutes a sense of self vary across cultures. These differences in conception about what a person is create a deep layer of mind distance and make cross-cultural communication more difficult because, as the late American anthropologist, Clifford Geertz, noted:

> The Western conception of the person as a bounded, unique, more or less integrated motivational and cognitive universe, a dynamic center of awareness, emotion, judgment, and action organized into a distinctive whole and set contractively both against other such wholes and against its social and natural backgrounds, is, however incorrigible it may seem to us, a rather peculiar idea within the context of the world's cultures.[6]

As we will explore in more detail in chapter fifteen, our identities and sense of self develop through our lifetimes, and adults can always utilize the brain's plasticity to learn new, more satisfying ways of perceiving, feeling, thinking, and behaving.[7] Attachment researchers and therapists are discovering it's not only the experiences we had as children, but the sense we make of them that is crucial for a healthy sense of self and the feeling of a life well lived.[8] Having a secure attachment is not essential for one's well-being, and many people have been able to find ways to heal early wounds and realize their potential.

Culture Shock

Banu's idyllic childhood came to an end when she was twelve. Early marriage is still common for girls in Iran, but her father wanted something better for his daughters. He knew how limited life was for girls who married young, and he wanted Banu and her sister to have the opportunity to learn more languages and develop a wider view of the world. After months of careful research, he presented them with a short list of three boarding schools outside Iran. Banu and her sister were to choose which one they would attend. Banu was torn. She hated the idea of leaving her mother and family, but she was thrilled with the prospects of growing up and going out into the wider world she had been dreaming about. In 1971, just after the Christmas holidays, Banu and her older sister arrived at their new school in Geneva.

Those first days in Switzerland were chaotic and frightening. Classes were taught in English and French and while Banu's English was more limited than she had realized, her French was non-existent. As a result, she found herself performing poorly. She was shocked and embarrassed as she had always been one of the best students in her classes. Now she was on par with the worst students and she dreaded being asked questions she could not understand. Worst of all, she felt alone and homesick. She hadn't yet made any friends and with her limited English skills that seemed impossible. Isolation like this was new to her and it seemed unbearable.

She had only been at the school for a few weeks when the teachers took the students on their annual ten-day ski trip. Banu was confused and anxious because she had never skied before and couldn't understand the French ski instructor. Trying to keep her balance on the two long skis that seemed intent on going in different directions was nerve-wracking. Making her way down the slopes without crashing was one long, terrifying experience. By the end of each day she was exhausted from the emotional and physical challenges.

Following dinner, after another long day on the ski slopes, she decided to wash her hair to save time the next morning. Halfway through her shower, she heard someone yelling and banging on the door. She came out, surprised to find a red-faced female teacher shouting at her. The teacher ordered Banu to go to the dining room where a male teacher joined them. They told Banu it was against regulations to take a shower after 10:00 p.m. Banu, confused and filled with shame at her transgression, was tearfully trying to explain that she did not know about that rule. The teachers countered that all rules were explained during the orientation and there was no excuse for her behavior. Due to her limited English, Banu had not understood the instructions. In fact, it was only that night she added the word *shower* to her English vocabulary.

As punishment, they gave her a broom and ordered her to sweep the dining room while they stood watching. With her hair still wet, shivering and crying, she did as they demanded. She never told her parents because she was too ashamed. She had hit the lowest point she had ever experienced in her short life. As a child, she could not yet understand that the Swiss and Iranians tend to view rules differently. All she knew then was that she felt broken.

But now, looking back as an interculturalist, she realizes this was an example of what some theorists call the "universalism-particularism distinction," which is closely bound up with the self-group dilemma.[9] People everywhere must balance the obligations they have towards family, friends, and colleagues (insiders) with those they have toward the society as a whole. Universalists believe certain social rules and principles apply regardless of context.[10] What is right is right and should be applied equally to everyone across the board. To be fair is to follow the rules by treating everyone alike and not playing favorites. The universalist perspective is common in Switzerland and many central and northern European countries where it is expected people will leave personal feelings aside when making decisions that affect society. By minimizing insider/outsider distinctions and treating everyone equally, universalists hope to create more social cohesion.

But Banu grew up in Iran, which is imbued with the spirit of particularism. People who take a particularist point of view believe your actions should be governed by relationship and context. From their perspective, what is right in one situation may be wrong in another. Particularists expect exceptions to be made and they use affection and personal feelings as important criteria for making decisions. For them, the relationship one has with another is the crucial criterion and one should always try to help insiders.[11] Fairness means seeing the uniqueness of each person and situation and then acting accordingly. Banu couldn't understand why these teachers were treating her so harshly. Surely they must hate her. But what had she done to deserve such hatred?

It took her a long time to get over that episode, but something deep within her was stirring. Perhaps it was anger or perhaps it was shame at being perceived as bad that made her vow to improve her English and learn French. Whatever it was, it drove her to study harder. One day in physics class, because she understood the universal language of math, which she had learned in Iran, she was able to solve a difficult physics problem that no one else could. Banu saw that the teacher was both surprised and impressed and she started regaining her self-respect.

Looking back as an adult, she now believes that scary night as a humiliated and shivering child was when she began developing the emotional resilience that would help her weather the tragedies that lay ahead. This resilience also helps her stay within her window of tolerance when cultural differences are creating emotional storms in the groups she works with.

Arnold Mindell refers to the ability to respond wisely while listening to opposing viewpoints as being able to "sit in the fire" of conflict and diversity. [12] What Arny and Banu both know is that nothing creates safety for others like the ability to join their reality, that is, to empathize with their feelings and understand their point of view. To sit in the fire of diversity requires both self-control and equanimity, key elements of emotional intelligence.

Getting Intelligent About Emotions

Daniel Goleman's 1995 publication of *Emotional Intelligence* was part of a larger trend that brought the study of emotions out of the shadowy corners of academia and into the mainstream. Despite numerous studies, there is still much we don't understand about emotions, and significant controversies exist within the scientific community about the role emotions play in our lives. [13] For instance, one important question is whether or not emotions are universal. In other words, is the fear experienced by an American the same as the fear experienced by people from another culture, say a Chinese or a Trobiand Islander? The experts disagree.

What about surprise? Is surprise an emotion or is it something else altogether? Again, the experts disagree. What about disgust and contempt? Are these two separate emotions or just two names for the same emotion? Opinions vary. What about pain or pleasure? Are these some sort of primal emotions? Some say yes, some say no. Disagreement about such basic questions abounds and there are many more questions to be answered, such as whether people whose language does not have a word for a specific emotion experience that emotion.

In fact, at this time it is impossible to define emotions in a way all researchers would agree with. Despite open questions, most researchers would agree we are emotional beings, thus making some form of emotional intelligence a prerequisite for a life well lived. This is doubly so when we encounter people who regard the nature and expression of emotions differently than we do. Such differences can easily trigger strong reactions in us.

Let's start with some indisputable characteristics of emotions. First, there are both subjective and objective components to any emotional experience. For example, if you walk around a corner and come face-to-face with a large pit bull foaming at the mouth and growling, noticeable physiological changes will occur within you. Your adrenal glands will shoot adrenaline into your blood stream and your heart will begin racing as your blood pressure increases. These changes can be measured objectively.

At the same time, correlated with these objective changes in your body and brain, you will experience a subjective "felt sense" or "flavor" that tells you what is happening inside you. You're scared! Your subjective experience of fear feels noticeably different from the joyful exhilaration of succeeding at a difficult challenge, and this feels different again from the heaviness of grief. What we call emotions not only affect our physiology, but our subjective experiences also differ depending upon the emotion.

Emotions also affect our thinking. To return to the example of the rabid dog: When you see the dog, you will let go of whatever you were thinking about before turning the corner and your attention will now be fixated on the growling menace in front of you. At the same time, your brain's inner team will be rapidly activating old memories that might relate to this situation. If you were bitten repeatedly by dogs as a child, you might now find old memories of panic and helplessness overwhelming you as you begin to turn and run. On the other hand, if you are an experienced veterinarian or dog trainer, your brain's inner team will probably be activating the knowledge and skills needed to handle this situation.

In short, emotions have both objective and subjective components that affect both our bodies and our brains, our feelings and our thinking. According to Antonio Damasio in his best-selling book, *Descartes's Error*, a unified perspective of emotions and cognition is emerging as the old dichotomy between thinking and feeling breaks down.[14] What Damasio and other researchers have shown is that without the emotions and arousal generated in more primitive parts of the brain, our ability to evaluate situations disappears and we become paralyzed with indecision. As Kenneth A. Dodge, a clinical and developmental psychologist, puts it: "All information processing is emotional, in that emotion is the energy that drives, organizes, amplifies, and attenuates cognitive activity and in turn is the experience and expression of this activity."[15]

This new way of thinking accords with the functional view of emotions taken by evolutionary biologists. From this perspective, emotions are seen as motivational states that generate impulses to act in ways that were useful for the survival of our ancestors. Seen this way, emotions evolved to motivate us to act in ways to solve life's recurring challenges.[16] Thus, the powerful urge to run away from the rabid dog tries to get us out of harm's way. While the basic emotional states generated by the sub-cortical areas of our brains are not as nuanced as the verbal expressions produced by our cortex, they have the advantage of speed: Far better to escape quickly and later discover the dog was not rabid than to reflect too long and get bitten.

Emotional states like hunger, thirst, and sexual desire motivate us to engage in certain behaviors. They do this by recruiting the appropriate members of our inner team to form a temporary motivational state, which then functions like a targeted project team. When the project is over, the team is disbanded. In the same way, emotions arise to motivate us and then dissipate as the situation changes. Fear makes us vigilant and prepares us to escape from danger; anger urges us to protect and defend ourselves and our interests; love and compassion encourage us to care for those we identify with; and sadness helps us process and learn from our losses before moving on. While emotions function as motivational states to help individuals navigate through the pleasures and dangers of the world, they are more than just individual phenomena. As we saw in chapter six, emotions also serve as enforcers of the moral and social orders we live in. At the same time, cultures, and the moral and social orders they construct, are also means for regulating the flow of emotion.

Emotional Resonance

When Banu received the invitation to her niece's wedding, she balked. Her grief was still deep and she craved solitude. Every day she put on her professional face and did the work necessary to keep her enterprise alive. She could put on a happy face for clients and associates, but she could not do that with her family. The idea of her grief weighing down what should be a joyous celebration was more than she could bear. But her family insisted and finally Banu agreed to go. Iranian culture, like most sociocentric cultures that emphasize the group over the individual, places great value on loyalty and duty. Banu put her own feelings second to the love she felt for her family. Pulling herself together, she left for the airport with a heavy heart.

   She had just begun checking into the hotel when she found herself surrounded by a joyous group of happy, exuberant cousins. They hugged and kissed her, welcoming her with open arms before grabbing her bags and sweeping her along with them to her room. For the next three days she was only alone when she was in the bathroom or sleeping. Her room was never empty. A small group of cousins, aunts, or siblings were always chattering away about this or that. After years of living in the solitude of a more individualist culture, Banu wasn't sure how she felt about being caught up in such a lively group again. But despite her ambivalence, she soon found herself laughing and resonating with the waves of happiness that rippled through the group. It was as if she were transported back to the safety and innocent joy of her childhood home. For the first time since the death of her husband, she felt the chains of grief begin to loosen. Banu began to hope again.

Humans are social beings and our ability to attune and share emotions, that is, to resonate with the internal state of others, has great value for groups. Long before humans developed language, they were sharing emotions in the form of nonverbal signals as a way to promote their survival and well-being. Basic nonverbal communication can be seen in many social species. Watch a herd of grazing deer. When a twig snaps the whole herd freezes and they watch one another carefully as they simultaneously scan the landscape for danger. When one deer spots a cougar and bolts, the whole herd is moving in a flash. Posture, gestures, facial expressions, and vocalizations of basic emotions such as fear, anger, joy, and sadness allowed our ancestors to alert one another to changes in the environment and can be viewed as the beginnings of our collective intelligence.

When two humans attend carefully to each other's nonverbal signals, something amazing happens: Their internal emotional states begin to attune. With the help of mirror neurons, social circuits in the brain attend to the intentions, movements, and emotions of other people, letting us intuit how they are feeling and what they are intending to do. The brain's social circuitry not only allows us to attune to another person's internal state, it also allows us to empathize with the other, a hallmark of human social interaction. By attuning to and resonating with another's internal state, we have a portal that allows us to get a direct sense of what is happening inside the other, making the black box a little less opaque.

Of course, there is more to empathy than that. If I don't like someone, I can be aware he is feeling miserable and take delight in it. This sort of malicious glee is what the Germans call *schadenfreude*—the pleasure of knowing someone I don't like is suffering. This ability to attune and know what the other is feeling is an ability we share with several of our primate cousins.[17]

The most highly developed form of empathy includes at least two additional abilities: The ability to care about how the other is feeling and the cognitive ability to take the other person's point of view. When all three parts are in place—state matching, concern for the other, and taking the other's point of view—we have the powerful form of empathy that makes us the ultra-social creatures we are.[18]

Sensing what the other is feeling breaks down barriers, helping us create deep and lasting relationships as well as communal identities. Seen from this perspective, emotional resonance serves as a sort of "social glue" that allows individuals to work together and generate the collective intelligence behind our greatest achievements. From the building of the pyramids to putting a man on the moon, from the development of languages and mathematics to the creation of our social institutions, all of humanity's greatest achievements involved groups of people communicating and cooperating intelligently. Underlying most scientific, social, and artistic achievements is the ability of humans to connect emotionally and work together for a common purpose. We can trace this collective intelligence to ancestral bands of foragers who realized that by working and living together they had more eyes and ears to scan for dangerous predators, more creativity to solve problems, and more joy in sharing and loving.

The Need for Boundaries

But just as emotional resonance helps us achieve amazing feats of collective intelligence, it also makes us susceptible to being influenced in destructive ways. For example, if a fire breaks out in a crowded theater, emotional resonance can amplify people's terror leading to mass hysteria and individuals being trampled to death. Emotional resonance can also fuel the hatred and fear that lead to lynch mobs and genocide. In *Shame And Pride*, the psychiatrist Donald Nathanson writes that, "Affective resonance is so powerful, so distracting a system of interaction, that infancy is the only period of our lives during which we are allowed free range of affective expression. In every society on the planet, children are speedily taught how to mute the display of affect so that they do not take over every situation in which they cry, smile or become excited."[19]

Emotions are as contagious as a virus and can quickly spread, influencing the perceptions, thoughts, feelings, and behavior of groups everywhere, both small and large. To avoid being overwhelmed by each other's states, individuals must develop healthy personal boundaries that allow them to attune with others, while at the same time remaining within their own window of tolerance.

In the same way, cultures develop rules and social boundaries to control the emotional resonance radiating outward in the form of nonverbal signals. As babies we tend to resonate with whatever emotional signals we are receiving, and then to express these same emotions openly, regardless of context. A large part of growing up is learning to send and receive emotional signals in socially appropriate ways. As social psychologist Carol Tavris puts it, "An emotion without social rules for containment and expression is like an egg without a shell: a gooey mess."[20] Often these norms and boundaries are explicitly formulated in the rules of courtesy, etiquette, and politeness that can be found around the world. But just as often they are informal and learned implicitly, for example, in the different ways we learn to use time and space to create both personal and social boundaries.

Think of the last time you were shopping and someone walked by too closely without saying, "Excuse me." How did you react? Or how about the time you were on a plane and nonverbally "negotiating" with your neighbor for the use of the armrest. As Edward T. Hall, the late American cultural anthropologist, showed, what is considered an appropriate distance to maintain when interacting varies from culture to culture.[21] While members of some cultures are more accustomed to crowding, others find crowding highly stressful. Even subtle differences in interpersonal distance can trigger surprising reactions.

Boundaries Are Embodied

Many years ago, when I was becoming more aware of the pervasive role emotional boundaries played in my life, my good friend, Dee Moulton, demonstrated how unconscious I was of my own personal boundaries. She did it in such a simple and vivid way I have never forgotten it. She asked me to sit in a chair so we might talk. As I sat down, she moved her chair in closer to me and we began talking. After a minute or so, she asked how I was feeling and I said, without really thinking about her question and wanting to be polite, that I was fine. Then she asked me to sense what I was feeling in my body. At first I noticed very little and was confused by her question. But as I began to observe my sensations I noticed a vague feeling of unease, perhaps a sort of anxiety. I told her this and she asked me where I felt it. This seemed an even odder question, but I did my best to locate it. As my awareness became more focused, I noticed a fluttery unease and clenching in my belly, as well as tension in my neck and shoulders.

Dee told me she had purposefully moved her chair in closer to me until, based on her observations of my body language, she knew she had made me uncomfortable. She had also noticed that I broke eye contact with her when she crossed an invisible line that marked my personal space. I had been as unaware of the change in my eye contact as I was of the tension in my shoulders and unease in my belly. Dee invited me to keep my attention focused on these areas and then moved her chair even closer to me. To my surprise the tension and unease increased and I was now clearly aware I was uncomfortable. I had also begun to breathe more shallowly. By intentionally ignoring my boundaries—boundaries I had not even been aware of—she was able to elicit a distinct emotional response from me which played out in my body and mind. Because I had not been paying attention to those emotional signals in my body, I was also unaware my eye contact had changed and, had this been a normal conversation, the incongruity between my words and behavior would have certainly affected the mood of the encounter.

Dee invited me to keep my attention on my discomfort as she began inching her chair away from me. To my surprise, the tension in my shoulders melted away as did the unease in my belly and a subtle, but pleasant sense of warmth and relaxation entered my arms. My breathing also slowed and became deeper as well. I was doing none of this, but my inner team was hard at work making internal adjustments to a changing context. By observing my body's nonverbal signals, Dee knew where to stop so we were now at a comfortable distance to talk. We stayed there for a minute to allow me to get a clear sense of what it felt like and then she moved her chair back several feet and asked me what I noticed. The pleasant warmth in my arms had disappeared and there was an uncomfortable sense of being disconnected and alone.

What Dee showed me in those few minutes was that communication is a whole-bodied undertaking and that even if we ignore the signals emanating from our bodies, they will still affect the other person, if only unconsciously. This shows that boundaries are more than abstract concepts. They are embodied and have visceral consequences on our relationships. When people get too close we feel unsafe, which can trigger the fight-or-flight response and we become more guarded. If they are too far away, they seem cold and distant and it is also hard to feel safe with them. Clear, healthy boundaries and congruent communication are essential for a trusting relationship. This is especially so when we are communicating across cultures.

As Hall and others have since pointed out, people in different cultures feel comfortable communicating at different distances. [22] People from Latin America and the Middle East often stand closer than people in the United States and Northern Europe. They also tend to touch more and this closeness and increased touching often triggers uncomfortable emotions in northern Europeans and Americans, whose desire for distance can come across to the Latin Americans and Middle Easterners as cold and aloof. Obviously such different reactions are not optimal for building trust.

Eye contact is also a crucial part of our interactions and I had not even been aware I broke eye contact with Dee. I was so focused on trying to be polite and think intelligently about what I was saying, I didn't notice my discomfort or the contradictory messages I was sending by talking and looking away at the same time.

Based on what I learned from Dee, I have since made a concerted effort to become ever more aware of what I am feeling in my body as I talk. This requires effort, but when I succeed I find I attune more with the other person in a way that respects both of our boundaries and leads to mutually satisfying conversations. When I lose that awareness of my body, different things can happen. Some of the more negative consequences I have noticed include the conversation becoming overly abstract and boring, ritualistic and mechanical, or even dogmatic and angry. While staying aware of feelings in the body is no panacea, it does help me talk in a way that better manages the respect and authenticity dilemma we examined in the previous chapter.

Many people will intuitively relate to the results of Dee's exercise. If it doesn't sound convincing to you, I encourage you to test it yourself. It can give you a clearer sense of how you respond somatically to changes in personal distance. If you don't notice any changes, it suggests you might be missing important nonverbal information when you are communicating. By attributing meaning to time and space, cultures create different contexts to regulate emotions and create social order. Paying attention to your feelings and bodily sensations will often give you quick insights to help you respond appropriately in diverse social situations.

Inside an Iranian Home

Banu has fond memories of her childhood home and the socializing that took place there. Hospitality in Iran has been developed to a high art and Iranians can become obsessive about ensuring the well-being of their guests, even to the point of causing themselves great discomfort. To promote hospitality, her family's salon was expensively furnished, filled with the family's prized possessions, and always kept spotless so an important guest could be received at a moment's notice. In a sense, the salon was a physical representation of the family's *aberou*, the Persian word for "face," and keeping it clean and beautiful was part of maintaining the family's reputation.[23]

Banu remembers listening with fascination as her parents and their guests engaged in *ta'arof*, the flowery, ritualistic style of polite speaking Iranians use to ensure that everyone's *aberou* is maintained. As she grew older, she too became adept at using the intricacies of this gracious, formalized conversational style. *Ta'arof* is like a complex verbal dance and everyone is expected to know what each move means and to master their part.[24] This includes managing their emotions to honor the rules of Iranian politeness. For instance, the host will almost surely ask the guest to stay for dinner, and the guest will just as surely decline, explaining with great regret that he has already eaten. Just as the host expected, and just as the guest knew the host expected. This is a game that is not a game, but rather a form of ritualistic graciousness Iranians use to show respect for one another, and to share meaning indirectly while respecting the *aberou* of all involved.

Aberou connotes far more for an Iranian than the word "face" does for an American. Social interactions and decisions in Iran center around issues of *aberou*. That includes not only the maintaining of one's individual reputation, honor, and position in society, but also the reputation and honor of one's family and the groups one belongs to.[25] Because face is such a central issue for Iranians, every utterance a person makes will be interpreted as an attempt to give, take, restore, or maintain one's own or the other's face. In Iran, the content level of communication is frequently relegated to the back seat while the relationship and identity levels drive the car.

How different *ta'arof* was from the more informal style of speaking Banu learned in the interior of the house. Traditional Iranian houses were divided into an area for receiving more formal guests, the *birun*, and the more secluded, private areas of the house, the *andarun*.[26] Traditionally the *andarun* was the area where the women stayed and only the closest family members were allowed entry. Here *ta'arof* gave way to a more relaxed and intimate way of speaking.

Openness and authenticity were expected, and to engage in *ta'arof* would indirectly signal anger or a lack of trust. As we saw in chapter eleven, cultures develop implicit assumptions and rules of politeness that are incorporated into speech styles. In Iran, the formality of *ta'arof* sends a signal of respect, whereas a more informal style of speaking implies an intimacy one would only share with insiders.

Different Emotional Languages

Personal windows of tolerance and social boundaries to manage the expression of emotions fit together like hand and glove. While growing up, children everywhere learn to regulate their internal states and manage powerful emotional urges. At the same time, they are learning the expectations members of their group use to judge emotional expression. For example, chapter six showed how disgust guides individual behaviors as well as regulates social boundaries. In other words, emotions are harnessed to regulate social boundaries and, conversely, we use social conventions and boundaries to regulate emotions.

Of course, individuals within a culture differ with regard to temperament. Some babies are more anxious and hesitant in exploring new environs, others are bolder, more energetic, and filled with movement. When these different inborn temperaments interact with the existing patterns of emotional expression in a culture, personalities begin to form. Just like the culture's shared verbal language, cultural expectations regarding emotional expression provide another language with which meaning can be shared.

Paul Ekman, the pioneering American psychologist who explored the connection between emotions and facial expressions, uses the term "display rules" to refer to the cultural conventions dictating which emotions are appropriate when, and how to express them.[27] Ekman suggests there are three general ways to display or express emotions: minimize, exaggerate, and substitute. Sometimes a group encourages its member to reduce the intensity and minimize the expression of an emotion, e.g., in the United States a subordinate is expected to minimize any show of anger he might feel towards a superior. Not to do so is to become unprofessional, a poor team player, or even "a loose cannon." At other times, cultures encourage individuals to exaggerate the expression of emotions, e.g., in Iran soccer fans intensify the fervor they feel for the national team and engage in wildly emotional displays as a sign of loyalty. If the team loses, tears of sadness are expected, even from men. If the team wins, loud demonstrations of excitement and joy are expected. At other times cultures expect individuals to substitute one emotion for another, e.g., in the United States, when one receives an unwanted gift, the proper response is not to express disappointment, but rather to smile and graciously pretend that one appreciates this wonderful gift.

While it is tempting to generalize and label whole cultures as minimizers, exaggerators, or substituters, social space is complex and personal, regional, class, gender, and generational differences influence the way emotions are expressed. Because our emotional conditioning is so engrained in us, we should not be surprised when our inner team presents us with a negative judgment about the way others are expressing—or not expressing—their emotions. If we keep in mind that different individuals and cultures speak different emotional languages, we are better able to hit the pause button and reflect on what the underlying message is. To minimize misunderstandings, the following points should be kept in mind.

First, don't mistake emotional display for depth of feeling. While empathy allows us to sense what the other is feeling, we are still looking in from the outside. We can't assume the other person feels exactly the way we would feel, if we were expressing ourselves in the same way. People may feel passionately about something while minimizing expression, as we will see in the next chapter. Conversely, if you are a person who minimizes expression, people who are intensifying their external display may not feel nearly as passionately about an issue as you think. In other words, the manner and intensity of emotion a person displays is often a cultural convention and not a precise indicator of what a particular individual is experiencing.

Second, if you are a person who minimizes emotional expression and admires restraint as a sign of self-control and maturity, you are likely to judge those who are more expressive as childish, immature, or unprofessional. On the other hand, if you are a person who openly expresses or even exaggerates the display of emotions and admires animated, passionate discussions as a sign of conviction and commitment, you may judge those who minimize emotional expression as shy, indecisive, indifferent, or even cold-hearted. Such judgments are often inaccurate and rarely conducive to developing good relationships.

Third, learning to recalibrate your perceptions to better interpret the other's emotional language is a key to building better relationships. While it can be challenging, it can also be liberating to broaden your own emotional repertoire so you can "speak" different emotional languages.

The emotional languages cultures use to create social cohesion are a central part of the way they manage the self-group dilemma. Many of our emotions urge us to act in selfish ways. We have strong impulses to satisfy our needs, to seek revenge, and to compete for power. Other powerful emotions encourage us to care for others, to cooperate and share our resources, and to feel bad when we betray those who are close to us. In other words, the self-group polarity and the other dilemmas cultures must manage are not only inextricably entangled with each other, they are also linked to powerful emotions, making them all the more challenging to understand and manage.

Emotions and Authority

Today Banu is a respected interculturalist and educator for business leaders around the world. In addition to Farsi, her native language, she now speaks fluent English and French and has lived, worked, and traveled in dozens of countries. But she was not always so competent in managing cultural differences.

When she first arrived at her new school in Switzerland, Banu was shocked by the many differences she encountered. At home in Tehran, a large part of her schoolwork consisted of memorizing passages from textbooks, which she would then recite in class with other students as the teacher supervised. The student's duty was to recite and the teacher's job was to ensure the recitation was correct.

The student's other duty was to show respect for the teacher and the teacher was expected to behave in a way that was worthy of this respect. Students rose when a teacher entered the classroom and obeyed the teacher's orders without question. At a deeper, more emotional level, Banu and her fellow students transferred the respect and affection they felt for their parents to the teachers and this created an atmosphere of quiet discipline in the classroom.

How different her new school was in Switzerland. There, students remained seated when teachers entered and often whispered among themselves, even when the teacher was talking. And instead of memorizing passages and reciting them back to the teacher, here she was expected to discuss important topics and think critically. Her fellow students not only questioned each other's arguments, they even had the audacity to openly question the teachers. Banu was dismayed. Classes here seemed like a chaotic free-for-all and she couldn't understand why her teachers allowed this.

She was also surprised to discover most of the teachers expected their students to question them critically. In Iran, the higher one is in the social hierarchy, the more *aberou* one has to lose and teachers are accorded high status. But these teachers in Switzerland were acting like they had little sense of *aberou*. Where would this all end?

Inequality and Conversational Style

Social hierarchies exist everywhere and people's attitudes toward social inequality vary.[28] For instance, many middle-class Americans become uncomfortable if they are waited on when they visit Latin American countries, where servants are common. Rather than issue a direct order, they will often formulate their wishes as a request: "*May I have some water, please?*" Or they will insist on carrying their own luggage and sometimes even go into the kitchen to help out. This often causes confusion for the Latin American servant who does not understand why a high-status guest would behave so oddly. It's the same confusion Banu experienced when her teachers in Switzerland did not behave as she expected.

In contrast, many middle- and upper-class Latin Americans accept servants as part of the natural order. They are comfortable giving their servants polite, direct orders about what they should do, such as, *"Bring me some water, please!"* and would never think to carry their own luggage or help with household chores.

Members of cultures with a wide disparity between the upper and lower classes often assume inequality is part of the natural order. Many emphasize that a hierarchy organizes social space and creates law and order. For instance, many note that decision-making is faster and less confusing with centralized power and clear chains of command. Many also like the sense of security that comes with strong and trusted leaders they can admire and respect. They often fear that without a strong social hierarchy, chaos would result.[29] Some even take the position that hierarchy is not only natural, it is the result of God's design for humanity. Such beliefs lead to emphasizing status and class differences and to behaving in a way that accords with one's station in life, i.e., higher-status people deserve to be accorded more privileges and rights than lower-status people.

In contrast, members of more egalitarian cultures tend to view humans as basically equal in terms of inherent dignity. They tend to minimize differences in status and rank by treating people more equally. They also tend to view hierarchies as just a convenient option for organizing society and assume that people in the lower ranks of hierarchical cultures are frustrated, unhappy, and dreaming of being liberated. As we will see in the next chapter, this is not always true and it is possible to enjoy being dependent upon and cared for by a trusted person in a higher position. I am not arguing for the myth of the happy slave, but when people are cared for and respected by those of higher rank, inequality becomes less of an issue.

In their attempts to create a more equal atmosphere by acting in an informal manner, people from more egalitarian cultures often overlook the fact that they are perceived as violating valued social boundaries. For instance, because informality implies intimacy in Iran, it should only be used by a person whose relationship would allow such intimacy. Thus informality, on the part of Americans who view it as a sign of equality, can easily be interpreted as disrespect in a country like Iran.

Regardless of your personal preferences and moral judgments regarding equality, others may feel differently than you do. They will assume their feelings and beliefs are morally justified, just as you assume yours are, and this can create tension. Be prepared for this. This is especially so if you find yourself working with someone from a culture different in terms of hierarchy and social structures. Regardless of whether you are in the position of superior, subordinate, or peer, you would do well to educate yourself about the different expectations this person has about power and equality.

Along with the social hierarchies and division of labor that accompanied increasing social complexity came different social roles and these, too, play important parts in regulating the flow of emotion within a culture. We Americans often think first of our professions when asked about our identities, but more pervasive and emotional are the social roles and identities determined by gender and a culture's kinship system.

Gender and Emotionality

Banu's first days at her new school were filled with one shock after another. The beginnings of adolescence can be very challenging. Our identities are balanced precariously on the cusp between childhood and adulthood and we are often not sure which direction we want to go. To be separated from one's family and dropped into a new culture at such a precarious time represents a challenge that would be difficult for even the hardiest of us.

Making matters worse, Banu believed she would never make friends because her English was so rudimentary. And the apparent lack of respect for teachers and the social order shown by the other students extended to their adolescent explorations with the opposite sex. Banu was mortified to see boys and girls openly holding hands and even kissing secretly when they thought no one was looking. She didn't know what to think. In Iran two girls, or even two boys, might walk holding hands, but this was a sign of friendship, not sexual attraction. A boy and a girl who were attracted to one another would never dare to do anything so outrageous in Tehran. Switzerland was turning out to be far more frightening than she could ever have imagined.

Regardless of the position one takes towards the socially expected roles of males and females within a group, almost everyone agrees that emotions are fundamental forces in determining how those roles play out in daily life. From ancient times to the present, a central motif in stories everywhere has been how powerful emotions such as love, desire, jealousy, shame, and anger have motivated men and women to behave in ways that ended either happily or, perhaps more commonly, tragically.

Because erotic desire is so powerful, it can disrupt the social order by disrespecting social rules, roles, and boundaries—a classic motif found in many stories is of a man and woman who are forbidden to consummate their desire because they are married or belong to different social classes. To tame these powerful emotional forces, different cultures have resorted to various forms, some subtle and some extreme, of social and psychological control. For example, sexual behavior may be defined as sacred, as a purely biological activity, as something degrading, and more. Accompanying these different conceptions of sexuality are different social roles for males and females. Such differentiated roles, coupled with different social norms and expectations, become reinforced by the emotional attachment that can be found in families of all cultures.

For example, in *Against Love – A Polemic*, cultural critic and university professor Laura Kipnis suggests that emotions and relationships between men and women in the United States are managed so as to accord with the dominant economic and political structures in the country.[30] Her account provides more compelling evidence that cultures are self-organizing systems that generate the sorts of personalities needed to replicate themselves from generation to generation.

Speech Style as Boundary

Just as our personal boundaries interact with the social boundaries of the cultures we grew up in like cogs on gears, so, too, do our personal ways of talking accord with socially sanctioned speech styles. Because the socially constructed aspects of male and female roles and speech styles are often not rationally reflected upon, gender roles that we are familiar with can seem self-evident. We then expect those familiar differences between males and females that we consider "biological" and "natural" to appear everywhere in the world. When they don't, we are often shocked and can easily become judgmental about what seems to be unnatural or immoral. This becomes clear when we compare the behaviors of men and women in Iran with the expectations of men and women in the United States.

If an American watches a number of Iranian movies, he will discover noticeable differences between Iranian and American emotional expression. It is not only that Iranians are, across the board, more gregarious, louder, and more emotionally expressive than Americans, though that seems a valid generalization.

What closer examination shows is that Iranian men are often more openly emotional than Iranian women. Heterosexual Iranian men express emotions that would make most American men cringe: They show affection for one another by embracing and holding hands in public and may cry openly if they suffer loss. They may also get into a loud shouting and pushing match and then, often with the help of third parties, make up with a kiss on the cheek. Iranian men are also prone to rely more on their intuition than logic when making decisions. If an Iranian man does not show enough emotionality, his compatriots will suspect an essential aspect of his humanity is missing and view him as undependable.[31]

Iranian women, on the other hand, are expected to be emotionally less intense and more pragmatic. In fact, Edward Hall quoted an American foreign service officer who was stationed in Iran for many years as saying: "If you will think of the emotional and intellectual sex roles as reversed from ours, you will do much better out here."[32] I suspect Banu would agree with this assessment and would point to her own parents as evidence. While highly educated, her father was a charming, charismatic story teller and the life of the party who was quick to follow his inclinations. Her mother was a smart, practical, and nurturing woman of many talents who was always ready to help solve the complex math problems Banu brought home from school.

The three universal tensions—self-group, equality-hierarchy and masculine-feminine—are central to the human condition and have become inextricably entangled with each other and with our emotions. Cultures have had to manage this complexity for thousands of years. By creating and maintaining social roles and expectations that are linked with the expression of certain emotions, cultures control the flow of emotional energy, which in turn creates social order and promotes social cohesion. For example, in most countries, power resides with the police and the military, so it is no surprise that a marine corps drill instructor in the United States is expected to use his anger to terrify and train his troops to be successful warriors. While we don't expect much gentle kindness from warriors, we do expect it from our nurses, just as we hope for detached impartiality from our judges.

Emotions also play a central role in the great spiritual traditions—Buddhism, Christianity, Confucianism, Hinduism, Islam, Judaism, and so on—that grew out of particular cultures. Each of these provides wisdom, ethics, and principles for managing emotional and moral dilemmas. Seen from this perspective, the ethical and moral systems that all cultures have developed can also be understood, in addition to their other functions, as attempts to domesticate and manage our emotional impulses.[33]

Born to Be Moral

In fact, mounting evidence shows many of our moral principles are based on our emotions, especially our more altruistic emotions.[34] Other evidence indicates we aren't the only creatures on the planet to have such altruistic emotions. In *The Age of Empathy*, a fascinating study of the animal kingdom, Frans de Waal provides detailed accounts of the way chimpanzees share food, care for each other, become upset when resources are not shared fairly, and support one another when injured. What this implies is that our highest moral behaviors have deep biological roots.

This does not mean systems of morality are the same everywhere, or only biological just because they are deeply anchored in our nature. It does mean our evolutionary past prepared the soil in which the socially constructed seeds of morality would be sowed by different groups and cultures. As David Brooks, *New York Times* columnist and best-selling author, notes, babies are born equipped to learn language and, in the same way, we are all born equipped to become moral beings. But what language we learn will depend on the language spoken around us. In the same way, we are born prepared to adjust our inherently moral emotions to fit the moral systems of our families and cultures.[35]

Cultural moral systems—in both their explicit and implicit aspects—teach us how to manage emotional impulses, express our emotions, and behave towards one another. As such, emotions and the moral systems built upon them create norms and boundaries that guide an individual's thoughts and behaviors. These norms and boundaries tell us how we are expected to talk and communicate with one another, how we should share goods and resources, how we should resolve disagreements, how we should show respect to one another, how we should treat members of the different sexes, and more.

Banu's students often ask her questions starting with "How do I know .....?" or "What's the best.... ?" In essence, these students are asking whose rules and whose boundaries they should use, and Banu, like all good interculturalists, knows the answer is always some variation of, "It all depends upon who you are and what you want. There is no one best way. There are different ways and which one is best will depend on the context. Pay attention to the situation, know where you are, and who you are with. Only then can you decide how to proceed." This is not what her students want to hear. They want a foolproof algorithm that will work everywhere. Banu's many experiences have taught her that there are no magic formulas.

For my part, I knew exactly how to respond as I heard her resolve to put her grieving behind her and find her joy again. I cheered. How could I not? Her budding joy and determination were infectious, proving the old maxim that shared joy is twice the joy, shared suffering half the suffering.

Conclusion

Emotions are driving forces in our lives that we must understand if we are to develop the mindsight we need for our success and well-being. We humans are emotional beings who use reason for various purposes. We are not purely rational, calculating beings as traditional economists and social scientists had long assumed. Emotions are not only powerful, they are also difficult to understand because they often operate below conscious awareness. Recent research offers a clearer picture of our emotional nature, allowing us to better understand ourselves and peer deeper into the black box.

On an individual level, emotions move us to act in ways meant to promote our well-being and they can be studied both objectively and subjectively. A key social skill is the ability to recognize another's emotions and then influence their emotional state. People who are good at this are perceived as charming or popular and tend to have greater social success.[36]

Human brains are structured to attune to one another and emotional resonance functions as a sort of social glue that can generate both collective intelligence and collective ignorance. Because emotions are so powerful, all cultures develop ways to regulate them and maintain social cohesion. Cultures do this in two primary ways.

On the one hand, they develop boundaries, conversational styles, and display rules regulating how adults are expected to manage and express their emotions. When individuals ignore these boundaries and rules, others gossip about them, laugh at them, punish them, and even ostracize them. When individuals obey these rules they are rewarded with respect, status, popularity, and other forms of social and economic success.

On the other hand, parents and adults transfer their own emotional conditioning to their children, thus replicating emotional patterns from generation to generation. This happens first via attachment to the primary caretaker who provides the child with core skills in emotional self-regulation. This conditioning continues as the child grows and internalizes the emotional patterns common in his family, community, and culture. In this process of internalization—also known as socialization or enculturation—the child begins developing the personality and behaviors that will allow him to become a member in good standing of his culture.

A culture's strategies for managing emotions are most noticeable in its social structures and boundaries, as well as in its preferred conversational styles and display rules. By taking time to become familiar with these boundaries and styles, the astute communicator can reduce mind distance and increase the odds of building satisfying relationships.

But what happens when people from cultures with different boundaries try to communicate and attune with one another? Because we grow up with different understandings of what emotions are, we should expect misunderstandings and emotional disconnects when dealing with people from other cultures. As we'll see next, anger is a common reaction when boundaries are violated. The bottom line is this: If we don't recognize the other's emotional boundaries, we can't respect them.

Thirteen

When the Fire Explodes

Anyone can become angry - that is easy, but to be angry with the right person at the right time, and for the right purpose and in the right way—that is not within everyone's power and that is not easy.

—Aristotle

The seventeen months Jean Briggs spent living in northern Canada with a small band of Inuit called the Utku were punctuated by a series of misunderstandings, some small, others more serious.[1] For example, her lack of fluency in their language and her inability to read their subtle nonverbal cues made the Utku an enigma to her. They appeared to be perpetually cheerful, but were they really? The Utku value equanimity above all else and controlling one's emotions is at the core of Utku morality. For the Utku, even thinking an angry thought is considered almost as dangerous as the open expression of anger, which is socially stigmatized.[2] Instead, the Utku are expected to exorcise anger and consistently express good cheer. In this way, emotional control mitigates the resentment and animosity that could threaten the survival of this nomadic people.

The environment in the Canadian Artic is harsh and unforgiving, with temperatures in the winter dipping down to minus sixty degrees Fahrenheit. During the long winter months, food becomes scarce and the lack of heat and light makes life above the Arctic Circle precarious. At that dark time of year, the Utku spend much of their time huddled together in their small igloos.

When families of four and five people must spend day after day together in such a cramped space, hostility and other negative emotions could easily become toxic. To alleviate this potential danger, Utku culture encourages all adults to develop a degree of equanimity and willingness to help each other that exceeded anything Briggs had ever experienced. While she was no more emotional than the average *kapluna* (white person), her individualistic, i.e., "selfish" behavior became more and more challenging for her Utku hosts. Try as they might, they were not successful in educating her about the proper behavior for a mature adult.

The Directness of *Kaplunas*

Briggs was an anthropologist and intent on learning to understand the Utku so she asked them many questions about their language and customs. While her intentions were good, her directness distressed the Utku, who made it a practice not to ask direct questions of one another. Even worse, her struggles to master the complicated Utku language made her feel incompetent. Although they would never show it—it was part of the problem that the Utku always smiled gently and tried to help her when she got upset—her displays of frustration and annoyance at her own failures upset the Utku.

Briggs also learned the Utku feared people who were not willing or able to transform their negative feelings into smiles, laughter, jokes, and other shows of good will. In fact, the Utku often interpret unhappiness as hostility and a moody person is viewed with suspicion.[3] Not able to read the subtle nonverbal clues that pointed to how distressful her behavior was to the Utku, Briggs soldiered on.

Her research was to serve as the basis for her doctoral dissertation and she was determined to see her project through, despite the harsh environment and challenging conditions. Her lack of fluency in their language made it even harder for her to use the indirect hints and subtle innuendo to express criticism and make requests as the Utku expected. Only Utku children asked for things directly, and among adults conversations were punctuated by long silences because it was considered rude to ask too many questions. One should wait for news, not blurt out a question like a small child. But as an anthropologist it was her job to ask questions and this, combined with her clumsy use of the language, only made her more of an outsider for the gentle Utku.

Her lack of fluency also contributed to her awkward use of the indirectness the Utku use to refuse a request and thus avoid resentment. And her inability to make the graceful verbal repairs the Utku expected led to her becoming even more frustrated. Despite her best attempts to control herself, her frustration leaked out in tiny gestures. While someone from New York or Berlin would have paid no attention to these brief flashes of volatility, they were like the deafening roar of a shotgun to the Utku.

In addition to her need to carry out her research project, her independent ways, common for a *kapluna* woman, made it hard for her to play the role of "adopted daughter" in her host family. Inuttiaq, an Utku man with a strong personality, had adopted her when she arrived in the Back River wilderness and generously invited her to live with him and his family. But her determination to do what needed to be done for her research often put her into conflict with Inuttiaq's expectations of her, though he did his best not to show this.

According to Briggs, Inuttiaq himself was a bit of an anomaly among the Utku. In general, Utku society was organized in an egalitarian manner and the men took great care not to give commands or order each other about. But Inuttiaq had the vitality and strong will of a natural leader and his emotional intensity meant he had to work hard to hold himself back from trying to dominate the others. At the same time, female Utku were expected to nurture and care for the children and home as well as to obey their husbands and fathers. All these expectations influenced the relationship between Briggs and her "adopted father."

After being in the Back River region for many months, and despite the Utku's outward restraint and gentleness, Briggs began sensing an undercurrent of hostile feelings and tension towards her volatile emotionality and strong-willed independence. It was only in the most innocent of remarks or a slight flash in the eyes that she sensed these feelings. They were so subtle she was not sure if she was not just imagining them. But when she got upset with the *kapluna* fishermen in August of 1964, it became painfully obvious.

The Final Straw

The *kapluna* sportsmen would fly in during the summer months to catch the abundant fish in the local rivers. The Utku were fascinated with the material wealth and abundance of food the fishermen brought with them. Because the Utku found it difficult to decline when asked directly for help, they always agreed when asked by the *kapluna* to lend their two canoes, even though this left them stranded on their side of the river. Due to their calm, cheerful reserve, Briggs was not sure what the Utku were feeling, but she sensed they were not happy about this arrangement. People seemed unusually lethargic and passive; their indirect remarks about going fishing when the *kaplunas* left made her suspect they were not thrilled with the situation. Then one of the two canoes was returned with a hole in its side, making it unusable. Briggs was incensed and felt protective towards her Utku friends.

She tried to convince Inuttiaq and the others that they did not have to lend their last canoe to the fishermen. When the *kaplunas* were not there, Inuttiaq strongly expressed his desire not to lend the canoe. Briggs was prepared to refuse the fishermen's request, but when the guide returned, Inuttiaq acquiesced once more. As the only moderately bilingual person present, Briggs was expected by both groups to serve as an interpreter, a mediator role that caused her great inner conflict. When Inuttiaq again agreed to lend his canoe, Briggs tried to keep her voice calm, but inside she was furious at both Inuttiaq and the *kapluna*. When she told the guide he could have the canoe, her voice was icy. Then she turned abruptly and strode back to her tent where she wept silently.

Though it took her several days to notice it—the Utku were still friendly and smiling towards her—she was now being ostracized. Her demonstrative show of displeasure and open anger had been too much for the gentle Utku. From their perspective they had done all they could to educate her in the ways of a mature adult, but she continued to behave like a temperamental child. Then, due to a fluke, unseasonal snowstorm, the fishermen left the day after Brigg's display of displeasure. This unexpected early departure may have upset the Utku even more. Briggs was now being avoided whenever possible, the worst form of punishment, short of murder, that the Utku mete out.

Although Briggs ended up cutting her stay with the Utku short, the story has a happy end. Just before she left, the Utku realized she had deployed her anger on their behalf. They had not understood her motivations. As so often happens, when people's intentions are not clear, confusion results. [4] When an Inuit from another tribe who better understood *kapluna* psychology was able to explain the intentions behind Briggs' behavior, her Utku hosts quickly forgave her. As they said their final goodbyes, her departure was marked by sadness on both sides.

Briggs' extensive report of her time with the Utku, *Never In Anger,* is rich with insights for anyone who wants to understand how cultural misunderstandings can exacerbate mind distance. Before leaving Back River, Briggs learned that Inuttiaq and the other Utku did indeed get annoyed and angry, but they either hid it so completely it remained invisible to her untrained eyes, or they expressed it in ways she was not used to. For instance, one sign that an Utku was upset was lethargy or sleeping a lot during the bright summer nights when the rest of the band would stay up late, talking with one another. As Carol Tavris so aptly suggests, "People everywhere get angry, but they get angry in the service of their culture's rules." [5]

Managing Anger

Anger is a powerful, potentially destructive emotion. Like other small bands of traditional peoples in the harshest regions of the planet, the Utku live a life on the edge. They have few possessions and their main security is the group, making belonging a primary edict of survival. No matter what danger pre-literate foragers encounter—extreme cold or heat, drought, dearth of food, illness or injury, attack by wild animals or other humans—their first and last line of defense is their group.

Members of these small bands are completely dependent on each other and for this reason, social cohesion is of utmost importance. As a result, they go to great lengths to make sure this cohesion is maintained.

The Utku indulge their youngest children's whims and rarely discipline them. Young children are also given large amounts of tender, loving, protective care.[6] Then, as the children grow older, adults begin gently urging them to restrain their displays of anger while at the same time encouraging them to smile, laugh, and joke playfully. By raising their children in this gentle way, the Utku reinforce the group's display rules that serve as emotional firewalls to prevent the spread of anger. These display rules, in conjunction with the Utku values of equanimity, good will, generosity, and helpfulness, create strong emotional bonds and social boundaries that allow the Utku to survive.

Other bands of foragers have developed different values and display rules to manage anger. For instance, the !Kung people of the Kalahari Desert have developed a mode of ritual bickering and complaining they use to regulate anger, distribute resources, and ensure harmony among members of the group.[7] Still another approach is that of the Mbuti who have refined the use of humor to defuse anger and conflict. When rational discussion breaks down and a quarrel ensues, Mbuti disputants begin mocking and caricaturing one another until both the disputants and the bystanders are all rolling in laughter.[8]

While the conventions for managing anger may vary, all cultures develop rules to regulate this powerful force. If not managed well, anger can spread rapidly in a group, triggering behaviors that destroy relationships and wreck social cohesion. If unchecked, anger can escalate into open violence, mayhem, and even war.

But managing anger is not easy. If we completely repress or dissociate from our anger, we risk losing our natural vitality and become lifeless pushovers. But if we express our anger whenever we are triggered, we run the risk of destruction and violence. The different ways individuals and cultures manage anger is another source of mind distance. Briggs's displays of frustration and irritation—ways of expression that would seem harmless to most North Americans of European descent—must have seemed as hostile and dangerous to the Utku as a disease-causing virus might seem to us.

As we explored in the previous chapter, it is part of the brain's design to become aware of and align with the emotional states of other brains. Whether we call this attunement "affective resonance" or "emotional contagion" is not crucial.[9] What is crucial, is to remember that our brains are social organs designed by nature to attune to one another. When individuals use the same display rules and respect the same social boundaries, their brains find it easier to connect in a harmonious manner.

There is much we still have to learn about the resonance circuitry of our social brains and how this resonance is managed when individuals interact, but there can be little doubt that skillfully managing emotional resonance is a major part of healthy self-regulation, as well as part of becoming a mature member of a group. What is also clear is that how much we are willing to attune with another person will have much to do with our intentions and expectations, our identity, and the relationship we have with the other. If we are willing to attune and authentically connect with the other, that is, to let ourselves be influenced by the other's internal state, we are in what Martin Buber called an "I-You" relationship.[10]

I-You Relationships

In an I-You relationship we allow ourselves to resonate with the other person, to feel what they are feeling, and to take the other person's point of view. By doing this, our experiences overlap, we reduce the mind distance between us, and we feel more identified with the other. In effect, we have temporarily joined the other's subjective reality. In principle, we can have I-You relationships with anyone, but experience shows they occur far more regularly in private relationships between insiders and less often between outsiders in public situations. But this is not inevitable and there are numerous instances of people aiding strangers who need help or who are suffering. As the remarkable events in chapter fifteen demonstrate, even former enemies can overcome their fears and suspicions to connect empathically, find their common humanity, and create community.

Buber contrasted I-You relationships with I-It relationships. In an I-It relationship the participants restrain their willingness to attune and empathize as they maintain, or even exaggerate, the mind distance that exists between them.[11] In such cases, one treats the other as just a social function or role, or, in extreme cases, as a lower form of life or even an object devoid of feelings. Dehumanization is an aspect of extreme I-It relationships, and as we saw in chapter six, this is often accompanied with feelings of disgust and contempt. When we see another person as just an object, we can deal with them in a more detached, impersonal manner.

A pure I-You interaction versus a pure I-It interaction can be thought of as the two poles of a continuum representing the mind distance that exists in every human relationship. At its most pure, an I-You interaction is a form of communion between two people. For example, when a loving mother and her child are attuned, laughing, and playing we have an example of I-You at its purest. Another example of I-You communion would be making love in such a way that two partners trust, attune, and open up so they seem to merge and become one for a short time. While such I-You connections can be intensely satisfying, in certain cases, too much attunement can violate boundaries and trigger a sense of danger if one is not used to such openness.

Contrast such deep, intimate connections with the emotional restraint that marks relationships in public space. Such interactions are often marked by civility and even affection, but in such interactions we restrain attunement and connect as our culture's display rules dictate. Such containment allows us to honor social boundaries and fulfill our social functions. For instance, while we all want our surgeons to be concerned and empathic, we don't want them to be so attuned that they go into shock when they are required to operate on the victim of a severe accident. Ideally, professional interactions combine the appropriate elements of both I-You and I-It relationships and are located somewhere in the middle of the continuum.

What, then, about a confidence man fleecing an unsuspecting innocent, or a violent rape where the perpetrator ignores the experience of the victim? Or a soldier coldly calculating how best to kill or torture the enemy? The gut-wrenching examples of genocide and terrorism the world has witnessed in the last hundred years are all examples of I-It interactions at an extreme. An enormous span of mind distance separates these two poles of profound communion (lovingly attuning and identifying with the other) and hate-filled dehumanization and destruction (absolute refusal to attune and acknowledge the other's essential humanity).

It is a tribute to our development as a species that most of our interactions are marked by civility, rather than by hate-filled attitudes. The ability to attune, empathize, and cooperate are the hallmarks of human cultures and we have our social intelligence to thank for this achievement. These abilities allow us to attune and treat the other as a You, and not as an It, but attunement alone is not enough. For instance, if we are just attuned, we are more susceptible to being triggered by negative emotional signals. We also need healthy boundaries to buffer us from the emotional turbulence the other person may be experiencing.

Boundaries Revisited

Because emotional resonance can trigger such strong reactions, individuals with either underdeveloped or overly rigid personal boundaries find highly attuned connections challenging. Such attuned connections can make them feel like they have lost control or have become exposed and vulnerable, experiences they do their utmost to avoid. Developing a mutually satisfying relationship with such people requires sensitivity to their needs and inner states so as to find just the right balance of I-You connection and I-It detachment. This may not always be possible.

The difficulty of finding just the right mixture of closeness and distance is illustrated by the classic metaphor of two porcupines trying to get close together to stay warm on a cold winter night. If they get too close, their quills prick each other, triggering pain and an urge to recoil. But at the same time, if they can't get close enough to keep each other warm, they may both end up freezing to death. This basic approach-avoid situation is challenging enough, but when one of the porcupines has longer quills than the other, or one is more sensitive to cold than the other, things get more difficult. Longer quills in this case represent stronger autonomy needs in one of the porcupines, while more sensitivity to the cold represents stronger needs for belonging and connection. This simple metaphor captures the essence of the self-group dilemma and our needs for both autonomy and belonging that all relationships and groups must manage.

Expectations, conversational styles, and display rules about how anger and other emotions are to be expressed are part of the way groups create boundaries to manage the self-group dilemma. By guiding the expression of such powerful emotions as anger, fear, grief, and sexual desire, these boundaries create safety and protect us from being overwhelmed by a tsunami of raw emotional force. When respected, such boundaries create the safety we need to balance our desire for autonomy as mature individuals and, at the same time, connect and join with one another in healthy, mutually satisfying relationships. But what if two individuals or cultures have differing notions of what constitutes healthy boundaries?

Visiting the United States

Soon after he first arrived in the United States, the Japanese psychiatrist Takeo Doi was visiting an American home.[12] His host, to whom he had just been introduced, asked if Doi would like some ice cream. Doi was hungry, but rules of Japanese politeness made it difficult for him to say so. He replied no, expecting his host to offer again, or even insist he eat something. He was surprised and disappointed when the host accepted his refusal at face value.

In *The Anatomy of Dependence,* Doi says a Japanese host would have empathically intuited that Doi was hungry and given him something to eat without asking. This would have been a manifestation of *amae,* a quality that permeates the traditional Japanese world view. Doi shows how "the prototype of *amae* is the infant's desire to be close to its mother, who, it has come vaguely to realize, is a separate existence from itself."[13] In the broader sense, *amae* is "the attempt to deny the fact of separation that is such an inseparable part of human existence and to obliterate the pain of separation."[14] In essence, *amae* is the desire to be loved and cared for unconditionally and, by extension, it is the presumption that one can depend on the other's good will.

The importance of *amae,* an everyday word in Japan, testifies to the great value the Japanese place on attuned, I-You connections. We have no comparable word in English and Doi suggests this is because most European languages do not distinguish between active and passive love and therefore have no common word to express and promote the concept of passive or dependent love.[15] Doi suggests a possible translation for *amae* might be "dependence," but for many Westerners, the idea of being dependent on someone is not viewed positively, nor is it always associated with affection.

But in Japan, where the parent-child relationship is idealized, relationships become deeper and more positive the more they approach the warmth and closeness of a parent-child relationship.[16] In the traditional Japanese world view, a world filled with *amae* would be "a truly human world."[17] This idealization of passive love and dependence can be seen in the reverence accorded to the Emperor of Japan, who was traditionally thought of as the father of the country and the Japanese people as his children.[18]

Self-Group Revisited

Many Japanese find it difficult to understand the ideal of individual freedom and their translators struggle to find an equivalent term. The word *jiyū* is usually used when "freedom" must be translated into

Japanese. But as Doi points out, *jiyū* implies a sense of capriciousness and therefore a negative connotation because it denotes behaving as one pleases with no sense of consideration for others. In contrast, for Westerners the word "freedom" implies the dignity and rights of autonomous citizens as contrasted to a slave's lack of rights.[19] As Doi states, "whereas in Japan where human relations of a dependent nature are worked into the social norm, in the West they are excluded, with the result that *amae* developed in the former and not in the latter."[20]

If *amae* and the sense of loving dependence became central pillars in the Japanese psyche, the rights and dignity of the individual became central pillars in the Western psyche. These ideas are institutionalized in the democratic political structures of Western cultures that aspire to liberty and equality. In contrast to the obedience accorded the Emperor as the "father of Japan," the "founding fathers" of the United States are men like George Washington, who fought the Revolutionary War and enshrined the ideals of freedom, equality, and individual responsibility in the Constitution and Bill of Rights.

Amae and the I-You relationship it implies is woven together with the strong sense of group identity that is common in Japan. Doi suggests it is this willingness to identify with the group that accounts for Japan's rapid industrialization, as well as the country's phoenix-like rise from the rubble of World War Two. Within a quarter of a century after its unconditional surrender, this tiny island nation had become one of the world's great economic powers.[21]

This willingness of the Japanese to depend upon and become part of the group is also demonstrated by *wa*, the concept of group harmony. In *You Gotta Have Wa*, a fascinating analysis of American baseball players playing professionally in Japan, Robert Whiting points out that American individualism is frowned upon. Even the word for individualism, *kojinshugi*, is perceived negatively.[22] Japanese fans are passionate about baseball and Whiting's report of American players in Japan is a fascinating description of an ongoing cultural clash. Take, for instance, the behavior of one of Japan's all-time great baseball players, Sadaharu Oh, who would break into a smile as he hurried back to the bench after striking out. His behavior was greatly admired by Japanese fans who viewed it as a form of respect for the team's collective peace of mind, their *wa*. In contrast, American players were known for their outbursts of temper.[23]

Presumably, the American players were not throwing their bats and kicking their helmets around to intentionally upset the Japanese fans. Far more likely is that they viewed their displays of anger as normal manifestations of personal frustration caused by their passion, determination, and desire to perform to the best of their ability.[24] From their perspective, not to have been angry would have indicated a lack of commitment. Would they have changed their behavior if they were able to see things from the Japanese perspective? As the next case makes clear, understanding the assumptions that display rules, speech styles, and social boundaries are based upon is invaluable in managing conflict.

A Transatlantic Blowup

Things came to a head during a conference call and stories about the argument spread quickly through the organization. There were differing accounts about what triggered it, but all were in agreement that both the German and the American involved probably saw themselves as the future leader of the global project team.

Everyone also agreed the intensity of the argument was beyond what was considered acceptable in this corporate culture. While we often think of gossip as a pernicious waste of time, telling stories about other people is ubiquitous, not only because humans love stories, but also because gossip is a powerful tool groups use to suppress selfishness and regulate their members' behavior.

Because most of us care deeply about what others think of us, we go out of our way to seek praise while avoiding behaviors that will lead others to talk about us in a negative fashion. Jonathan Haidt suggests our pre-occupation with others' opinions played a central role in the development of our social emotions. As he notes, even Charles Darwin emphasized the role played by "the praise and blame of our fellow-men" in the development of our moral systems.[25]

As the story of the argument spread, more and more people in positions of responsibility concluded that something had to be done to resolve the conflict. At this point I was called in to help the team understand what role cultural differences played and help them develop more skillful means to manage those differences. Cultural differences were not the primary cause of this blow-up and the members faced numerous challenges as they struggled to create a seamless global team. In addition to the technical, marketing, and organizational challenges, the largest problem was the recent departure of their former manager.

People from more egalitarian cultures often focus on the negative consequences of social hierarchies, of which there are many, but they also overlook the value of a hierarchy for maintaining order and managing conflict. The power vacuum on this team was a major cause of the blow-up between these two men. And while cultural differences were not the principal cause, they exacerbated an already unstable situation. To help team members become aware of these differences, I agreed to lead a workshop for them.

In the morning session I compared and contrasted the different cultural values and attitudes that inform communication in the United States and Germany. As team members realized the other side was just following their own culture's conventions and did not harbor bad intentions, the atmosphere in the room became less chilly.

But it was in the afternoon session when we explored German and American speech styles and display rules that they really got it. Rather than just seeing John, the American who had engaged in the shouting match, as an out-of-control hothead, or Klaus, the German who argued so forcefully against John, as overly combative and domineering, team members began to realize the blow-up had been shaped by their cultural scripts.

For example, an assumption common among educated Germans is that as long as you cannot prove my claim wrong with a rational, evidence-based argument, I am entitled to maintain my position. The Germans readily acknowledged that this was indeed a common assumption. Many of them claimed it was an excellent way to get to the truth. They also agreed that they valued clarity and directness in communication for the same reason. When they had all the facts and knew what the truth was, they believed they were in a better position to move forward. They saw their efforts to get at the truth as signs they were good team players.

They also acknowledged that this right to defend a position was easier to implement among equals. While they were accustomed to giving their managers more pushback than Americans did, the Germans avoided pushing too much. Because the members of the temporary leadership committee were officially of the same rank, the Germans felt freer to defend their opinions.

The Americans had been operating on different assumptions and this caused misunderstanding and tension. It wasn't that they didn't value the truth, they did. But they were less inclined to dissect every assumption under the microscope of intense debate. For them, getting a general understanding was enough, and then they wanted to move on. For them, the German style was not only abrasive, it seemed a waste of valuable time and they were frustrated with what they saw as unproductive, long-winded discussions.

Emotional Speed Limits

The Germans agreed the meetings had been stressful at times, but attributed it to the language barrier and what they viewed as American vagueness. They often thought the Americans showed up without having done their homework, unprepared for the level of detailed discussion the Germans expected. This perception, coupled with the challenging issues they had to resolve, led the Germans to think they needed to be more vigilant than usual to ensure the success of the project. But they had not realized the Americans were frustrated with the length of the meetings, or that the Americans viewed the Germans' style as abrasive.

As we saw in chapter ten, when communicating in professional settings, Germans are expected to use a detached, impersonal style of speaking that focuses on the content level. When not used skillfully, this style can turn meetings into long debates and often comes across as abrasive to cultures that focus more on the relationship and identity levels. Because remaining matter-of-fact and focusing on content seem to be most effective to the Germans, they often miss how these strategies make others uncomfortable.

And while Germans make a clear distinction between public and private contexts and change their style accordingly, Americans tend to blur this private-public distinction and tone it down while placing more emphasis on the relationship and identity level of communication in general. For the Germans this comes across as vague and wishy-washy.

In line with their more personal approach, Americans often downplay disagreement, for example by making a humorous remark intended to defuse the tension. Because Germans tend to become even more matter-of-fact when there is a disagreement, they view such humor as a distraction. While Germans rarely smile in situations marked by disagreement, they are generally more comfortable showing signs of irritation or frustration. For example, when Germans are disagreeing among themselves they often raise their voices, the muscles in their faces become more tense, and their gestures become quicker and more forceful. And although they all agree it is better not to interrupt one another, when a disagreement occurs they often do exactly that. Because they have grown up with this direct, content-oriented style of confrontation, they feel familiar with it and can maintain this level of intense interaction, staying within their windows of tolerance for hours on end without losing control.

For the Americans, this level of intensity was too much. One of the Americans likened it to the stress he felt in the dense traffic on a German *autobahn* where there is no upper speed limit. He found it stressful to be driving over eighty-five miles per hour with another car close behind him waiting to pass. Just as we get used to the style of driving that we grow up with, so, too, do we get used to the level of emotional intensity in our speech styles. When people with different emotional speed limits try to interact, it is often stressful for both sides.

What made the situation worse was that Klaus was poor at reading nonverbal signals, particularly when he was intent on defending his position. Then he became so focused on making his point that he failed to notice the signals indicating the other person was getting upset. I suspect ignoring the other's emotional signals was part of the way he maintained his own personal boundaries and stayed within his window of tolerance. Ignoring their own feelings and the feelings of others is one way some people maintain emotional and behavioral control. While this style helps them stay within their own window of tolerance, it often creates a rigid and impermeable emotional wall that makes it hard to connect with others in a mutually satisfactory way.

Judging from his posture and the abrupt, angular movements he made when he spoke, Klaus was tense, too, but he was probably so used to this level of tension he didn't accord it any importance. For him it must have seemed like business as usual.

Daniel Goleman suggests that the ability to recognize and then to influence others' emotional states is a core social competency. Because Klaus focused on making his point and often ignored the emotional states of those he worked with, he was poor at influencing their emotions in a positive way and this weakened his leadership ability. Even the Germans, who were used to a more direct and impersonal style of talking, found Klaus hard to take. Because he ignored their feelings, they sometimes felt disrespected, but the convention to remain matter-of-fact made it hard for them to tell him this. Klaus did not seem to realize one of the easiest ways of making a disagreement worse is to deny the other's experience. Although his intentions were justifiable, by ignoring the emotional states of the members of the leadership committee, he was co-creating the stress that made the situation worse.

While Klaus failed to recognize and respect the emotions of his partners, John had a different weakness. He was not able to contain his agitation and listen attentively when others talked. When others said things he disagreed with, his brows would pull together as his jaw tightened, classic nonverbal signals of anger. Part of his anger may have been triggered by the malicious intentions he attributed to others.

For instance, John hinted to me that Klaus might be out to make him look bad so Klaus could assume leadership of the team. Based on his reactions, this thought was enough to make John feel threatened. As we saw in chapter five, when our sympathetic nervous system is triggered, we find it almost impossible to listen empathically to other people. While we still hear their words, our brains have shifted down from the social engagement system to the sympathetic nervous system, which is preparing us to defend ourselves against danger.

John may be one of the many poor listeners who confuse understanding another person's point of view with condoning it. Because poor listeners do not distinguish between understanding and agreeing, they find it hard to remain calm and understand the other person. It's important to note that many of us have this problem. I know when someone is saying something I disagree with, I also find myself becoming agitated. I'm afraid if I understand the other, I will also end up agreeing with her and this somehow seems dangerous. This subjective sense of danger can then agitate me even more, making it all the more difficult to listen with the intent to understand.

What poor listeners don't realize is that listening empathically is a powerful speech act well worth learning. To learn to listen more skillfully, it helps to understand why we get upset when we hear things we don't agree with.

Anger in America

As Carol Tavris points out in her insightful book, *Anger*, America is rife with ambiguity and misunderstanding about this fiery emotion.[26] On the one hand, we see that anger can be an effective solution in certain situations and on the other, we also know how destructive it can be. This ambiguity leads to confusion for individuals when confronted with the choice between expressing or suppressing angry feelings. What an individual chooses to do will depend greatly on her beliefs about the nature of emotions in general, and anger in particular.

Since Plato the Western world has viewed reason as superior to feelings.[27] Feelings were often seen as dangerous, irrational eruptions that jeopardized the smooth flow of reason. Seen from this perspective, feelings of all kinds needed to be kept on a tight leash. This was also the attitude of the Puritans who settled in America, and it undergirded the Protestant ethic. In this ethos, the sign of good character, at least in a man, was to live life "dry of eye and stiff of lip."[28]

But there has been a different, more positive view of emotions in the West as well, typified by the European Romantic movement, which opposed rigid rationalism. This more positive view of emotions is represented by the research of such scientists as Charles Darwin, Paul Ekman, Antonio Damasio, and others. When Darwin showed that human emotions are closely related to emotions in animals, they became a serious subject for biologists to study. This tendency to look more closely at the true nature of emotions was strengthened by Freud's focus on the unconscious and the role of repression in the psyche.

Freud's work spawned many imitators. While Freud viewed repression as a defense mechanism essential for civilization, many of those who popularized his ideas ignored this detail. As a result, it has become common to believe that not expressing emotions is always a bad thing that can lead to serious psychological problems, even to psychosomatic illness. In this view, emotions should always be expressed.[29]

Given these different beliefs about emotions, when and how it is healthy and appropriate to express them is a controversial issue. It's easy for Americans to become confused or ambiguous towards our emotional responses. We believe, on the one hand, that emotions are primitive and irrational, motivating us to behave in ways we shouldn't. Therefore we must control them, or at least ignore them. And on the other hand, we also believe that not expressing emotions is the sign of an emotionally repressed person who is more likely to suffer from high blood pressure and other psychosomatic illnesses. We also believe we should be polite and respectful to others and, at the same time, we see those who get angry and complain loudest often get the rewards we would like for ourselves. It seems we must choose between two courses of action: Either we "turn the other cheek" or we must demand "an eye for an eye." This social ambiguity towards anger, as well as towards other emotions, makes it harder to know how to manage them. Should we repress, suppress, or express? This is hard enough, but when we have to deal with people who use different display rules and have different expectations about anger, we face additional challenges.

Part of our confusion stems from either/or thinking that only sees two possibilities: either I express my emotions or I suppress them. There are other options and as we will see in the next chapter, by becoming aware of and naming our emotions, we can actually tame them. Many people are afraid that if they even allow their emotions into conscious awareness they will be overwhelmed, but actually the opposite happens.[30] Whether we like them or not, our feelings are important members of our inner teams and when they are marginalized, it creates internal dissonance. By becoming aware of what we are feeling, we become more able to use the information these feelings provide to make better decisions, as well as harness their energy to accomplish our goals. In so doing our inner team becomes more integrated, allowing us to remain within our window of tolerance. If both sides in this German-American conflict were more aware of the power of emotional resonance, they might have been able to avoid the blow-up they experienced.

For instance, if the Germans had been more aware that their matter-of-fact style did not place enough emphasis on the identity and relationship levels the Americans needed to feel comfortable, they might have been able to adjust their style accordingly. And if Klaus had been paying more attention to his partners' nonverbal signals, he would have realized how his actions were pushing the team into the danger zone.

Similarly, if John and the other Americans had realized the Germans were following the speech styles and display rules of their own culture, they might not have taken it so personally. If they had also understood there were rational reasons for the Germans' way of communicating, i.e., the belief that a direct, impersonal discussion about issues is the best way to ascertain the truth and that the truth provides the best basis for making decisions that will benefit the group, the Americans would have been in a better position to accept the German style without feeling disrespected.

At the same time, if the Americans had been aware their own style of speaking was just one style of speech and not an absolute standard by which to judge politeness, they would have been able to be more detached and impersonal themselves. Awareness of these differences would have also allowed the team to make the speech styles themselves a topic of conversation and then to discuss how these differences were causing misunderstandings.

By doing just that in our afternoon session, we were able to defuse enough of the tension for the group to resume its work. The willingness of the participants to reflect upon the actual intentions that lay behind their different speech styles helped them begin the slow process of reconciliation.

The Nature of Forgiveness

While anger and the desire for revenge are anchored in our biology, so, too, are altruistic traits such as forgiveness, love, loyalty, empathy, caring for others, and cooperation.[31] Many people believe our selfish, aggressive sides are more real while our more social, altruistic qualities are moral virtues we must impose on our authentic selves. From this perspective, altruistic behaviors are exceptions to the rule, either self-delusions or hypocritical veneers covering our true nature. But, as two leading psychologists, Martin Seligman and Mihaly Csikszentmihalyi, point out, there are other ways of understanding human nature:

> It has been a common but unspoken assumption in the social sciences that negative traits are authentic and positive traits derivative, compensatory or even inauthentic, but there are two other possibilities: that negative traits are derivative from positive traits or that the positive and negative systems are separate systems.[32]

More and more evidence from the life and social sciences shows the cynical view towards human altruism as biased.[33] In fact, conflict and aggression lead to stress, anxiety, and disease and we have a built-in, physiological willingness to forgive and reconcile. What this means in practice is that it not only feels good to forgive, it also relieves stress and improves our health—our heart rate slows, blood pressure sinks, we sweat less, and muscular tension relaxes.[34]

Forgiveness has social benefits as well: When we forgive we preserve valuable relationships and other social capital. Evolution seems to have equipped us with an instinct to forgive that provided our ancestors with reproductive, social, and economic advantages. This forgiveness instinct is at work when you find yourself caring for someone who has hurt you, when you remember the value a relationship has for you, or when you once again feel safe around a person who hurt you. The flip side of this is also true: If we don't care for someone, if we don't view the relationship as valuable, and if we don't feel safe, we are less willing to forgive.[35]

Our instinct to forgive depends on who did the harming and what kind of relationship we have with them. We are predisposed to forgive those we know and love and we find it easier to let go of grudges and forgive our spouses, children, siblings, friends, and neighbors. But when we are harmed by outsiders, people who are different, or long-standing enemies, we find it easier to seek revenge. Unfortunately for interculturalists, this tendency to categorize people as insiders or "us" versus outsiders or "them" seems to be "innate, powerful and automatic."[36]

This tendency makes it all the more difficult to have satisfying, productive conversations between people with different expectations, communication styles, and world views. To have such conversations we need to find new ways of talking, ways that are both safer and more truthful than the ways we have used until now. But we humans tend to discover new ways of doing things through trial and error. We get an idea and we try it out, fumbling around with it until we get it right. But can we afford to risk fumbling around when discussing limited resources, climate change, poverty, prejudice, and all the other big problems facing us as a species? If it's natural to make mistakes as we learn new ways of doing things, and if it's harder to forgive outsiders when they make a mistake, who is going to have the courage to try a new way of talking that will provide both the safety and the truth we need to manage our dilemmas?

People *can* forgive outsiders if they choose to. Just because many of our emotions and moral impulses are anchored in our biology doesn't mean we don't have a choice as to how we express them. In the same way, just because social boundaries and display rules exist everywhere, doesn't mean we need be imprisoned by them. These socially constructed conventions can be improved upon to make life more fulfilling for all of us. By learning to forgive more readily, we can reduce our own stress, while at the same time developing healthier relationships that promote peace and cooperation. One common way to trigger the forgiveness instinct is by apologizing.

Speech Act Extraordinaire

Our perception of speech acts and communication styles depends upon our frame of reference, and this is certainly true for apologizing. In Japan, for example, apologies are ubiquitous in daily discourse and almost everyone is quick to say "I'm sorry." Both parties expressing regret serves as a social lubricant. Takeo Doi talks about the "magical power" of a heartfelt apology to promote reconciliation and restore the social harmony so valued by the Japanese.[37]

Despite the efficacy of an apology to heal wounds, repair relationships, and promote social harmony, many of us find it hard to do. Few of us enjoy admitting we made a mistake, and it is even more difficult when emotions are running high, our reputations are on the line, or the moral and financial consequences significant. Perhaps we're afraid apologizing makes us look weak or vulnerable. Or perhaps we don't want to accept responsibility for what we did because of the shame and guilt we might feel. Or perhaps we think to apologize would mean we had "lost" and the other person "won." Regardless of the reason, many people go to great lengths to avoid apologizing. In fact, Marshall Goldsmith, a leading executive coach, cites the inability or unwillingness to apologize as one of the most common failings of successful business people.[38] While apologizing is a powerful social tool, its use requires courage and integrity.

Neither Klaus nor John apologized that day, but they did begin to act more contrite as they expressed interest in the role cultural differences played in their blow-up. This was a step in the right direction, but I suspect an apology from either John or Klaus would have gone even further towards healing the rift.

For some individuals and cultures, the willingness to apologize may be seen as a sign of weakness. Perhaps this explains the readiness of American women to say "I'm sorry" more than men. Studies show that both girls and boys in the United States learn to speak in ways to create rapport and negotiate status, both essential aspects of the identity and relationship levels of communication. But girls tend to practice building rapport, whereas boys focus on negotiating status.[39]

Deborah Tannen suggests that the simple phrase "I'm sorry" and its variations is more commonly used by American women than men. While American women tend to apologize as a ritualistic way of expressing concern and building trust, American men tend to avoid it because it seems to put the speaker in a one-down position.

While an apology can be a powerful speech act, expectations and perceptions of apologies vary. Where one person may perceive an apology as an admission of guilt, another may see it as an attempt to create trust. In the same way, the act of apologizing, or the lack thereof, can be viewed as a sign of confidence and good character, just as it can be seen as a sign of weakness and submission.

Taking the time to discover the protocols for apologizing in those cultures you are dealing with on a regular basis is a wise investment. Mistakes are part of cross-cultural conversations and acknowledging responsibility and expressing regret are essential skills for repairing harm and building trust. Not only can a skillful apology help reduce your own stress, it is also a way to keep disagreements from destroying valuable relationships.

But while individuals and cultures use different rituals and verbal formulations to apologize, a few generalizations seem valid everywhere. [40] First, taking responsibility for your actions and acknowledging the harm you may have caused is essential for an apology to work. While it may help to explain your intentions, this can sometimes come across as a denial of responsibility. Second, an effective apology will express regret for any harm your actions caused. Sincere regret means you feel bad about what happened. This helps the harmed party feel safe.

Feeling safe is a primary requirement for people to forgive. If we don't feel safe, we find it hard to let go of our negative thoughts and hurt feelings. For this reason, it is also useful to express your intent to do better in the future. A sincere apology is one of the best ways to build more trust. It is also an effective way to develop a good character—we hear ourselves acknowledge our own shortcomings and are often motivated to become a better person.

Conclusion

This chapter focused on anger to deepen our understanding of emotions and the central role they play in our lives, both as individuals and communities. We could just as easily have explored fear, shame, love, grief, joy, or any of the other emotions that motivate our lives. But because anger is both universal and potentially destructive, learning about it is invaluable for successful cross-cultural communication.

Our brains are social organs that attune to one another, and emotions can spread from one person to another in the blink of an eye. To manage and channel emotions, all cultures develop display rules and social conventions that maintain social cohesion. As children grow up, they internalize these conventions by developing their own personal boundaries that they use to regulate their feelings. One of the key distinctions between children and adults everywhere is that adults are expected to be able to control their emotions in ways that children can't. When our own boundaries are both strong and flexible, they allow us to interact more satisfactorily with people whose display rules and boundaries are different.

When anger emerges, it is a sign some boundary or expectation—either personal or social—has been violated and the angry individual probably does not feel safe. Expressed anger is often an attempt to restore safety, though just as often it has the opposite effect. Anger also indicates a person is not behaving as the angry person thinks the other "ought" to behave. This "ought" points to anger's moral and policing function in the group. Seen from this perspective, anger is a signal that some social rule or norm has been broken and the social order is being endangered. Because anger can be used to maintain the social order, it is often the prerogative of the higher-ranking person to get angry while the lower-ranking person is expected to contain her ire.

Display rules and social boundaries influence our intuition about how attuned we should be to the other. If we become either too attuned or too detached we run the risk of violating boundaries, which can trigger anger and other negative emotions. Given the variety of ways in which emotions are managed and expressed, it is inevitable that misunderstandings and disagreements will occur. For this reason, knowing how to take responsibility for our actions and say "I'm sorry" is a powerful tool for reducing hurt and repairing harm.

Part Four

Mindsight and Identity

A human being is a part of the whole, called by us "Universe"; a part limited in time and space. He experiences himself, his thoughts and feelings as something separated from the rest – a kind of optical delusion of consciousness. This delusion is a kind of prison for us, restricting us to our personal desires and to affection for a few persons nearest us. Our task must be to free ourselves from this prison by widening our circle of compassion to embrace all living creatures and the whole of nature in its beauty. Nobody is able to achieve this completely, but the striving for such achievement is in itself a part of the liberation and a foundation for security.

— Albert Einstein

Fourteen

The Power of Mindfulness

While consciousness lies in the no man's land between religion and science, claimed by both yet understood by neither, it may also hold a key to the apparent conflict between these two great human institutions.

— B. Alan Wallace

Much to his father's consternation, Steven Anthony Young, a mediocre student at best, was worst at math and science. In fact, Steve hated math and science and was scattered and impatient, bouncing restlessly from one activity to the next. That was bad enough, but the D's and F's in math and science most upset his father and ignited arguments every time Steve brought home his report card. Those days became times of emotional crisis in the Young household. Who would have guessed that this young man would go on to receive an honorary doctorate for his efforts to promote the cross-fertilization of Western science and Eastern meditation techniques? The transformation started, as it often does, with a story. In this case it was a story about samurai warriors.

That was 1958 and America was in the throes of a post-war economic boom with rock and roll at center stage in the lives of many teenagers. But as young Steve sat in the tiny theatre in downtown Los Angeles with his best friend, Gerald Takahashi, rock and roll was the furthest thing from his mind. Enthralled by the samurai film set in seventeenth century Japan, it seemed as if he had been transported to another time and place. He dreamed of being a samurai warrior.

Inspired by the film, he threw himself into learning all he could about Japan. When he found out there was a Japanese language school in Los Angeles, he talked his parents into letting him attend. He spent every weekend at the school learning the language, customs, and culture of Japan. When he later discovered that he would never be able to fully understand Japanese culture without understanding the influence China had had upon it, Steve enthusiastically began studying Chinese. Still later, after realizing the formative influence of Indic Buddhism on China, he began studying Sanskrit. By the time he graduated from high school, he was fluent in Japanese and spoke basic Chinese and Sanskrit.

While it may have been just a teenage fantasy that sparked his interest, by the time he was ready for college, that fantasy had morphed into something more practical: He entered UCLA, intending to become an Asian scholar. He spent his senior year of college in Japan, deepening his understanding of the language and culture.

Returning Home

The year in Japan was a dream come true. While he occasionally attended classes to improve his Japanese skills, he preferred to wander around Tokyo absorbing the sights and sounds of Japanese life. Back then, it was rare for a foreigner to speak fluent Japanese so Steve only had to begin talking and doors would open. The Japanese were surprised and delighted that a "big nose" had made the effort to learn their language and they went out of their way to welcome him.

Although it was not exactly the same as the samurai films he had come to love, he discovered hidden corners of Tokyo that seemed untouched by time. Some of his favorite spots were the temples and monasteries that exuded tranquility and peace. Visiting them was like traveling back to an earlier age before Japan modernized under the influence of the West. That year in Japan passed quickly, but when he returned to Los Angeles he was blindsided by the challenges of readjustment.

When perceptual, cognitive, and behavioral patterns that we learned in our home culture do not function well in the new culture people experience stress. In essence, the new cultural context pushes us out of our window of tolerance and triggers the stress response. If this happens frequently enough, the stress becomes chronic and people find themselves sliding into unpleasant states of depression or nervous agitation, referred to as culture shock.

In chapter eleven we saw some of these effects: During her adjustment to life in Switzerland, Banu experienced a painful sense of isolation, loneliness, and self-doubt. Insomnia, increased reactivity, and lack of motivation are also common among sojourners in foreign cultures. As a result, it is not uncommon for expatriates to experience strained relationships, lowered job performance, and substance abuse problems. But, as we also saw in Banu's case, experiences abroad can also make us more resilient while broadening our identities. This is now received wisdom among interculturalists and the term culture shock has become part of the general vocabulary. As a result, people have come to expect it.

It seems counter-intuitive that we would need to go through an adjustment period upon reentry, but, in fact, returning home can be as challenging as adjusting to a foreign culture. For one thing, an extended overseas experience can change us so much that we are not the same person as when we left. When people spend time in another culture, they often develop parts of their potential that had lain fallow. In this regard, it is worth noting that people can be well-adjusted to a particular culture and still not lead a full and satisfying life. If their culture of origin does not allow them to develop their potential, life can seem either boring or frustrating.

When the time spent in a different culture allows an individual to develop unrealized potential, a person's identity grows and he comes to think of himself differently than before. Expecting a returning sojourner to slip easily back into his well-adjusted but significantly smaller identity is like expecting a growing child to wear the shoes it outgrew a year ago.

Returning home is also challenging if the returnee now views his home culture with an outsider's perspective. Having broadened his point of view, the returnee often sees contradictions he had not noticed before. This new perspective sets him apart. This makes relationships more difficult with those natives who cannot see what he sees. A distressing sense of alienation is often the result.

At the same time, life has gone on and home is no longer the same place. All of this can have an unsettling effect. Having changed and grown so much during his year in Japan, Steve now saw America from a new angle that made it difficult for him to fit back into his old identity. He had expected his life would pick up where it had left off and when it didn't, he sank into a deep depression.

Because of the war then raging in Vietnam, Congress had appropriated money for American students to study Buddhism. Steve saw graduate school as his opportunity to return to Asia. His new goal was to become a professor of Buddhist studies and he chose Shingon Buddhism for his dissertation topic.[1] Not only was it an unoccupied niche in American academia at the time, it would allow him to visit the Japanese monasteries he so enjoyed. His plan seemed perfect.

When he returned to Japan in 1970 he went to the Shingon monastery at Mt. Kōya to begin his research. At least he tried to begin his research. He approached the abbot of the monastery, Zenkyo Nakagawa, and asked for permission to study the customs of the Shingon tradition. The abbot politely refused. Steve was consternated. This research was essential to his career plan and to be turned down was the last thing he expected.

He persisted in asking and the abbot persisted by responding with polite but evasive replies. The essence of his evasions was this: Talking about the meditative experience is like trying to explain colors to a blind man. What we do here is far beyond thinking verbally and if you want to understand it, you have to experience it. There is no other way.

Steve saw no choice. Learning to meditate was the last thing he wanted, but to complete his research he was going to have to learn. He reluctantly agreed to Abbot Nakagawa's demands, was ordained as a

Shingon monk, and given the name Shinzen. So began the most important transition of his life. Instead of returning to the States after a year abroad as he had planned, he stayed at the monastery for three years practicing the meditative techniques his teacher was now glad to show him. Steve Young faded into the past as did his dreams of becoming a college professor. In their place, Shinzen Young, a modern mindfulness teacher, emerged.

Mindfulness

Mindfulness is a clear, nonjudgmental state of mind that allows a person to feel, think, and perform better. Developing more mindfulness will not only increase your self-awareness and make you a better communicator, it can also increase your sense of personal well-being. Understanding how mindfulness improves both performance and well-being also provides valuable insights into the workings of our minds.

Mindfulness can be developed in various ways.[2] While you don't have to meditate to develop this clarity of mind, meditation is one of the most powerful ways I know for increasing self-awareness and developing more mindsight.[3]

Just as you don't have to be Italian to drive a Ferrari, you don't have to become a Buddhist to use these powerful mental technologies. Meditative practices were developed and refined for millennia in Eastern religious contexts, but in recent years the underlying principles have been extracted from those contexts, secularized, and are now spreading rapidly around the world.[4] Today, business leaders, engineers, journalists, marines, and even politicians are practicing mindfulness meditation to improve their personal sense of well-being and increase their professional abilities.[5] In addition, numerous scientific studies confirm the ability of mindfulness to improve well-being and performance.[6]

My own experience indicates it's an excellent investment of time and effort. Paradoxically, the more time I spend practicing mindfulness, the more time and energy I seem to have and the less driven I've become. You don't have to spend years in a monastery to reap the benefits. Just practicing ten or twenty minutes a day on a regular basis is enough to reduce internal dissonance, develop more mindsight, and connect more satisfactorily with others.

The three awareness skills that Shinzen teaches in his mindfulness classes—clarity, equanimity, and concentration—are powerful tools for promoting our personal growth. For one thing, they allow us to develop more of our potential, which enables us to liberate ourselves from cultural conditioning as well as from constraints imposed by context. As we saw in chapter four, the ability to freely choose our attitude is essential for growing our inner power. At the same time, these three skills also allow us to grow our identities. As we will see, enlarging our identities enables us to communicate in a more attuned, efficacious manner with people who are different from us.

Clarity, equanimity, and concentration can be thought of as meta-skills that can be used to enhance any other practice. These inner skills for the mind are analogous to strength training for our bodies. By lifting weights on a regular basis and in the proper manner, an individual can increase his physical strength. This can then be used in a variety of physical activities, from playing tennis to moving a heavy couch.

In the same way we can strengthen our brains and minds, thereby improving any activity we choose. Even better, these skills form a synergistic triad with each one supporting and reinforcing the other two. Let's look at each of them in turn to discover how they can help us become better communicators.

Clarity

Imagine a landscape painter who has gone into the countryside on a warm September day. After choosing an appealing location, he sets up his easel and prepares his paints. Then he turns his attention to the landscape, noticing as many details as he can. Because he wants to create a realistic, photograph-like painting, he pays careful attention to every aspect before him so as not to embellish or delete anything he sees. This precise attention to detail is at the heart of sensory clarity.

Sensory clarity can be thought of as the ability to distinguish differences in the incoming flow of sensory input, e.g., "those leaves are a slightly darker shade of green than those leaves and the leaves on that branch are showing signs of changing to a yellowish orange." To make accurate distinctions, one needs to be sensitive to the nuances of sensory data. At the same time, if the painter wants to ensure that he is creating a truly realistic image, he must pay attention to "just what is" and not add details from his imagination.

This development of sensory clarity is sometimes referred to as developing the witness function. Just as the perfect witness to an event neither adds nor leaves out any relevant information, so, too, does the mindfulness meditator. Of course, what is considered relevant information is dependent on the context and intention of the meditator.

Because we can direct our attention to anything we choose—a person, a book, a star, or even a garbage can, as well as to internal phenomena, such as our thoughts and feelings—we have the ability to develop sensory clarity towards both external and internal phenomena. We also have the ability to choose which sensory channel to focus our attention on. When painting, the painter will use the sense of sight, while a musician composing a new piece would be focused on the auditory channel, and a chef baking a cake more focused on taste. Regardless of which channel or channels we choose, by aiming to notice "just what is" we can improve the accuracy of our perceptions.

When it comes to creating safety and speaking truthfully to people who are different, the accuracy of our perceptions is essential. All too often our desires, fears, memories, stereotypes, and more get entangled with our perceptions so that we are not perceiving "just what is," but are projecting our own subjective meaning onto the incoming perceptual information. Such subjective projection is a normal part of the way our brains try to make sense of our experiences, but it often distorts our perceptions, which then creates problems, especially when we are trying to build a healthy relationship.

Ellen Langer is a professor of social psychology at Harvard who has been studying mindfulness since the 1970s.[7] She suggests a simple exercise to show how sensory clarity can improve our relationships: The next time you are with someone you think you know well, try to notice five new things about this person you never noticed before. Perhaps you will notice a fleeting facial expression or a way they use their voice or a particular phrase. Try to find five things about them, no matter how small or unimportant, that you had not noticed before. If you attempt this you will find that you are engaging with them in a more conscious, less mechanical manner that promotes the attuned communication we explored in previous chapters. Often the other person will respond positively to your more attuned approach and the social motor will begin turning in a more productive direction. Intentionally seeking sensory clarity in another person's behavior and appearance also has the power to make us less defensive and to weaken negative stereotypes, as we will see later.

Seen from this perspective, sensory clarity implies an openness to experiences that allows us to become a better witness to "just what is." But to do this well, we also need a second attentional skill, equanimity.

Equanimity

Equanimity is a subtle concept that is easily misunderstood. Some people equate it with indifference, apathy, or even repression of particular thoughts and feelings. Others fear that becoming equanimous implies giving up deeply held values and their sense of right and wrong. Still others fear they will lose the sense of pleasure in their lives. None of these views captures the essence of equanimity, which is an attitude that allows us to maintain our sense of psychological and emotional balance in challenging situations. In fact, having an equanimous attitude towards our experiences makes those that are painful and unpleasant less problematic, while at the same time allowing our pleasurable experiences to become more satisfying and fulfilling.

When we turn our attention inward and observe our thoughts and feelings with genuine curiosity and gentle acceptance for whatever arises within us, we catalyze the growth of equanimity. By noticing our thoughts and feelings we are bringing sensory clarity to them. Noticing them with an attitude of equanimity means allowing them to arise in our mind and body without interfering with them. By neither trying to suppress them nor identify with them, we grow our ability to hit the pause button so we can choose how we will respond to a given situation. This allows us to use our thoughts and feelings to motivate and direct our behavior, but without either over- or under-reacting.

Observing experience with equanimity requires practice. Some thoughts and feelings are inherently pleasurable when they arise in our mind and body. We pursue them like a hunter chasing game. Perhaps it's the thought of a promotion, the image of an attractive person, or a hot fudge sundae. Whatever the thought and associated feeling, if it is pleasurable, it will grab our attention and chain-react into another thought and then another as we get caught up in it and identify with it. But if we can let pleasurable thoughts and feelings arise while observing them with equanimity, they are actually more fulfilling than when we chase after them. The more we can notice our thoughts and feelings as they arise and then fade away without reacting to or identifying with them, the more we gain the power to hit the pause button and behave in a skillful manner.

While members of the inner team automatically pursue pleasurable thoughts, they recoil just as automatically from negative ones. When a thought arises that triggers anxiety, jealousy, sadness, or any other unpleasant feeling, members of our inner team try to pull away from it.[8] This recoiling from a negative thought or feeling can easily turn into denial or repression and keep us from attaining the flow states of optimal experience we all yearn for. But if we practice the same sort of equanimous observation of these negative thoughts and feelings instead of fighting them, something interesting happens. They begin to lose their power over us and we start to develop an inner fearlessness. This is especially valuable for an interculturalist, because the more we are able to watch our own thoughts and feelings with equanimity and clarity, the more we are able to listen to others and communicate without overreacting.

For example, in chapter three I described how being interrupted once knocked me out of a pleasurable state of flow and almost caused me to overreact. The incident left me shaken and my mind was torn between feelings of anxiety and guilt on the one hand, and my rational belief I had handled the situation well on the other. One of equanimity's great advantages is that the more of it we have, the less we need to engage in self-deception. Because equanimity makes cognitive dissonance and negative emotions less problematic, we are able to accept their messages in a rational manner, rather than shoot the messenger. It's not that equanimity reduces the dissonance, but rather the dissonance becomes less distressing and loses its power to drive our thinking. This allows us to notice and accept all parts of ourselves, including those parts we have marginalized. As we will see in the next chapter, when we are able to acknowledge and accept all members of our own inner teams, good things start to happen and we become more able to communicate and connect with people who are different.

Equanimity grows with practice and the more we practice, the more we grow our window of tolerance. As we do, things which would have once caused us to become reactive become just more thoughts and feelings passing through our bodymind. By mindfully observing these thoughts and feelings with an attitude of curiosity and acceptance, we become less reactive and life becomes more enjoyable.

In addition, when observed with equanimity, dissonance can become a source of "aha" moments that give us insights into our basic nature and why we feel, think, and do as we do. Sometimes these "aha" moments actually resolve the dissonance while providing valuable insights, custom tailored to our own needs and situation.[9]

One of Shinzen's important insights was that emotional experiences are a tangling together of thoughts in the mind and sensations in the body. By mindfully observing each of the different subcomponents of his emotions, he was able to use a divide and conquer approach to develop what he calls "skill at feeling." By focusing his attention on the various sub-components of these emotions, that is, on the internal self-talk and visual images in the mind, as well as the physical sensations in the body that are the building blocks of all emotional experiences, he discovered that the intensity of his negative emotions decreased and became less capable of triggering unwanted behavior.

In addition to equanimously noticing our emotional experiences, we can further reduce the power they have over us by naming them. "Name it to tame it," is how Daniel Siegel refers to this technique.[10] One traditional exercise encourages mindfulness meditators to do exactly this. As he sits and observes his thoughts and feelings passing by in his stream of consciousness, he names those emotions or their sub-components. For some still-unknown reason, by first noticing and then naming our emotions, we are more able to let them flow past without becoming attached to them. As they flow by, so too does their emotional charge and thus our reactivity. Neuroscientists are now trying to understand why this technique works.

At UCLA, David Creswell and his colleagues used functional magnetic resonance imaging technology to watch the brains of subjects as they looked at pictures of male or female faces making emotional expressions.[11] Below some of the pictures was a male or female name, e.g., "Sally" or "John." Below other pictures were two words denoting a negative emotion such as "angry" or "fearful" that could describe the expression. The scientists asked the subjects to choose which of the labels was most appropriate for the picture they were looking at.

The researchers discovered that when the subjects were asked to choose between emotion words, activity in two parts of their brains changed: The right ventrolateral prefrontal cortex, which is associated with using words to think about emotional experiences, became more active. At the same time, activity in the amygdala, which is a sort of emotional alarm signal for the brain, calmed down.

In contrast, when the participants only chose a gender-appropriate name for the person in the picture, no such changes were noted.

Labeling an emotion turns out to be a highly effective tool for calming the brain and helping us become less reactive. As Matt Lieberman, another member of the UCLA research team expressed it: "In the same way you hit the brake when you're driving when you see a yellow light, when you put feelings into words, you seem to be hitting the brakes on your emotional responses."[12]

This study shows that by developing what Daniel Goleman calls "emotional literacy," we can liberate ourselves from the influence powerful emotions have upon us.[13] Emotional literacy is not only an awareness of what we are feeling, it is also a vocabulary to think and talk about our feelings. Developing emotional literacy increases our equanimity and allows us to more easily hit the pause button. But to make optimal use of equanimity and clarity, we need to develop the final skill in this powerful triad.

The Power of Concentration

If you have ever watched a master performer in any field—Rafael Nadal playing tennis, Margot Fonteyn dancing, Anatoly Karpov playing chess, or Keith Jarrett playing piano—you have seen the power of concentration in action. A hallmark of all master performers is their ability to focus completely on their activity. This one-pointed concentration allows them to pursue their goal while ignoring distractions that might otherwise interfere with their performance. Concentration, then, is an essential skill for high performance and, like any other skill, it, too, can be developed.

To understand the power of concentration we need to distinguish between two types of attention, what psychologists call "top-down" and "bottom-up" attention. Top-down attention refers to choosing what to pay attention to and it is associated with the prefrontal cortex. Top-down attention is also called "executive attention" and is the attention that we, as leaders of our inner teams, use to accomplish our goals. It is top-down, or executive, attention that gives us the ability to concentrate.

Bottom-up attention is also known as "stimulus-driven" attention and refers to how members of our inner team can become activated by something other than what we, as team leader, have chosen. When a member of our inner team directs our attention towards one thing and we are trying to focus on another, we feel torn and lose the one-pointed focus that we need for optimal performance. For example, if you are playing tennis and are just about to serve when a nearby car backfires, the loud noise may startle you and this distraction may cause you to serve poorly. This startle response is an example of bottom-up attention. Another example of bottom-up attention would be if a member of your inner team remembered a time in the past when you were in a similar situation and you double-faulted. As this memory gets activated, it, too, can distract you and cause you to serve poorly.

Based on these examples, we might presume that top-down attention is always good and bottom-up attention is always bad, but that would be simplistic. Imagine the situation where you are working at your computer and you smell smoke. If you were to remain focused on your work, the results might be disastrous.

In a similar vein, sometimes athletes are so focused on their goals that they end up with severe injuries because they aren't listening to their bottom-up signals. Analogously, we all know people who exhibit amazing focus on their work goals, but end up becoming workaholics who are unable to enjoy the rest of their lives. These examples point to the importance of developing not only our ability to concentrate on our goals, but also our clarity and equanimity to help us discern what is truly important to focus on.

That being said, there is more and more scientific evidence showing that concentration is a key component to becoming happier and more successful. Writing in a recent *Harvard Business Review* article, Matthew Killingsworth notes that[14]:

One major finding is that people's minds wander nearly half the time, and this appears to lower their mood. Wandering to unpleasant or even neutral topics is associated with sharply lowered happiness; straying to positive topics has no effect either way. The amount of mind-wandering varies greatly depending on the activity, from roughly 60% of the time while commuting to 30% when talking to someone or playing a game to 10% during sex. But no matter what people are doing, they are much less happy when their minds are wandering than when their minds are focused.

Based on this and other evidence, the message is clear: Developing our ability to concentrate is an effective way to improve both our performance and the quality of our lives. The ability to concentrate will become increasingly important as the global information economy continues to expand and the Internet connects more of our lives. As the world grows more complex and bombards us with more and more information and attractive distractions that can pull us away from the things we need for our true well-being, it will become ever more important to have both equanimity and concentration to help us make wise decisions. Who has not gone onto the web to research one question for work, only to find themselves still sitting there an hour and a half later, mindlessly surfing?

While our brains may have evolved in simpler times when the sea of information that surrounds us today did not exist, they did evolve the power to learn so that we could change and adapt. We all have areas in our lives where we would like to see improvement and we can combine the power of intention and goal setting with the meta-skills of sensory clarity, equanimity, and concentration to develop our potential and find the flow and happiness we all yearn for.

Developing Our Potential

For example, when I began practicing mindfulness in 2005, I hoped to better manage my anxiety and impatience.[15] Within months after beginning, I started noticing positive changes in my life. In particular my increased equanimity and sensory clarity helped me realize I had not been as honest with myself as I had believed. My coping strategies for handling stress and time pressure, especially in my relationships, were less than ideal and I decided to change. Thanks to the synergistic effects provided by increased clarity, equanimity, and concentration,

I've become less anxious, less compulsive, and less impatient. Happily, I've also become more empathic, as well as more truthful with myself and others. As a result, my personal and professional relationships have become more satisfying and my life is now more fulfilling than before.

Of course, developing mindfulness does require practice. Just understanding how resistance training strengthens muscles does not result in increased strength. You must actually lift the weights for that to happen. But people who practice mindfulness on a regular basis agree it has improved their lives and the scientists who study meditators' brains concur. To give you a better idea how each of these three skills can be used, here's how Shinzen used them to cure a phobia and develop unused potential.

When he discovered neuroscientists had begun studying meditators' brains he got excited. Shinzen was convinced mindfulness and related mental practices were the pinnacle of what Asian culture had to offer the world. He was also convinced mindfulness would help anyone improve their life, while simultaneously reducing ignorance and suffering. Developing skills of attention, which could be turned inward to discover one's deepest nature seemed to him a highpoint of human achievement.

At the same time, he was also aware his old nemesis, mathematics and science, represented an equally important pinnacle in human achievement. Science and the powerful technologies discovered by scientists ushered in the modern age and it seemed to him these two different technologies, one developed in Asia, and the other in Europe, were like two poles of human civilization. What would happen, he wondered, if these two different sciences, one focused on developing the internal powers of the mind, and the other focused on understanding the world, were combined? The question left him no peace. To answer it, he would have to face his childhood fears.

He began by teaching himself mathematics. In the past when he had tried to solve a math problem, he would try once or twice and if he couldn't solve it, he would give up. Now, thanks to his increased capacity for one-pointed concentration, he had staying power. It did not matter whether he needed to return to the same problem ten, twenty, thirty, or even more times. He kept working on it until he got it. Of course, he didn't start with calculus. He went back to multiplication and division and did them over and over until he mastered them. Then he moved onto the next level. Step by step he developed his math skills until he was able to understand graduate-level mathematics. By breaking up the challenge into smaller, easily achievable steps, he was more successful and able to keep his inner team motivated.

As he achieved the realistic goals he was setting for himself, he also began to enjoy the sense of competency and flow he got as he worked his way through a tough math problem. As we saw in chapter eleven, a key component of flow states is the feedback the experiencer gets with regard to attaining his goal.

In Shinzen's case, both the goal and the feedback were clear. His goal was to solve the math problem he was working on and the feedback was equally clear. Either he got the objective answer expert mathematicians had worked out before him or he didn't. Such clear feedback made it almost impossible for him to engage in self-deception, either by deflating his abilities when he actually succeeded or by inflating them when he didn't.

While his increased concentration was essential for his success, it alone was not enough. He had a negative self-concept regarding his math abilities and distressing emotions would rip into him in the form of a critical voice and unpleasant bodily sensations every time he sat down to do a math problem: *Who am I trying to kid? I can't do this stuff! I hate math. I always have and always will. This is a waste of time and I'm just torturing myself!* Not only was this critical voice filled with self-doubt, it was also charged with intensely negative memories of anger, fear, and sadness left over from the countless family fights when he failed math as a child. But this time Shinzen had the equanimity and "skill at feeling" that allowed him to deconstruct this negative self-image and its distressing bodily sensations.

Each time the critical voice and negative feelings arose, he would turn his attention from the math problem and direct it to the basic elements of the emotional attack going on inside him. Using equanimity and sensory clarity, he was able to observe and name the different elements of his emotional experience. This allowed the critical self-talk and negative images in his mind, as well as the unpleasant sensations and feelings in his body, to play themselves out. Rather than fight against or try to suppress these feelings and the negative self-talk, he was, in his own words, "loving them to death" and the more he did this, the less they attacked. Eventually they disappeared.

While unpleasant thoughts and feelings are part of human experience, we are actually creating unnecessary internal dissonance when we use mental force to suppress them. When we direct our attention to these thoughts and feelings with an attitude of curiosity and acceptance—after all, they are just thoughts and feelings in our minds and bodies—we begin the process of mastering them. While this tactic may temporarily increase the sense of unpleasantness, this quickly subsides and we end up increasing our long-term well-being.

Growing an Identity

When Shinzen was teaching himself how to do challenging math problems, he not only used his skills of clarity, equanimity, and concentration to stay focused on his goals and master his negative emotions, he also used them to become a better listener and enlarge his identity.

When he was a teenager, mathematicians and scientists were the last people he would have wanted to associate with, but now he began seeking them out. He was still unable to understand conceptually what they were talking about, so he didn't focus on content. Instead, he used his attentional skills to focus on the sights, sounds, and other nonverbal signals of these men and women as they spoke passionately about their work. Becoming so attuned to another person as they are talking is to become absorbed in them and is almost like falling in love. It allows us to open up and drop the defenses we normally use to keep people at a distance. As he engaged in this highly attuned, nonverbal mode of communicating, he found himself experiencing the same joy and excitement about mathematics that the others were feeling.

As this happened, he felt himself connecting with them so completely it was almost as if he were merging with them. These experiences began affecting his own sense of identity. It was as if a part of himself was becoming a mathematician and he found he was even more able to solve difficult math problems. At the same time, the more he attuned and connected with them, the more he enjoyed being in their company. More and more he came to realize that mathematicians and scientists were fascinating people in their own right. And more and more, he came to accept that he was one of them.

Shinzen's experiences with the mathematicians exemplify the power of attuned communication to create I-You relationships and to enlarge our own identities as we tap into our potential. While it can be scary to disarm our defenses and open our hearts and minds so completely to others, as we will see in the next chapter, when we are able to do this, wonderful things result.

His success at math was a first step towards realizing his dream of helping the best of East and West cross-fertilize each other. Today in his work as a teacher of mindfulness, Shinzen divides his time between deepening his own skills, teaching his many students,[16] and working with psychologists and neuroscientists at Harvard, Carnegie Mellon, and the University of Massachusetts. These scientists are using modern technologies to study meditators' brains to better understand why mindfulness is such an effective method for improving human functioning and reducing suffering.

Being a savvy interculturalist, Shinzen has worked hard to translate the ancient, sometimes arcane terminology and obscure wisdom of various Eastern meditation practices into secular terms that are easier for Westerners to understand. His clear and precise use of language to describe how we can use the skills of clarity, equanimity, and concentration to improve our lives have made him a favorite teacher among scientists, professionals, and academics. Not only has he created a modern, secular framework to describe and teach mindfulness, he has also made it as culture-neutral as possible. For example, he has reformulated one ancient insight into what sounds like a mathematical equation: "Suffering equals pain multiplied by resistance." In other words, when we stop resisting our pain and learn to take a more relaxed, more equanimous stance towards our experiences, our suffering is reduced. All of this helps explain his growing popularity among his many students from around the world.

Conclusion

Mindfulness has entered the mainstream and research scientists from around the world are currently studying its many benefits. Thousands of scientific studies have already been conducted that demonstrate the power of mindfulness for our health and well-being.[17] To name but a few, mindfulness meditation has been shown to have beneficial effects for people suffering from stress, depression, drug addiction, and more. It has also been shown to reduce loneliness, boost the immune system, and help improve GRE test scores. Perhaps most importantly, these studies are helping us better understand how the mind works and thus increasing our collective mindsight.

Because it is precise and easy to understand, I've used Shinzen's definition of mindfulness as comprised of three core attentional skills: sensory clarity, equanimity, and concentration.

Sensory clarity is the ability to accurately perceive "just what is" without projecting subjective meaning onto our perceptions. The more sensory clarity we can develop, the more we can separate facts from interpretations to better test our assumptions. When we are able to perceive "just what is," we are better able to understand and communicate with people who are different from us.

Equanimity is an accepting, welcoming attitude towards the thoughts and feelings that arise within us. The more equanimity we develop, the more we are able to stay within our window of tolerance and hit the pause button rather than reacting unskillfully. If we also develop a precise vocabulary to think and talk about the emotions that would otherwise anger, frighten, sadden, or embarrass us, we are able to achieve even more self-mastery.

Concentration is the ability to place our attention on the target of our choice, and then to keep it there for as long as we deem appropriate. Concentration is essential to harness the power of intention and to reach our goals. It is also essential for becoming a good listener, a key competency for every interculturalist.

These three meta-skills can be developed separately, but when they are practiced together they strengthen and reinforce one another, allowing us to develop more of our potential while increasing our well-being. Developing these three skills also promotes the development of more mindsight, allowing us to reduce both internal dissonance and the need for self-deception. As we will see in the next chapter, when we are willing to let go of needless self-deception and become more truthful, good things begin to happen.

Fifteen

Descent into Hell

If we could read the secret history of our enemies, we should find in each man's sorrow and suffering enough to disarm all hostility.

—Henry Wadsworth Longfellow

As the United Nations van headed towards Osijek in eastern Croatia, Arlene Audergon and Lane Arye stared out the van's windows at charred houses destroyed in the war.[1] In Osijek not a single house had been left untouched by bullet holes or artillery fire. They took a deep breath and exchanged a short, silent glance before climbing out of the van.

It was 1996, the fighting had stopped and the war was officially over. But fear, mistrust, grief, and depression lingered on in the survivors who were trying to put their lives back together amidst the devastated infrastructure and emptiness left by lost loved ones. Lane and Arlene were invited to Osijek to serve as facilitators for a communal process of reconciliation and rebuilding. For the next four days they will meet and work with a large group of doctors, nurses, teachers, lawyers, mayors, city administrators, and social workers who have come from different regions in Croatia and Bosnia. These forty participants represent a microcosm of the ethnic diversity in these countries: Serbs, Croats, and Bosniaks form the bulk of the group, but other ethnic backgrounds, such as Hungarian and Roma, are also present. The idea is that if these participants can work on the traumas and post-war issues that exist among themselves, they will be better able to help the rebuilding processes in their towns and communities.

For some of the participants, it's the first time since the war they are meeting with members of the other ethnic groups. The atmosphere is charged and words are chosen carefully. People are even hesitant to say their full names because it would identify them as Bosniak, Croat, or Serb. If they mention where they are from, other participants may imagine a whole story about them and what they did during the war.

Deep Democracy

Arlene and Lane are accomplished practitioners of Process Work as well as highly experienced group facilitators.[2] Although they were born in the United States, they have extensive experience living and working abroad, qualifications that make them excellent interculturalists. Process Work offers a number of pragmatic tools for dealing with differences, one of the most useful being the concept of "deep democracy." While many groups and cultures use some form of democracy as a way to make decisions and to manage the self-group dilemma, conventional democracy usually means the majority in a group controls the decisions. One consequence of such decision-making is that people on the peripheries tend to be marginalized. Their viewpoints are often considered to be too radical, too idealistic, too frivolous, or simply irrelevant.

In contrast, deep democracy, as conceptualized by Arnold Mindell, calls for all voices to be heard.[3] In this regard, deep democracy is similar to a core assumption of Ken Wilber's integral psychology that assumes everyone has a piece of the truth, while no one has the entire truth.[4] Neither Mindell's deep democracy, nor Wilber's integral model, assumes that everyone is equally right. As we all know, some people's views are more accurate than others about different parts of reality. But what deep democracy and the integral model both insist upon is that everyone have a place at the table

This assumption that every voice needs to be heard is also common among many of the skilled practitioners within the dialogue movement. For example, here is what Kerry Patterson, a leading business consultant and proponent of dialogue, says about the importance of letting all voices be heard:

> People who are skilled at dialogue do their best to make it safe for everyone to add their meaning to the shared pool of meaning—even ideas that at first glance appear controversial, wrong, or at odds with their own beliefs. Now, obviously they don't agree with every idea; they simply do their best to ensure that all ideas find their way into the open.[5]

Deep democracy exemplifies the power of both/and thinking to help us better manage the dilemmas we all face. For the pragmatic communicator, this means that no matter how different a person's point of view, there is something valuable and true in that viewpoint that needs to be heard if we hope to create a better world. What this meant for Lane and Arlene was not to push the survivors to talk about what had happened during the war or about their ethnic differences. When the two facilitators tried talking about these differences on the first morning, the group became charged and agitated. A conventional facilitator might have pressed ahead at that point, convinced that avoiding these issues was not healthy. But Arlene and Lane, following the principle of deep democracy, switched gears and allowed the members of the group to voice their fears.

Talking about Differences

At this point Lane and Arlene faced a challenge all interculturalists struggle with: Cultural and ethnic differences are at the heart of many conflicts, but often people don't know how to acknowledge or talk about those differences in a safe and productive way. What to do? Believing in the innate wisdom of the group, the facilitators acknowledged and validated the group's fears while allowing the group's needs to determine the direction and timing of the discussion. At the same time, they began directing the group's awareness to this atmosphere of fear and tension so that its influence became part of the discussion. What the group knew—and what Arlene and Lane quickly learned by allowing all voices to be heard—was that ethnic and cultural differences had been politically manipulated and distorted with misinformation during the wars to encourage the different groups to fear and hate each other. The appalling atrocities and ethnic cleansings could not have happened without these manipulations.

Talking about differences can be challenging and there are many reasons for this, not least because there are so many types of differences. Some differences are obvious, but so trivial as to be irrelevant. For instance, you like to eat spinach and I don't. No big deal. You eat what you want and I'll eat what I want. At the other extreme, differences can seem so depraved and dangerous as to appear evil. For instance, you believe God created some people to be the slaves of others and I find slavery abhorrent. Now we have a problem. Because differences of one sort or another are a fundamental aspect of most human interactions, learning to talk about them in a skillful manner is essential for successful dialogues. Lane and Arlene knew this and they knew that sooner or later, this issue needed to be processed if the group was to heal.

They decided to help this happen by offering to work with just two people from different groups who wanted to talk about their relationship. Two old friends, one a Serb and one a Croat, volunteered. As experienced process workers, Arlene and Lane felt at home dealing with personal relationships and were more relaxed working with these two women. Before the war these women had been friends, but since the war's end, they had not been able to talk openly about their experiences as members of warring groups.

They were distanced from one another and both knew they were avoiding the deep issues separating them, fearing what might happen if they talked openly. Both women regretted this loss of intimacy and they wanted to reclaim their friendship and trust. With Lane and Arlene's help, they began talking about their feelings for each other. When they reached a hot spot, Arlene and Lane would help them navigate through the delicate issues in a way that allowed them to listen to each other. With the help of the facilitators, these women were able to talk respectfully and truthfully in a way that allowed them to listen empathically to each other's stories. When what the other said hurt or triggered intense emotions, the facilitators were there to help them work through it.

These women not only wanted to talk about their friendship and their feelings for one another, they also wanted to talk about their identities as Serb and Croat and what that meant to them. This made their conversation not only deeply personal, but also highly political. The other members of the group sat transfixed as they watched this conversation unfold. Afterwards one of the participants, a man who had been a fighter on the front lines during the war, rushed up to Lane and Arlene. He was amazed and wanted to know how it was possible that a Serb and Croat could talk so openly without becoming inflamed and violent. He hadn't believed something like this was possible. This was life-changing, but also potentially threatening. This was confirmed by another participant who told the facilitators that if some of the people from her own community knew she was engaging in such conversations with the other side, her safety would be at risk.

While this conversation impressed many of the participants, fear still had the upper hand. Every time anyone would bring up the war, a heavy silence would come over the group. The silence was like a thick fog descending on the room and the facilitators decided to amplify this silence as a way to help everyone become more aware of what was happening. The facilitators personified the tense silence by acting it out and giving it a voice, saying, "Don't talk about the war" and "Don't talk to people from the other side or else." Soon the participants joined in this social drama, adding other warnings and threats: Don't talk about what divides you, it's far too dangerous; don't open up old wounds, it could inflame the conflict all over again; talking about your experiences will open up too much pain.

The role play triggered a discussion in which some said talking about anything political must be avoided. What they needed to focus on was humanitarian issues for a better future. We are here, they said, to rebuild our country and that is what we must discuss. Their need and intention to rebuild their communities was a fundamental part of the group's identity.

Exploring Identity

Understanding the central role of identity in human affairs and how our identities grow and develop is invaluable for anyone who wants to communicate well. Such understanding must include one's own identity as well as a basic awareness of the other's identity. It must also include understanding how people's personal identities are impacted by the group(s) they belong to and identify with.

Most psychologists agree that human development occurs sequentially, that is, healthy development follows a general direction.[6] Put metaphorically, mighty oak trees start as acorns and crowing roosters start as eggs. In the same way, we see regular patterns of sequential development among humans in areas such as physical growth, kinesthetic development, emotional self-regulation, cognition, needs, morals, social skills, and more. Evidence suggests that as we grow and develop, our sense of who and what we are and who and what we identify with also grows and develops sequentially. Parallel with this growth in identity, our moral sense of what is right and wrong also grows and develops.[7] Babies start out with an identity that is undifferentiated from its environment—a baby has to learn that if it bites its blanket it does not hurt, but that if it bites its thumb it does.[8] As babies we also have a strong fixation on our own needs.

In this initial stage, which is sometimes referred to as the egocentric or pre-conventional stage, both our identity and our sense of right and wrong are based predominantly on our own needs, feelings, and bodily sensations. What's right is what makes us feel pleasure, wrong is what causes pain or discomfort. We gurgle and smile when happy and cry and rage when we are hungry with little regard for whether those around us are sleeping. At this stage of development, we see the world through our eyes alone and tend to feel and think in the "language of me."

But as we continue to grow and develop, we begin to realize other people have feelings, too, and we start taking their points of view into account. Different researchers refer to this growing ability as the conventional, conformist, or sociocentric stage of development.[9] In this stage, individuals internalize the values, world views, morals, and norms of the group they belong to. At this point in the process of enculturation, the child is learning how to balance the "language of me" with the "language of us." During this phase she is learning when and how she may continue to be egocentric or "individual" and when and how she must conform to the norms of the group if she wants to be accepted as a good member. Because humans have deep needs to belong to a group, most children quickly adapt their behavior to the norms of their group, that is, to what the group deems to be normal, natural, and good.

This transition does not take place overnight, but rather the egocentric identity is slowly transcended and integrated into a larger, sociocentric identity. This means an adult's behavior is a blend of egocentric and sociocentric traits and that at any particular moment an adult may be more "selfish" or more "groupish." We all know those moments of decision where we must decide whether we will pursue our own individual desires or obey the norms of the group. As the healthy child grows and matures, the incidence of selfish, egocentric behavior lessens and the child begins to behave in more group-oriented ways. Helping children transition from a purely egocentric to a larger, more balanced group identity is a challenge the self-group dilemma presents to all cultures.

When we have reached the sociocentric stage our morals, expectations, and behaviors are strongly influenced by our notions of loyalty and our sense of belonging to a particular group. For people in the sociocentric stage, being a good and moral person means following the rules of their group. This also means those people who do not follow the group's rules are often considered bad, criminal, or evil. It is the most normal and natural thing in the world to want to be considered a good person by one's in-group, and the vast majority of humans strive to do so.

This growth and movement from the egocentric stage to the sociocentric or conventional stage involves a growing emotional attachment, first to our caretakers—usually the mother—and then to our families. As we continue to grow, our circle of contacts also grows. As it does, we can become emotionally attached to our extended families and our friends, to our tribes and local communities, to our ethnic and speech communities, and even to our entire nation. These feelings of attachment often manifest as a strong sense of affection, loyalty, and obligation to family and group.

For many individuals—and for the majority of the world's population—this growth stops at the sociocentric stage.[10] For them, managing the self-group dilemma means finding a way to balance and harmonize their own individual needs and desires with the needs and morals of their in-group. Why and exactly where this growth of emotional attachments stops depends on many factors and it is not important for our purposes here.

What is important is to realize that at this stage people identify with and feel attached to certain people, while viewing others as outsiders towards whom they do not feel much emotional attachment. Individuals whose identity stops at this sociocentric stage see and judge the world through their group's values and world views. Often, owing to past conflicts and negative experiences with other groups, members of out-groups are distrusted and even despised, while members of in-groups spend a great deal of time with their own group with whom they typically share resources quite generously.

World-centric Identity

For some individuals, growth of identity does not stop with a particular group, but continues to develop towards the inclusion of more and more humans. Ultimately it reaches the stage where it identifies with all human beings. This stage of identity development is sometimes referred to as the universal or world-centric stage by researchers.[11] People at this stage of development tend to speak in the language of "all of us" and say things like "I am a human being, nothing that is human is alien to me."[12] This famous quote from the ancient Roman playwright, Terence, emphasizes the common aspects of the human condition.

As a person's identity begins to grow beyond the sociocentric stage, several things begin to happen. For one, the individual begins to examine her own group's traditions, beliefs, and values more rationally, often calling them into question when they seem too narrow or distorted. For another, individuals begin to develop valued relationships with members of other groups and to widen their world views. By considering the other group's beliefs and values they learn to switch points of view and perceive the world from various perspectives. As one's world view expands and one discovers that members of other groups are also decent, caring human beings, one's capacity to empathize with them also grows. As this ability to empathize with wider circles of people continues, our sense of identity grows. We become more compassionate and caring towards ever larger groups of humans. We have more understanding and are more willing to help and support ever larger numbers of different people until our own identity encompasses all of humanity.

When our sense of identity grows, it does not exclude our earlier identity and connections, but rather transcends and includes them. That is, my identity and emotional attachment to my family, close friends, and community need not weaken, but rather my sense of empathy and care extends to ever larger groups of humans. Nor does growth towards a world-centric identity mean I can no longer feel strong affection, loyalty, or concern for the communities, organizations, or nations I grew up in or belong to. What it does mean is that as we begin to transcend our resistance to people who are different, we also transcend and move beyond the fears, disgust, and hatreds that fuel tribalism, ethnocentrism, racism, and aggressive nationalism.

This growth of our identities through a process of transcend and include can be represented visually as follows:

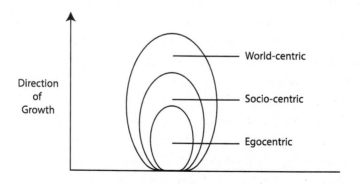

Figure 15.1 — Stages of Identity Development

It is essential to recognize that sequential development is not the same as linear development, though it is easy to confuse the two. This underlines the need for precision in how we use language to explain our experiences. Linearity implies a straight line connecting two points. Sequential development only implies a starting point, a direction, and an end point, for example, a birth, a life, and a death. But how one gets from start to finish, from birth to death, can be filled with loops, spirals, and all manner of nonlinear patterns.

When we look at the development of an individual's identity, directionality implies that we start at an egocentric level, move towards sociocentric and then, hopefully, to world-centric. Just as nobody starts old and grows younger, so, too, no one is born with a world-centric identity and then proceeds towards egocentric. But this path towards a larger, more inclusive identity can be filled with starts, stops, and detours along the way as context plays its inevitable role and the individual does her best to deal with the contingencies with which she is confronted.

Seen from this perspective, sequential development does not exclude the possibility of regression or setbacks. Individuals and groups may reach a higher stage of identity and then, for various reasons, regress to an earlier stage. This seems to be the case with the former Yugoslavia, which was characterized by inter-ethnic cooperation and where inter-ethnic marriages were common. Bosnia, and Sarajevo in particular, had an admirable reputation for being multi-cultural, cosmopolitan, and inclusive. But when hatred and misinformation were manipulated by some leaders for political purposes, it stirred up old fears and created new ones, leading to a vicious downward spiral into ethnocentric warfare and all its horrors.

Despite regressions and detours, the long arc of social evolution also exhibits this directionality. Today more people around the planet have developed world-centric identities than ever before. Support for this tendency to become ever more inclusive and supportive of equal rights, justice, peace, and care for all humans is exemplified by most of the world's recent humanitarian leaders and heroes such as Aung San Suu Kyi, Dag Hammarskjöld, Mahatma Gandhi, Nelson Mandela,

Mother Teresa, Maya Angelou, Albert Schweitzer, Eleanor Roosevelt, and Martin Luther King, Jr., to name but a few of the most well-known. Such role models inspire us to imitate them and many people—as individuals and as groups—have been encouraged to become more inclusive and tolerant. This desire to work together for a common future was the primary identity of the group at Osijek.

Marginalization

One Process Work method for working with groups is to notice not only what a group identifies with, but also what they avoid identifying with.[13] Based on what the group in Osijek was saying as they avoided talking about the war, this group's primary identity was: "We are all humanitarians here. We are the tolerant ones. We like each other and are not the ones who created the conflict. We want to build a peaceful society for all our peoples." This strong identification with tolerance and rebuilding communities was something these people cared about deeply. And their common-sense fear that talking about differences might inflame old conflicts and cause more pain fed into it. The group aspired to a more inclusive, universalist approach as a way to bridge their differences and avoid conflicts.

But Arlene and Lane also noticed contradictory signals that indicated this primary identity was not the whole story. If they were really so tolerant and accepting, why was there so much fear and tension in the group? And why, despite all the good will, did small groups of people always form along ethnic lines? Why were the conversations during the coffee breaks always Serbs with Serbs, Croats with Croats, and Bosniaks with Bosniaks?

Just as strongly as the group identified with "we are the humanitarians," it also avoided identifying with "the intolerant ones," the ones who manipulated and distorted the ethnic and cultural differences and who triggered the violence that led to the horror and atrocities. But while the group at Osijek consciously distanced itself from those who were intolerant and sociocentric, they themselves were acting ethnocentrically during the breaks. In this sense, the group was a microcosm of the larger society around them that wanted a more peaceful future, but was also stuck in fear of the old conflicts reigniting. In communities throughout Croatia and Bosnia at this time, there was a general atmosphere of depression punctuated by occasional outbreaks of local violence.[14]

Although safety first, truth second is not an explicit principle of Process Work, Lane and Arlene had intuitively been following this principle in their facilitation of the group's process. By using Mindell's notion of deep democracy, which actively worked to include all voices, they had created safety for each individual participant. In their wisdom of allowing the group to move at its own speed and direction, they had created a further sense of safety for the participants. When the group saw the conversation between the two women, they were given further evidence that Croats and Serbs could actually talk safely about the war without becoming violent. Finally, by validating the fears that were keeping the group silent, Arlene and Lane had built enough safety for the group to move forward.

Reigniting the Fire

The facilitators knew that for the group to truly rebuild their lives and communities that had been so damaged and traumatized, they needed to find a way to talk about what had happened without reigniting the violence that had almost destroyed them. They again trusted in the wisdom of the group and waited for the step forward to emerge. On the morning of the third day something simple and amazing happened: One woman courageously and tentatively acknowledged that perhaps, maybe just a little, she might find it slightly more comfortable to be with her own people.

This simple admission, one that on the surface seems so natural and harmless, lit the fire and brought it to a roaring blaze in a matter of seconds. Now Lane and Arlene had their hands full to keep the blaze from consuming the group. This woman's small remark triggered outrage among some of the participants: See, they said, we knew we couldn't trust you!

At this point personal stories began pouring out and Arlene and Lane facilitated the interaction. One after another, different individuals stood up and told of their experiences during the war. Their pain and suffering was hard to hear and some couldn't listen. As one story detailing the intense suffering of one group finished, another story from a different group came to explain how their suffering had been just as awful. And as stories of the brutality and atrocities by other groups were told, others rushed in to tell stories of the good deeds their own groups had done. Behind the pain and intense emotions of these stories were implicit accusations, which made it even harder to listen.

Finally, the group was speaking personally and authentically. As they told what they had experienced during the war, the reality of what it meant for the different ethnic groups to sit together for the first time in this post-war situation was highlighted. The conflict was out in the open and the group had reached a new stage in their process. This was a critical point for the group and Lane and Arlene needed to make sure the fire did not rage out of control. Somehow they needed to help the group find a way to manage the mind distance—the pain and the trauma created by these intense experiences—that kept them divided. At the same time they needed to help the group respond to the accusations and distrust that were now visible for all to see.

The Numbing Power of Distance

One of the small groups that had formed during the breaks was composed of individuals from Sarajevo. They had become close and were perceived critically by some in the larger group for having become a clique. But the Sarajevans had a different perception and one of them, a woman, accused the rest of the group of keeping them at a distance. While all of the participants had experienced traumas and losses due to the war, Sarajevo had been the center of a siege lasting from 1992 to 1996 and had only recently emerged from the hell of war. This woman accused the rest of the group: "You keep us at a distance. You look at us like museum pieces. You look but you don't touch." Her pain and desire for connection were obvious to all and in response, one courageous Croat woman stood up, walked across the room, and spoke to her directly.

"It's true," she said, "I remember keeping you at a distance when I watched Sarajevo on television. At that point the war in Croatia had stopped and, though I lived only two hundred kilometers from Sarajevo, I watched it on television and it seemed so far away. I couldn't feel anything. I remember thinking I was glad it was there and not here." As she finished tears filled both women's eyes. This truthful acknowledgment, both honest and courageous, had bridged the distance separating them. By now, everyone in the room, including the facilitators, had tears rolling down their faces. The interpreter apologized for her tears and her inability to remain professional. When assured by the facilitators it was okay to cry, she collapsed weeping on the floor. Others jumped into to help with the interpreting so the process could continue and no one would be left out. The differences, distrust, and fears that had separated the group were melted by the tears at this profound moment of public intimacy. Others now stood up and admitted how they too had kept others at a distance as a way to avoid their own fears and pain. In acknowledging how they remained aloof and isolated themselves, they also told how they had kept their own feelings and experiences at a distance.

Any overwhelming experience can create deep memories in the human nervous system and psyche, but the traumas of war leave some of the deepest scars. As we saw in chapter five, our autonomic nervous system is composed of three circuits of different evolutionary ages. It is the oldest of these three circuits that is responsible for triggering the so-called freeze or immobility response. In those moments when our experiences are so terrifying or so overwhelming that we perceive no chance to either fight or flee, our nervous system triggers this immobility response and we react as if paralyzed. In such moments we lose our ability to move and talk and we feel frozen like the proverbial "deer in the headlights."

While people don't remain physically paralyzed after an overwhelming event, they often dissociate their memories of the event as a way to protect themselves and to continue functioning as life demands. As a result, there is often a mechanical quality to their behavior and internally they often feel numb, powerless, and like shadows of their former selves.[15] While the overwhelming experiences are horrible in their own right, the internal splitting-off of memories and the sense of powerlessness that follow the initial event are a double whammy that can imprison people for decades.

This internal separation of traumatic memories and experiences, as well as the fears and sense of helplessness that many individuals experience after such an event, is not confined to just individuals. When overwhelming events, such as war, are experienced communally, the internal splitting off of feelings and memories in individuals can have profound effects on the entire culture.[16] The more such traumatic experiences are split off and not talked about openly, the more likely these dissociated experiences are to be re-enacted in the form of widespread depression and feelings of powerlessness, as well as in outbreaks of violence. For this particular group in Osijek, these unprocessed traumatic experiences manifested as the tense silences and avoidance of talking about the war and the differences that divided people.

Fortunately, our understanding of both the physiological basis of trauma as well as our methods for healing traumatic experiences has grown rapidly in the last decades.[17] While much of the initial work with PTSD was done to understand the suffering and disabilities of Vietnam veterans, research into the nature and effects of trauma has grown by leaps and bounds. PTSD is becoming part of our common vocabulary. Most encouraging, evidence shows that just as we are biologically predisposed to heal our wounds when cut, we are also predisposed to liberate ourselves from the effects of trauma and return to mental and emotional well-being. As this knowledge becomes more widespread and as more accomplished therapists and group facilitators become available, we can realistically hope that we might free ourselves from the prisons of trauma that individuals and groups find themselves in.

By supporting the creation of more and more safety within this group, Arlene and Lane were able to help its members face the traumatic experiences from which they had distanced themselves. Once safety had been created, it took only one truthful acknowledgement—I do feel a little more comfortable with members of my own group—to trigger the outpouring of truth in the form of feelings and stories of suffering and loss. And as everyone in the group confronted the communal horror and terror of their past experiences, it was once again the courage to be truthful—yes, I did keep you at a distance—that helped bridge the gap.

That night true unity appeared in the form of local wine and a guitar. The group sat singing together until the early morning. Songs from all parts of the former Yugoslavia and in all the different languages were sung as the entire group celebrated its common humanity. The mood was filled with the joyful vitality of life celebrated after a long illness.

Conclusion

Dealing with different points of view is a challenge we all face. Mindell's notion of deep democracy and Wilber's view that "everyone is right" suggest everyone has a piece of the puzzle and we need to fit all the pieces together if we want to find the larger truth. While we may all be right, we are not all equally right. We all have part of the truth, but we don't always know which parts of our truth are accurate and which are distorted.

When we forget how we are all prone to self-deception, it is easy to believe our truth is the only truth and to stop listening to other points of view. When we do this, we create more mind distance. While some people react with vehemence to the idea that the voices of people they despise need to be paid attention to, being willing to listen empathically to people with radically different points of view is an essential skill for good interculturalists.

This ability to take other people's points of view is a skill we can all learn. It grows in parallel with the growth of our personal and social identities. As we progress from egocentric beings, focused primarily on getting our own needs met while speaking the language of "me," to more conventional beings who think and speak in terms of "us," our ability to take other people's points of view grows. Some individuals tend to stop growing as they reach the level of conformity with the world views and mores of their own ethnic and cultural groups. They can only speak the language of "us" which they define by contrasting "us," the good people, with "them," the people who are not quite so good or who may even be considered depraved and evil. People whose identities stop growing at this level find it hard to listen to the points of view of "them." But there is no inherent reason that growth of identity need stop at this point. As researchers continue to study the human experience, we can expect to gain a better understanding of why some people develop world-centric identities, while others do not.

When people get trapped in the numbing paralysis of trauma, they feel helpless, hopeless, and unable to take responsibility for their feelings, thoughts, and actions. Much human violence is a reenactment of unresolved trauma from past conflicts. If we are to transform these old traumas and let our more elevated emotions gain the upper hand, we will need to debunk the old myths that cause so much mind distance and suffering. That is the subject of the next chapter.

Sixteen

The Ladder of Trust

We have met the enemy and he is us.

—Pogo (Walt Kelly)

Six months after the first post-war forum in Osijek, Lane and Arlene returned to Croatia, this time to the ancient coastal city of Split on the Adriatic Sea. At one session, some Serbs accused the Croats of abusing returning Serbs.[1] During the war, ethnic Serbs had fled Croatia to find safety elsewhere and when they returned home after hostilities had ceased, they were persecuted by some of the Croats. These Serbs wanted someone to be held accountable for the suffering they experienced in 1995.

The Croats were stunned and outraged at being accused of not welcoming the returning refugees with open arms. What did the Serbs expect? Given the atrocities committed by Serbs against Croats in 1991, it was, from the Croats' perspective, only natural to seek revenge.

Some of the Serbs countered this charge by accusing the Croats of having committed atrocities against them during World War Two when the Croats had aligned with the Nazis. Members of both ethnic groups were soon pushed beyond their windows of tolerance and began shouting accusations of, "Your side started it!" and, "No, your side started it!" Within fifteen minutes accusations were being made about events that had taken place during the fourteenth century! Such is the power of our stories to trigger disagreement and intense emotional reactions.

Unfinished Business

When people get caught up in disagreements about unresolved conflicts, it is easy for them to become fearful and angry. Emotions are contagious and when members of a group become reactive, their fear and anger can infect others, causing a group to polarize before people realize what is happening. This is particularly true in situations where groups have been in conflict with one another and where unresolved trauma and suffering exist.

When ignored, unresolved conflict has a tendency to recycle, surfacing again and again in new forms. Often these conflicts are triggered by accusations of blame. Blaming, in this context, can be understood as an attempt to transfer the blamer's emotional suffering onto the accused.

The same is true for individuals and families who do not know how to process the emotional hurt left over from previous arguments. Our inner teams are always assessing the intentions of others. If we get emotionally hijacked, it is natural to assume the other person is acting maliciously. When we do, the next step is just as natural: We treat the other person as if he had bad intentions. When we do this we are, whether we realize it or not, encouraging him to reciprocate. This reciprocal exchange of accusations is at the heart of the blame game that we explored in chapter six.

Such symmetrical blaming causes the social motor to accelerate towards the danger zone, triggering fear and anger and making it more probable that individuals will defend themselves or try to escape. Because such reciprocal blaming can easily spiral out of control and result in verbal, emotional, and physical violence, we must tread carefully. But when managed with skill, empathy, and compassion, confrontations can be turning points in the process of repairing past harms and helping both sides heal and grow.

Human history is littered with brutal violence, torture, and other appalling atrocities. While we may want to put those ugly parts of our past behind us, our past remains alive in the stories we tell. In this forum at Split, old, divisive stories emerged as the emotional intensity of the interaction increased. These old stories, often distorted and loaded with disinformation, were used by members of the different factions to justify their actions.

The Same Old Story

We humans are storytellers. We use our stories to make sense of our world, to justify our actions, to teach, inspire, motivate, entertain, and more. We are also beings who are prone to self-deception and the stories we tell are often less than accurate. Because our stories play such a central role in our lives, it is easy to become hypnotized and mistake them for reality. When we do, especially when they are not true, we suffer the consequences.

Telling one-sided stories and outright lies to promote fear and hatred of outsiders is a powerful and pervasive way to create social cohesion within a group. When people are afraid, they look to one another for guidance and they bond together to protect themselves. Unenlightened leaders have long used this tactic of telling biased stories about "them, the enemy over there who wants to destroy us and our way of life" as a way to consolidate their power and keep members of a group in line.

This time-tested method of creating a common enemy was used often as the former Yugoslavia disintegrated and broke apart into warring enclaves. By arousing and encouraging people's fears and hatred of other ethnicities, ethnocentric leaders were able to increase their own political power. As old lies and twisted stories emerged, the country spiraled downward into violence and multicultural areas like Sarajevo, which had been characterized by interethnic cooperation, were ripped apart. It has been said that truth is the first casualty of any war, and this was certainly true in the former Yugoslavia. As safety disappeared, so, too, did the truth.

Because they were so caught up in the powerful emotions generated by their own stories, neither side was able to listen to the other. If they had been able to hit the pause button and take a broader viewpoint, they might have noticed what had become apparent to

Arlene and Lane: Both sides were telling the same story, only the roles were reversed. Both Serbs and Croats were telling how cruel, heartless killers were responsible for the war, the atrocities, the horror, and the suffering. Lane and Arlene also recognized the killer was a role no one wanted to take on. Like unconscious assumptions, unoccupied roles often remain invisible in the stories we tell. Because they can have a strong influence on group dynamics, good interculturalists and group facilitators learn to notice them and make them visible.

In Process Work theory, unoccupied roles are referred to as ghost roles.[2] Arlene and Lane knew that making these roles more visible was an effective way to help the group raise its awareness, create shared meaning, and reduce mind distance. The two facilitators asked the group for permission to occupy the ghost role. While such a role play might be challenging to witness, they said it could help stop the vicious cycle of blame. After receiving permission, Lane and Arlene took on the role of the killer: They began swaggering around the room, extolling their great power as warlords, and bragging about killing the enemy and anyone else who would stand in their way.

The group sat entranced, shocked by this naked portrayal of a power-drunk killer. One woman woke from her shock, stood up, and announced that she knew this killer. She told how a brutal warlord had invaded her home, forced his way into her kitchen, and threatened her and her family. After she told her story, Arlene and Lane encouraged her to take on the role of this warlord. With their encouragement, she overcame her trepidation and began strutting and swaggering around the room, spitting out hatred and bravado as she made loud threats to people in the group.

The participants watched, mesmerized, as this woman took on the role of a powerful, violent killer. Then they, too, began waking from their shock, reacting forcefully against this killer. As the group expressed its rage, terror, and grief at the losses and suffering caused by the killer, the woman left the role and rejoined the group. Now, united against brutality, violence, and killing in general, they were able to find their common humanity.

While this forum's emotional intensity is extreme, it shows once again the importance of creating safety if we want to free ourselves from old stories and reduce the mind distance separating us. Had these individuals expressed their horror at the atrocities during the actual war, their lives would have been endangered. To cope and stay alive, they had to distance themselves from their more compassionate parts. Marginalizing these parts enabled them to function and survive the horrors of war, but it left them feeling less than whole. Only when they found themselves in a place of safety could they reconnect with these split-off parts of their inner teams.

By opening up and empathically feeling the pain, suffering, and unresolved grief both sides had lived through, they were able to begin healing and find the reconciliation they all desired. By being truthful and identifying the real enemy—the atrocities, violence, hatred, and lies perpetrated by members of both sides—these individuals were able to liberate themselves from old, divisive stories. Now they were able to experience a bigger sense of identity that allowed them to tell a more honest, human story, a story that included them all. We need courage to challenge the myths that claim people are inherently evil and that war and killing are inevitable, but that is our challenge as interculturalists. Fortunately, new scientific research supports this more positive view of human nature.

Newer, Truer Stories

Thanks to the development of new empirical methods and a growing international community of researchers from various disciplines— sociology, economics, biology, neuroscience, anthropology, developmental psychology, primate behavioral ecology, and more—a more holistic, more nuanced picture of human nature is emerging. Here's what Joan B. Silk, a professor of anthropology at UCLA, has to say about this new story:

> In a time when we have all too much evidence of the harm that humans can do to one another and to the planet, it is ironic that

striking developments within the human sciences have highlighted our capacity for cooperation, our concern for the welfare of others, and our altruistic social preferences. It is extremely exciting to see the human sciences converging on the question of how humans evolved to be such an altruistic species.[3]

As this more holistic picture emerges, it shows us to be emotional beings to the core. Long before we learned to use symbols to think and communicate, emotions had evolved to motivate and guide us.[4] While we have since developed science and sophisticated systems of logic to make our symbolic thinking more rational, efficacious symbolic thinking is impossible without the underlying emotions that fuel and guide all information processing in the brain. For example, when we communicate, our ability to attune to one another, intuitively sense the other's intentions, and interact based on empathic understanding would be impossible without both the emotional and social circuitry of our brains.

When encouraged to develop in a healthy manner, our propensity for empathy serves as the basis for the compassion that is at the heart of the collective intelligence exhibited when we are functioning at our best. What is becoming ever clearer is that to be at our best, most of us need to feel safe. Feeling safe enables the limbic and social engagement systems in our brains to function optimally, allowing our inner team to perceive "just what is" and make better decisions, rather than getting caught up in a biased story that leads us astray. When we feel threatened, we are more apt to trigger the stress response, which changes our perceptions, making it harder to develop trusting relationships.

Because we are such complex, multileveled beings, what we interpret as threatening often has little to do with our physical safety. For instance, we have all seen how otherwise intelligent adults react irrationally to claims that challenge their beliefs, their identities, their reputations, and so on. When our emotional agendas are running the show, we may do our best to appear civil, but we often sense we are not operating with the intention of supporting the highest good of all concerned. At such moments our identities and world views are contracted into a more one-sided, more selfish perspective.

How much more satisfying would our interactions be—in the classroom, the boardroom, or the bedroom—if we were to develop more emotional intelligence? Then we could integrate our emotions into our lives in more productive ways, rather than try to exorcise them or pretend they don't exist. That we are emotional beings with the ability to think symbolically has deep implications for our future. If we are to live up to our potential as a species, rather than fall prey to our fears and hates and the unnecessary wars they generate, we need to develop more mindsight and devise better emotional agendas.

Our ability to use symbols and logic has enabled us to create the powerful technologies that are now changing the world, but it is our emotional agendas that will determine how these technologies get used. Whether we turn the countries of the world into corrupt, oppressive police states on cybernetic lockdown or into vibrant, humane economies with freedom, justice, and opportunities for all depends on our emotional agendas and the stories we tell. When our fear, anger, envy, and other challenging emotions are denied or ignored, they only seem to disappear. In actuality, they continue to motivate us from behind the closed door, influencing our actions for the worse. Conversely, if we have the courage to explore our more challenging and painful feelings, we also gain more power to experience our more elevated emotions such as enthusiasm, gratitude, care, compassion, awe, forgiveness, and love.

Not only are researchers in the human sciences expanding our understanding of how our brains and minds function, growing communities of practitioners—interculturalists, facilitators, teachers, psychotherapists, coaches, mediators, negotiators, consultants, social activists, and more—are spreading this new knowledge and pioneering new ways to apply it. Innovative and insightful new methods are being tested to help people not only develop more mindsight, but also to use them in our daily lives to liberate us and bridge the mind distance that separates us.

Process Work is just one of these new methods. Countless others are being developed and with time we will discover which ones work best in which contexts. Humans learn by trial and error, often fumbling around in our attempts to solve our problems. Because we still have much to learn, mistakes will be made, and we will need to be truthful about them as well. When we are courageous enough to acknowledge our errors and express our regrets, we reduce the need for self-deception and open the door for more truth and transformation. As the following example shows, transformation often begins when we are willing to take responsibility for our actions and errors.

Truthfulness Begets Truthfulness

At one of the post-war forums, a Croat woman did something that was both unusual and courageous at the time. She acknowledged the brutality her own side had engaged in.[5] She stood before the group and spoke about a Croat soldier who had killed a Muslim mother and her child. This Croat woman acknowledged she had been in favor of the war in order to liberate the occupied parts of Croatia. "That was war," she said, "but I did not want Savka and Jovan to be thrown into the well."

After the Croat woman spoke, a Serb woman stood up and responded. She was on the verge of tears as she spoke: "No one can tell me that an eighty-seven year-old Croat man should be made to suffer at the hands of Serbs. I graduated from the best university. But I still can't explain to a Croat mother why her four year-old had to die. Why did they beat up an eighty-seven-year-old man? How can I learn to forget this?"

The pain and suffering expressed by these women was almost unbearable, but the participants listened because they needed to hear these stories, reconnect with their deepest feelings, and take responsibility for their own actions. After acknowledging the atrocities committed by her fellow Serbs, this same woman continued by saying, "It's not that I'm personally guilty, because I am not. But if I were silent, I would not be taking responsibility. By speaking I take responsibility."

As this example illustrates, one truthful admission often encourages another person to reciprocate. If reciprocity, in the form of symmetrical blaming, gets the social motor turning towards the danger zone, then acknowledging responsibility and expressing regret can encourage the other to reciprocate and start a virtuous cycle of increasing trust. Truthful self-disclosure of our inner states also makes it easier for the other to better understand our point of view. By reducing mind distance, such acts of self-disclosure assist in the creation of more trust and understanding as illustrated below:

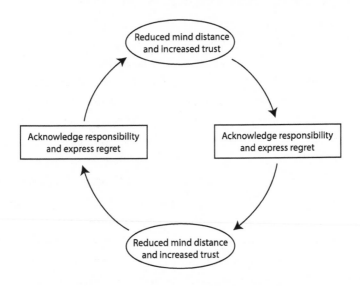

Figure 16.1 — Virtuous Cycle of Growing Trust

These truthful acknowledgments of responsibility changed the direction of this particular forum. Participants began discussing, first in sub-groups, and then in the entire group, how they could take responsibility and assume leadership roles in their own communities. People began to see their own war experiences in a new light and to reframe who they were and how much personal power and responsibility they had. They were drawing new conclusions and creating new stories to heal themselves and grow. By separating guilt from responsibility, they found hope and empowered themselves to act differently in the future. One woman said she had been a teenager when the wars started and she could not do anything, but then she added, "But now I see that my feelings then—my hatred—contributed to the atmosphere that led to war, and that has led to wars throughout history."

This woman grasped intuitively what science is now proving: The social circuitry in our brains connects us, allowing our intentions, feelings, and moods to be communicated nonverbally, even when we are not consciously aware such communication is occurring. When we couple such insights with courageous acts of truthfulness such as these women displayed, we can stop conflicts from spiraling out of control. By acknowledging our own feelings, thoughts, and deeds, as well as those of our groups, we have a tool to reduce reciprocal blaming, while bringing forth more truth and compassion. We can also, both individually and collectively, free ourselves from the prisons of our past.

Enduring overwhelming experience—both natural in the form of floods, famines, epidemics, and other disasters, as well as that created by humans in the form of torture, genocide, war, and other atrocities—has long been part of the human condition. While there is little we can do about earthquakes and volcanic eruptions, much of human history has been written in blood and the atrocities of past wars have left deep scars on the psyches of individuals and groups. Not only do victims of violence find it difficult to lead joyful, healthy lives, they often pass their unresolved experiences on to the next generation in the form of both stories and unconscious nonverbal communication. Learning how to heal trauma allows us to reclaim marginalized parts of ourselves and take responsibility for our own lives while helping those around us.

Just as most communities have experienced some form of suffering and trauma, so, too, most individuals have been hit by their share of the "slings and arrows of outrageous fortune." To be sure, some have led more protected lives than others, but we all have feelings that get hurt, we all get sick at one time or another, and we all must face the inevitability of death. Whether our painful experiences come at the hands of imperfect parents, racist teachers, schoolyard bullies, or any of the countless ways in which we can be harmed, we all get hurt, and we all draw our own conclusions to explain our plight and cope with our pain.

Because we drew many of our core conclusions about human nature when we were children, simplistic over-generalizations affect many areas of our lives. Countless false conclusions can be drawn by our young minds. When we believe such conclusions as adults, for example, "I'm a failure unless everyone likes me," or, "a perfect solution must be found for every problem," or, "people are liars who can't be trusted," and then act accordingly, we not only limit our development, we also generate unnecessary stress.

Because of the autonomous nature of our inner teams and the way memory works—both implicit and explicit—these conclusions, and the stories they are embedded in, get replayed over and over again. As they do, they become so automatic we no longer notice them as they recycle in the background of our minds. But because thoughts and feelings work in conjunction with one another, the automatic retelling of these old stories holds our emotional suffering in place.

No matter what conclusions we've drawn, if they are inaccurate and remain untested, they distort our thoughts, feelings, and perceptions, as well as our decisions and actions. But if we have the courage to test our assumptions, we can not only reduce suffering and mind distance, we can also free ourselves from their grip, develop our potential, and build more trusting, productive, and meaningful relationships.

The Ripple Effect

At the second forum in Split, one young woman sat silently.[6] She felt oppressed and helpless. She was preoccupied with fears about the government's plan to build a nuclear waste dump in her town. A common conclusion, especially among traumatized individuals, is, "I am small, weak, and helpless." When we are overwhelmed by powerful forces beyond our control, we experience what it's like to be weak and helpless, but if we then conclude we are weak and powerless in general, or that we will always be weak and powerless, it's easy to become depressed and give up hope.

But when this same young woman returned to the next forum six months later, she told an inspiring story. At Split she had been amazed to discover people could talk truthfully about their differences without becoming violent, could cry and grieve with one another and end up respecting, and even loving, each other.

Witnessing these transformations had a powerful effect on her. When she returned to her home town, she began organizing a campaign to stop the nuclear waste dump. She collected thousands of signatures and met with the mayor, who told her he was too small to do anything. The girl told the mayor she disagreed and was amazed by her own audacity: "Imagine me, a young woman, telling the mayor that he is not small! Now I feel much more powerful and free, because in spite of all odds, I have changed something in my community, and in my head." In effect, this young woman now had a new story about who she was and what she could accomplish, a new story that empowered and liberated her.

This was the essence of many stories that Arlene and Lane heard at the different post-war forums they facilitated in Croatia. [7] Many participants spoke of these events as life-transforming experiences. They were thrilled to realize conflict need not end in violence, and this insight enabled them to draw a new conclusion: If they were willing to talk openly and take responsibility for their own thoughts and feelings, their differences could be used as a force for peace. They also learned that truthfulness helped them heal their wounds. By courageously opening up and telling what they had experienced, they helped unfreeze the traumas that had kept them imprisoned.

Participants formed strong friendships across ethnic and cultural lines as they collaborated on projects to rebuild their war-torn country. By talking openly and respectfully, they enlarged their own identities and created connections with those they had once kept at a distance. Transformed by their experiences, they took their new insights and attitudes home with them, thus spreading hope to their families and communities. As these more elevated emotions rippled outwards, they multiplied, creating even more trust and hope. The path from hatred, fear, and violence to respect, peace, and beyond is all about building more trust: Trust in ourselves, trust in others, and trust in something bigger than ourselves.

The Ladder of Trust

If we have the courage to turn our attention inwards, we can develop the self-awareness we need to take responsibility for our thoughts, feelings, and actions. Not only can increased mindsight help us reduce internal dissonance, it can also, if we share our thoughts and feelings in a safe and truthful way, help us reduce mind distance.

Of course, one person's truthfulness can be perceived by another as disrespect or even abuse. Such transparency can also be perceived as weakness and naiveté. But regardless of how much of our truth we decide to share, it is essential to be as truthful as possible with ourselves to avoid the trap of self-deception.

How truthful and authentic we choose to be with others must always be balanced by considerations of context and safety, as well as by cultural norms and personal values. But if our sincere intention is to be both respectful *and* truthful, we decrease the chances of misunderstanding. And if we are willing to acknowledge our errors and express regret, we need worry even less about making mistakes.

When we commit ourselves to both truthfulness and respect, we make it easier for others to reciprocate and increase the odds that mutual trust will grow. The propensity to empathize with and help others is anchored in our biology and we can use this knowledge to create safer contexts and virtuous cycles, encouraging more of the world's social motors to move towards peace and justice.[8]

As our sense of safety grows, it also allows our identities to expand. We discover we have more in common with the other person than we had first realized. This does not mean personal and cultural differences disappear, they don't. But rather than being sources of fear and hatred, they become variations on a deeper, more universal theme. As we begin connecting at this deeper, more universal level, we begin to grow towards a larger, more world-centric identity. As mutual trust grows, step by step, the social motor continues turning in the right direction so as to create even more trust, as illustrated below.

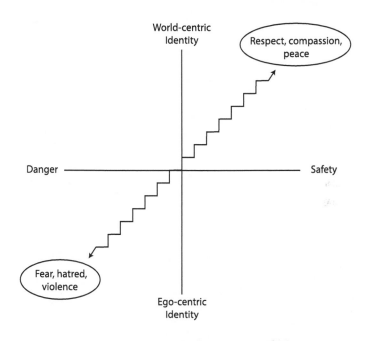

Figure 16.2 — The Ladder of Trust

This is what happened at the forums in Osijek and Split. As safety was created and people began to be more truthful, their sense of common identity grew and they began moving up the ladder of trust. Strong mutual trust does not grow overnight, but must be cultivated patiently as we each go about living our lives. As we saw in chapter six, when we are able to build trust, we can develop virtuous cycles to help improve the collective intelligence, performance, and morale of the groups we belong to. This is another reason why safety first, truth second is such an efficacious principle to live by.

Seventeen

Final Thoughts

Good, the more communicated,
the more abundant grows.

—John Milton

As we saw in the last chapter, the stories we tell ourselves have real consequences and when we choose to believe the wrong ones, we suffer. Believing the wrong stories also encourages us to expect others to be different than they are, which creates more misunderstandings.

Beliefs and choices go hand in hand, each one influencing the other. For example, I used to believe fasting was an efficient way to detoxify my body, so I chose to do a detox every spring for several years. I am no longer so sure about the efficacy of fasting—it may or may not promote detoxification, I simply don't know—and it's been decades since I did a long fast.

Nonetheless, I used to enjoy fasting for a number of reasons. For one, after two or three days my metabolism would shift gears and I would find myself feeling lighter and more energetic than usual while needing less sleep and getting more done. I also liked the idea I was purifying myself and I had a greater sense of self-control than usual. One year I went thirteen days without eating and was quite proud of myself.

But what always surprised me was how, once I started eating again, it was as if I lost the self-control I had during the fast, and if I were hungry and had to wait half an hour to eat, I would find myself getting irritable and impatient. What had happened to the self-control and the lighter, more buoyant feelings I had while fasting? And why couldn't I take an extra ten or twenty minutes to prepare a healthy meal rather than devour whatever I could get my hands on?

Such basic experiences speak volumes about the power of belief. When I was fasting, my choice was based on the belief I was helping my body. In contrast, when I got hungry in the course of a normal day, there was no good reason to restrain myself and hunger took control. I was driven to satisfy my hunger *now* and even though part of me was arguing for the healthier choice—a salad instead of the pretzels—desire often won out, leaving me in an unpleasant, conflicted state of mind.

Somehow making a choice and committing to it helps align our inner teams so we experience the flow states we all desire. But often, because our inner teams and our social realities are so complex, it's hard to get everything into alignment. For example, I was once in Namibia and touring one of the townships with friends. The poverty was abysmal by Western standards, but the residents were doing the best they could with the resources they had. I remember being impressed by their resilience and ingenuity. They had even found ways to create works of art out of discarded coke cans and other "trash."

Everywhere we went the residents were friendly and welcoming and when we were invited to stop at a street restaurant and eat, we did. Calling it a restaurant is overstating the case. It was actually a small shack next to which were erected some grills made out of old fifty-five gallon drums. And on the bare, dry ground there stood a few cheap plastic tables and chairs for guests to sit at. I wanted to show my gratitude for the warm welcome we had been receiving, so when I was offered one of the local delicacies, I found it hard to decline.

I'm not sure what type of worms they were—they were about the size of my thumb and had been grilled until they were crisp—but as I put the first one into my mouth, a part of me was ringing the alarm bell and screaming, *What are you doing, that's a worm! That's disgusting! Spit it out!* As you'll remember, disgust is one of the many social emotions groups use to condition their members and protect their world view and social order.

At the same time, my mouth was sending a very different message: This is delicious! I don't think I've ever tasted anything quite like this before, it reminds me a little of fried chicken. Give me more! I was torn between the thoughts in my mind and the taste in my mouth. But the delicious taste had a strong ally. I not only wanted to show my appreciation for all the good will we had been receiving, I also wanted to drop my culturally conditioned beliefs and grow my identity. I ordered another beer and kept eating the fried worms as I found myself connecting more and more with our hosts. Later some of the local children set up a boom box and entertained us with their dancing. The conversation, music, and dancing decreased the mind distance between us. Black and white, Namibian and American, for a short time those distinctions receded and I was part of something much larger and more joyous than my usual self.

If there is one key message in this book, it's this: To think and act like an interculturalist, we must choose to do so. No one is born with a world-centric identity. As we saw in chapter four, it is essential to harness our inner power if we hope to achieve our highest aspirations. To the degree that we make wise choices—as well as take responsibility for those less-than-optimal choices we also make—we can grow our mindsight and liberate ourselves from outdated conditioning as we pursue our highest dreams.

Getting clear about our intentions and setting smart goals is one key to the health and happiness we all desire. The same applies to dealing with differences. If we want to communicate and cooperate well with people who are different, we must choose to do so. That choice will help us hit the pause button when we find ourselves getting annoyed, confused, or stressed. Such moments are part and parcel of dealing with differences and without a clear commitment to your higher values, you will find yourself getting pulled back into the egocentric traps and ethnocentric conditioning we all struggle with. As one wise person once said, the best way to say no to a tempting distraction is to have a higher goal to say yes to.

A second key lesson of this book is that we are emotional beings who are designed to connect, but we need to feel safe to do so. Emotions are contagious and can spread like wildfire, either uniting and building up our relationships and communities, or polarizing and destroying them. To tame powerful emotions like fear and anger that can destroy empathy and trust, we must develop more mindsight, broaden our windows of tolerance, and learn to hit the pause button more skillfully. Emotions are not simply motivational, they are also moral forces guiding our way through life. In their attempts to manage humanity's core dilemmas, groups have devised different ways to employ emotions to promote survival and build social cohesion. As a result, differences often seem wrong and immoral rather than neutral.

We are designed to connect and attune, but mind distance separates us. When we don't know what others are feeling and thinking, we are more likely to deny their experience, reduce their sense of safety, and inhibit the growth of trust. Only when we allow empathy to work its magic and help us take the other person's point of view will we be able to structure our lives, relationships, and communities to support and promote our more elevated emotional states. Only then will we feel safe and free enough to express the love and compassion that are our birthright.

A third key lesson is that we are great story tellers who sometimes confuse our stories with reality. Our memories and brain maps are both malleable and fallible, and in our desire to tell a good story that presents us in the best light, we often engage in self-deception that distorts our perceptions. When that happens, we lose the ability to see "just what is."

Because so much of our brain's information processing occurs below the level of conscious awareness, it is essential that we have the courage to focus our attention inwards and test our expectations, assumptions, conclusions, and stories. Only then will we be able to develop the mindsight and emotional intelligence we need to detect distortions in our points of view.

Because we try to protect our beliefs the same way we try to protect our reputations, we are prone to emotional hijackings when others call our beliefs into question. Such reactivity limits our ability to think clearly, creatively, and compassionately. To avoid such emotional hijackings, we must be willing to test our beliefs and revise or let go of those that no longer serve us. This choice faces all of us and the more consciously we commit to it, the more we increase the likelihood of transcending our conditioning and finding fulfilment.

A final lesson is that the better you understand and like yourself, the better you will be able to understand and like others. We all have parts of ourselves we dislike and tend to marginalize. Much of this internal marginalization results from early experiences and the simplistic conclusions we drew as children. When we push these parts of ourselves aside and pretend they are not there, we not only impede the growth of our own mindsight, we make it that much harder to understand people who remind us of the marginalized parts in ourselves.

Part of the challenge of developing more mindsight is getting in touch with our outlawed parts and helping them become productive members of our inner teams. As we learn to understand, forgive, and accept these marginalized parts of ourselves, something remarkable begins to happen: We also find it easier to understand, forgive, and accept people who once seemed so different from us.

Conversely, we have much to learn from those who are different because they have an uncanny ability to tap into and trigger those parts of ourselves we most want to avoid. By waking up our marginalized parts, they give us the opportunity to get to know ourselves better. At the same time, people who are different from us have often developed creative ways to do things that we can learn from and use to improve our own lives. From this perspective, differences can be seen as another opportunity for us to learn, grow, and liberate ourselves.

Start Where You Are

I introduced this book by telling how a small, seemingly ordinary conversation changed my life for the better. I would like to end on the same note. While our social situations and personal obligations may not allow us to participate in large, transformational forums such as those held in Osijek and Split, we can, if we choose to do so, use any conversation to reduce mind distance, create more empathy, and find the optimal experiences we all desire. Great conversations and increased mindsight go hand in hand, allowing us to create virtuous cycles to improve our lives.

For instance, if we are willing to study and reflect honestly on our conversations, we can uncover the untested assumptions that motivated our words and actions. As we do, we gain more awareness of our thoughts and feelings, thus growing our mindsight and emotional intelligence. This, in turn, can reduce internal dissonance as well as the need for self-deception, allowing us to become more whole and lead freer, more satisfying lives.

Because other people's minds will always remain, to one degree or another, invisible to us, we will always be faced with uncertainty. Our uncertainty towards others is compounded by the parts of our own minds that exist behind a closed door we can't open. Most people find this uncertainty unpleasant, but if we pretend it's not there, we often think and talk in ways that reduce safety and promote defensiveness. In this regard, every conversation allows us to practice hitting the pause button and to grow our equanimity. The more we are able to tolerate uncertainty and ambiguity, the more we can use our conversations to empathize with others, take their point of view, and reduce mind distance.

While the various differences you encounter in your everyday conversations may not be as challenging as those found at Osijek and Split, mind distance exists, to one degree or another, between everyone we meet. If we practice listening attentively and with an open mind, we can reduce this mind distance and create healthier relationships. If we also use our conversations to practice speaking both respectfully and truthfully, even if it means admitting how much we don't know, we can create more shared meaning, truer stories, and stronger relationships. Not only will that enable us to lead more satisfying lives, it will also enable us to better manage our great diversity.

If we use our conversations well, we can also harness the ripple effect to share kindness, compassion, and love. As our mindsight and more elevated emotions ripple outwards, they help move us towards the more peaceful, deeply democratic world that is waiting to be built. Every conversation is an opportunity. All we need is the courage and willingness to accept the invitation.

Acknowledgments

I want to thank my friend and fellow interculturalist, Ruth Bleuze, for her tireless support and invaluable help. Ruth carefully and critically read every iteration of every chapter—and there were many—helping me ferret out the inconsequential and merely important to concentrate on the essentials. I also owe special thanks to Kevin Kelly whose incisive reading and critique of the entire manuscript helped me locate weak spots and highlight what was most valuable. In addition to their help with the content, both Ruth and Kevin offered support and encouragement at those times when the writing process seemed interminable. Thanks to them this is a far better book than I could ever have written alone and I am deeply indebted to both of them.

Ironically, finding the right title for this book was one of my biggest challenges and my conversation with Don Horton was fundamental in solving this problem. This was just one of our many conversations that clarified my thinking and for which I am deeply grateful. Many other friends read one or more individual chapters and offered valuable feedback. These include Denise Daniel, Christel Detsch, Eric Groon, Wendy Hoover, Pat Kirby, Kathleen Lawler, Greg Westerwick, and Zoe Zimmermann. Christel also helped me with important research in the early stages of writing. Special thanks to Michael Pacanowsky for his encouragement after reading drafts of the book's initial chapters, as well as for his mentoring which has made me a better coach and consultant.

I am deeply indebted to my editor, Erin Ferguson, for her help in focusing my writing and making it more precise and succinct. Her patience, skills, and light touch in offering constructive criticism have helped make this a better, shorter, and more readable book. I also owe special thanks to Kathryn Chapman for her thorough and conscientious proofreading of the final text.

I am especially thankful to Natalie Bolton for her great help in creating the cover and illustrations, as well as for laying out the book's interior. Her knowledge and resourceful pragmatism were essential in creating the book you now have in your hands. I also want to thank Al Wadleigh for generously sharing his expertise on the publishing process.

I have had the good fortune to encounter many wonderful teachers who shared their knowledge and skills with me and to four of them I owe a special debt of gratitude: Heinz Göhring, Arny Mindell, Kristine Fitch, and Shinzen Young. I know Heinz would have been delighted to read this book and it saddens me that he is no longer among us. I also want to thank Arlene Audergon, Banu Golesorkhi, Heinz Willebrand, Lane Arye, and Lee Shainis for allowing me to use their stories and for being good friends. Thanks are also due to my many clients and seminar participants who taught me so much by sharing their intercultural experiences.

On a more personal note, I want to thank Ursula Dreiner Kühlmann and her family for their love and support when I was a stranger in their country. Without their help, I would not be where I am today. I also want to thank my mother for teaching me to read, for sharing her love of books with me, and for listening patiently to all my progress reports on the status of this book.

NOTES

Chapter 1

1. Barnlund, *Public and Private Self*, 7.
2. Matsumoto, *The Unspoken Way*, 8.
3. Personal communication with Professor Heinz Göhring who spoke to Takeo Doi at an international conference exploring cultural differences.
4. Barnlund, *Private and Public Self*, 7.
5. I believe I first read the term "mind distance" in a SIETAR journal. Since then I have not seen the term used again and unfortunately I can no longer locate the actual journal in which I first read it.
6. Haidt, "The Emotional Dog and Its Rational Tail," 817.
7. Patterson, *Crucial Conversations*, 113.
8. Upon closer examination, smiling turns out to be far more complex than this simple analysis might lead one to believe. In *Emotions Revealed*, Dr. Paul Ekman provides a detailed analysis of different types of smiles and the various reasons we smile in social situations.
9. Much of the so-called mind-body problem can be understood as a dissociation of mind and body. Compounding this dissociation are semantic confusions resulting from the imprecise use of such terms as "mind" and "body." For an overview of this problem, see Chapter 14 of *Integral Psychology* by Ken Wilber.
10. Mindell, *The Leader as Martial Artist*, 8.
11. Personal communication with Arnold Mindell.
12. Siegel, *The Developing Mind*, 4, 70.
13. Cozolino, *Neuroscience of Human Relationships*, 7.
14. Goleman, *Social Intelligence*, 5.
15. Ibid., 312.
16. Sapolsky, *Why Zebras Don't Get Ulcers*, 164.

Chapter 2

1. This story is recounted by Dr. Siegel in *Mindsight – The New Science of Personal Transformation* and in his audiobook, *The Neurobiology of "We"*. Bruce is a pseudonym Siegel used to protect his patient's identity.
2. Becker, *Denial of Death*, 52.
3. Siegel, *Mindsight*, xi.

4. Ibid., xvi.

5. Throughout this book I will use the terms "nervous system" and "brain" to refer to physiological systems we can empirically observe, while reserving the word "mind" for the subjective and self-referential experience of being conscious.

6. Wilson, *Strangers To Ourselves*, 6.

7. Shaules, *The Intercultural Mind*, 54; Haidt, *The Emotional Dog and Its Rational Tail*, 819.

8. Doidge, *The Brain That Changes Itself*, 50; Wexler, *Brain and Culture*, 20.

9. Kandel, *In Search of Memory*, 147.

10. Ibid., 142.

11. Wexler, *Brain and Culture*, 20.

12. Hanson, *Buddha's Brain*, 6.

13. Kandel, *In Search of Memory*, 160.

14. Siegel, *Mindsight*, 73-4.

15. Siegel, *The Developing Mind*, 43.

16. Siegel, *Mindsight*, 146.

17. Ibid., 150.

18. Cozolino, *The Neuroscience of Human Relationships,* 129.

19. Haidt, "The Emotional Dog and Its Rational Tail," 828.

20. Schwartz, *The Mind and the Brain*, 117.

21. Kuhl, "Born To Learn," 5.

22. Ibid., 5.

23. Schwartz, *The Mind and the Brain*, 117.

24. Kuhl, "Born to Learn," 6.

25. Ibid., 5.

26. While it is difficult for an adult to learn to speak a new language without an accent, it is possible to retrain the brain to hear the sounds of a new language more clearly by creating new brain maps for these unheard sounds. See Doidge, *The Brain That Changes Itself*, 349, for a successful method of Japanese learning to distinguish the *r* and *l* sounds.

27. Some researchers refer to this process as socialization. While some draw a distinction between socialization and enculturation, for our purposes they can be thought of as the same basic process in which a child internalizes the physical and social environments in which it grows up.

28. Kuhl, "Born to Learn," 7.

29. Tavris, *Mistakes Were Made*, 42.

30. Tomasello, *Why We Cooperate*, x-xi.

Chapter 3

1. Siegel, *Mindsight*, 71.

2. Csikszentmihalyi, *Flow,* 52.

3. Childre, *Transforming Stress*, 45.

4. Csikszentmihalyi, *Flow*, 4.

5. Goleman, *Emotional Intelligence*, 14.

6. Siegel, *Mindsight*, 7.

7. Navarro, *What Every Body Is Saying*, 22.

8. Siegel, *Mindsight*, 222.

9. Damasio, *The Feeling of What Happens,* 93.

10. Siegel, *Mindsight*, 70.

11. Damasio, *Self Comes To Mind*, 101.

12. Ibid., 193.

13. McEwen, *The End of Stress*, 19.

14. Siegel, *Mindsight*, 137.

15 Ibid.

16. There are exceptions to this basic model, e.g., in states of deep relaxation and meditation. In addition, depression is sometimes linked to states of agitation, but in general this model of arousal works well to describe most normal states of mind.

17. The technical term for our ability to perceive what is going on inside ourselves is interoception. See Siegel, *Mindsight*, 127 for more details.

18. Fine, *A Mind of its Own*, 8.

19. For many people, cognitive implies such dissonance is only mental, ignoring the fact that dissonance can also be experienced emotionally and felt in the body, e.g., when people talk about having mixed feelings towards something or someone. There is nothing new about such internal dissonance as the famous line from Goethe's Faust indicates: "In my breast, alas, live two souls". For this reason I will sometimes refer to the state of internal disharmony as internal dissonance, inner conflict or simply dissonance.

20. Tavris, *Mistakes Were Made*, 13.

21. Ibid., 14.

22. Ibid., 19.

23. Ibid., 18.

24. Gladwell, *Blink*, 48.

25. Haidt, "The Emotional Dog and its Rational Tail", 814.

26. Ibid., 818.

27. Gladwell, *Blink*, 53.

28. Ibid., 57.

29. Brooks, *Social Animal*, 180.

30. Wilson, *Strangers to Ourselves*, 30.

31. Siegel, *Mindsight*, 137.

32. De Becker, *The Gift of Fear*, 346.

Chapter 4

1. Haslam, *Tyranny*, 139.

2. Zimbardo, *The Lucifer Effect,* ix.

3. Milgram, *Obedience to Authority*, 4.

4. Blass, "Understanding behavior in the Milgram experiment," 398.

5. Frankl, *Man's Search for Meaning*, 104.

6. Jones, "The Attribution of Attitudes," 1.

7. Barabási, *Linked*, 7.

8. Wilber, *Integral Psychology*, 166.

9. McCullough, *Beyond Revenge*, 225.

10. Sapolsky, *Why Zebras Don't Get Ulcers*, xi.

11. Kohls, *Learning to Think Korean*, 165-170.

12. Brooks, *The Social Animal*, 151.

13. Langer, *Mindfulness*, 182-183.

Chapter 5

1. Canton, "Cell phone culture."

2. Ibid.

3. Hofstede, *Culture's Consequences,* 11.

4. Hofstede, *Cultures and Organizations*, 280.

5. Haidt, *The Righteous Mind*, 16-26. Much of Moral Foundations Theory was inspired by the work of Jonathan Haidt's mentor, the cultural psychologist, Richard Shweder. After its initial conception by Haidt and Joseph, MFT was expanded upon and refined in collaboration with a larger group of researchers. While MFT was originally devised to measure differences between cultures, the publication of Haidt's book in 2002, *The Righteous Mind,* has served to popularize MFT as a way to better understand the current political and cultural battles in the United States and to explain the mind distance that exists between conservatives and liberals.

6. Ibid., 197-205. MFT was originally composed of five dimensions, the sixth, liberty, was added to better account for the empirical data the researchers were collecting.

7. Kluckhohn, *Variations in Value Orientation*. viii.

8. Hall, *Beyond Culture*.

9. Parsons, *The Social System*.

10. Trompenaars, *Riding the Waves of Culture*, 37.

11. We must also avoid confusing the map with the territory if we want to escape the trap of stereotypical thinking. One of the disadvantages of these big picture systems is they encourage us to label and categorize people, while overlooking the complexity of human cognition and the behavioral diversity that exists among individuals.

12. Canton, "Cell phone culture."

13. Ibid.

14. Porges, *Polyvagal Theory*, 54.

15. Ibid., 56, 64, and 250.

16. Sapolsky, *Why Zebras Don't Get Ulcers*, 353.

17. Porges, *Polyvagal Theory*, 11.

18. Goleman, *Social Intelligence*, 16-17.

19. Porges, *Polyvagal Theory*, 213-214.
20. Zimbardo, *Lucifer Effect*, 53.
21. I wish I could claim responsibility for creating what I am calling the social motor, but I was inspired by the work of Christoph Thomann and Friedemann Schulz von Thun. I first saw this model used to clarify human interactions in their excellent book, *Klärungshilfe*.
22. This simple model, as useful as it is, has a flaw: It downplays the apparent simultaneity of nonverbal signals being sent and received by both persons, nonverbal signals the threat assessment systems of both partners monitor continuously and attribute meaning to.
23. Van der Kolk, Foreword to *Polyvagal Theory*, xi.

Chapter 6

1. Douglas, *Purity and Danger*, xi.
2. Ibid., 40.
3. Ibid., 42.
4. Damasio, *Self Comes to Mind*, 117.
5. Elias, *On the Process of Civilization*, 464.
6. Kluger, *The Sibling Effect*, 44.
7. Haidt, *The Righteous Mind*, 170.
8. Haidt, "The Emotional Dog and its Rational Tail," 814.
9. Gladwell, *Blink*, 33.
10. Ibid.
11. Gazzaniga, *Who's In Charge?*, 204.
12. Gilligan, *Violence*, 105.
13. Ibid., 11.
14. Geertz. *The Interpretation of Cultures*, 5.

Chapter 7

1. To respect the privacy of my client, I have changed names and features in this story. The spirit of the story and the gist of my experiences are presented accurately.
2. Argyris, "Teaching Smart People How to Learn," 100.
3. Becker, *Denial of Death*, 199.
4. Gazzaniga, *Who's In Charge?*, 35.
5. Ibid., 85.
6. Ibid., 95.
7. Ibid., 82.
8. Damasio, *The Feeling of What Happens,* 187.
9. Haidt, "The Emotional Dog and Its Rational Tail," 814.
10. Fischhoff, "I knew it would happen," 1.
11. Doidge, *The Brain That Changes Itself,* 304.
12. Ost, James, "Crashing Memories and Reality Monitoring," 125–134.
13. Haidt, "The Emotional Dog and Its Rational Tail," 820.

14. Beck, *Cognitive Therapy and the Emotional Disorders,* 2-4.

15. Doidge, *The Brain That Changes Itself,* 87.

16. Jenkins, "Last of the Cave People," 139.

17. Doidge, *The Brain That Changes Itself,* 304.

18. Wexler, *Brain and Culture,* 5-7.

19. Van Berkum, "Right or Wrong?", 1092.

Chapter 8

1. Diamond, *Guns, Germs, and Steel,* 143.

2. Ibid., 306.

3. Guns, Germs, and Steel, DVD, Episode 1, Out of Eden.

4. Diamond, *Guns, Germs, and Steel,* 306.

5. Ibid., 270.

6. Ibid., 144.

7. Ibid., 13.

8. Ibid., 14.

9. Ibid., 298.

10. Ibid., 20.

11. Flannery, *Creation of Inequality,* 16.

12. If you are like me, you too have had friends or acquaintances who suffered from severe depression and chose to take their own lives. According to Dr. Christopher Murray of the World Health Organization, there is a growing epidemic of depression around the world. Such an unnatural trend should encourage all of us to pause and reflect on the deeper meaning of these numbers. "Spirit of the age," *The Economist,* 113.

13. Tavris and Aronson, *Mistakes Were Made,* 37.

14. Ibid., 32.

15. Ibid., 6.

16. Sapolsky, *Why Zebras Don't Get Ulcers,* 260.

17. Diamond, *Guns, Germs, and Steel,* 144.

18. Benko, "The People Who Walk With Reindeer," 66.

19. Buller, "Four Fallacies of Pop Evolutionary Psychology," 77.

20. Some anthropologists now prefer the term "foragers" in place of "hunter-gatherers" because evidence suggests that hunting contributed less to early humans' food supply than was previously believed.

21. Diamond, *Guns, Germs, and Steel,* 87-91.

22. Ibid., 88-9.

23. Ibid., 215.

24. Ibid., 123-24.

25. Ibid., 247.

Chapter 9

1. As in chapter seven, I have changed names and specifics to protect the privacy of my client.
2. Carneiro, "The Role of Warfare in Political Evolution", 88.
3. Diamond, *Guns, Germs, and Steel*, 268-69.
4. Buller, "Four Fallacies," 78.
5. Porges, *Polyvagal Theory*, 16.
6. Baron-Cohen, *Mindblindness,* 13.
7. Ibid., 14.
8. Robinowitz, *Modern-Day Vikings*, 71.
9. Ibid., 72.
10. It's worth noting that many of the countries that are typically ranked highest in individualism are also countries that have strong Protestant roots. Surely there are other factors involved, but Martin Luther's emphasis on each person being able to communicate directly with God would seem to promote a more individualistic world view. In effect, Luther's teaching encourages individuals to bypass the hierarchy of church and state to develop a direct relationship with the ultimate power in the universe.
11. Haidt, *Righteous Mind*, 162.
12. Johnson, *Polarity Management*, 82.
13. Ibid., 22.
14. Haidt, *Righteous Mind*, 49
15. Rousseau, "On the Origin of Inequality", 351.
16. For example, the individualism end of the self-group dilemma is also referred to as agency, self-orientation, independence, egocentric, detached, and separate by different researchers, while the group end of the pole is sometimes referred to as dependence, group oriented, interdependence, sociocentric, connected, communal, belonging, and enmeshed. Each of these terms can have a different meaning according to context and may trigger a different reaction depending upon whom you are speaking to.
17. Belt, "Sweden in Search of a New Model," 13.
18. Ibid., 34.
19. Sapolsky, *Why Zebras Don't Get Ulcers,* 364-5.
20. Ibid., 366.
21. *Polarity Management* by Rob Johnson posits many dilemmas that individuals and groups face. For a look at how different dilemmas influence business practices around the world, see *Riding the Waves of Culture* by Fons Trompenaars and Charles Hampden-Turner.
22. Frankl, "Psychotherapie mit Menschlichen Anlitz."
23. Robinowitz, *Modern-Day Vikings*, 5.

Chapter 10

1. Pearce, *Interpersonal Communication*, xv.
2. Patterson, *Crucial Conversations,* 21.

3. Ibid., 23.
4. Schulz von Thun, *Miteinander Reden 1*, 11-15.
5. Burgoon, *Nonverbal Communication*, 267.
6. Ibid., 242.
7. For a fuller treatment of German and American cultural differences and mindsets, see Nees, *Germany: Unraveling an Enigma*.
8. Hess, *The Expert Expat*, 168.
9. Nees, *Germany*, 50-52.
10. English formerly had such a system, but it went out of use many years ago. Remnants of this system can still be found, for instance, in the use of thou and thee in older versions of the Bible.
11. Goleman, *Social Intelligence*, 40-44.
12. Siegel, *The Developing Mind*, 68.
13. West, "Communication Accommodation Theory".
14. Siegel, *Developing Mind*, 334.

Chapter 11

1. I first met Lee around 2005, when I volunteered to teach English to a Mexican family. Most recently I presented introductory lectures on cultural differences to raise the awareness of new volunteers at Intercambio.
2. For more details on Intercambio, see their website: www.intercambioweb.org
3. Whitmore, *Coaching for Performance*, 55-56.
4. Csikszentmihalyi, *Flow*, 6.
5. Sapolsky, *Why Zebras Don't Get Ulcers*, 263.
6. Covey, *The 7 Habits of Highly Effective People*, 99.
7. Mindell, *Sitting In The Fire*, 55.
8. De Waal, *The Age of Empathy*, 79.
9. Searle, *Speech Acts*, 22.
10. Tannen, "The Power of Talk," 142.
11. Ibid.
12. Ibid., 140.
13. Patterson, *Crucial Conversations*, 40. As Patterson and his co-authors show, figuring out both what we want and what we don't want is also an effective way to avoid the downsides of either-or thinking.
14. Putnam, *Bowling Alone*, 135.
15. Tannen, "The Power of Talk," 144.
16. Ibid., 140.
17. Covey, *The 7 Habits of Highly Effective People*, 235.
18. Cialdini, *Influence*, 19.
19. Benkler, "The Unselfish Gene," 82.
20. Harris, *10% Happier*, 184.
21. Siegel, *Mindsight*, 259.
22. Harris, *10% Happier*, 184.

23. Siegel, *Mindsight*, 259.
24. De Becker, *The Gift of Fear*, 64-5; Cialdini, *Influence*, 28.

Chapter 12
1. Levine, *In An Unspoken Voice*, 137.
2. Siegel, *The Developing Mind*, 278.
3. Van der Kolk, Foreword to *Polyvagal Theory*, xii.
4. Siegel, *Mindsight*, 170.
5. Shaules, *The Intercultural Mind*, 104.
6. Geertz, *Local Knowledge*, 59.
7 Harris, *10% Happier*, 170.
8. Siegel, *Mindsight*, 171-2.
9. Trompenaars and Hampden-Turner, *Riding the Waves of Culture*, 39, view universalism and particularism as a separate dilemma from the self-group dilemma. This interpretation makes sense and may allow for a more detailed analysis. For the purposes of this book, I believe it is sensible to think of them as aspects of the larger self-group dilemma.
10. Ibid., 42.
11. McCullough, *Beyond Revenge*, 190. The distinction between insiders, one of "us", and outsiders, one of "them", seems to exist everywhere and evidence suggests this is an artifact of the way our brains process information. Research in this area is ongoing, but for the moment it is safe to say people generally behave differently towards insiders than they do towards outsiders. According to Koutlaki, *Among the Iranians*, 24, children in Iran quickly learn the importance of distinguishing between insiders (*khodi*) and outsiders (*qarib*), as well as between more public and private contexts, in order to know the appropriate ways to express their emotions.
12. Mindell, *Sitting In The Fire*.
13. Siegel, *The Developing Mind*, 122-3.
14. Damasio, *Descartes Error*, xii-xiii.
15. Siegel, *The Developing Mind*, 123.
16. Goleman, *Emotional Intelligence*, 4-5.
17. De Waal, *The Age of Empathy*, 208-9.
18. Ibid.
19. Nathanson, *Shame and Pride*, 110.
20. Tavris, *Anger*, 23.
21. In ground breaking books such as *The Silent Language* and *The Hidden Dimension*, Edward T. Hall described in exquisite detail what he called "proxemics", the ways cultures used space to organize themselves and promote social order and cohesion. Hall also showed how people view the area around themselves as if it were an extension of their body and how we react defensively when we perceive our space being invaded. Hall pointed out that while such contextual dimensions as time and space are used pervasively

in cultures around the world, people are typically unaware of how powerfully these dimensions influence them.

22. Hall, *The Hidden Dimension*, 131-164.

23. The use of the English word *face* to refer to a person's reputation, dignity, prestige, status, or honor originated as the translation of a concept used in China. Today the concept of face is used in many fields including psychology, political science, sociology, and sociolinguistics. Giving and receiving face require skillful management of the three core dilemmas we have explored up until now: Self-group, equality-hierarchy, and masculine-feminine. When these dilemmas are not managed well, face is threatened and with it a person's internal sense of safety. Needless to say, while creating and maintaining face and safety is important in all cultures, it is more important in some and the rules for giving and receiving face can vary greatly.

24. Koutlaki, *Among the Iranians*, 44-50.

25. Tremayne, "Face and 'Change' in Modern Iran," 26-28.

26. Koutlaki, *Among the Iranians*, 186-87.

27. Ekman, *Emotions Revealed*, 4.

28. Hofstede, *Culture's Consequences*, 77; Haidt, *The Righteous Mind*, 165-69.

29. Social hierarchies can tame our innate urge for revenge that can spiral out of control, leading to murder, mayhem, blood feuds, and warfare. For example, in *Beyond Revenge*, McCullough notes that murder rates fell dramatically in medieval Europe once governments began assuming a monopoly on force and developing systems of justice that were accepted by the populace. Laws that prohibited murder and revenge and that demanded victims present their cases to the laws of the land reduced the murder rates twenty to forty-fold in different European countries.

30. Kipnis, *Against Love*, 35-41.

31. Hall, *Silent Language*, 42.

32. Ibid., 43.

33. Goleman, *Emotional Intelligence*, 5.

34. Ibid., xii.

35. Brooks, *The Social Animal*, 285.

36. Goleman, *Emotional Intelligence*, 112.

Chapter 13

1. Briggs, *Never in Anger*, 1. The full name of these people is the Utkuhikhalingmiut,, but for simplicity's sake I will follow Brigg's lead and refer to them as the Utku.

2. Ibid., 48.

3. Ibid., 47.

4. Ibid., 238.

5. Tavris, *Anger*, 49.

6. Briggs, *Never in Anger*, 140.

7. Tavris, *Anger*, 52.

8. Ibid., 58.

9. Nathanson, in *Shame and Pride* refers to it as affective resonance while Goleman in *Emotional Intelligence* calls it emotional contagion.

10. Goleman, *Social Intelligence*, 107.

11. Ibid., 105.

12. Doi, *The Anatomy of Dependence*, 11.

13. Ibid., 75.

14. Ibid.

15. Ibid., 20.

16. Ibid., 36.

17. Ibid., 60.

18. Ibid.

19. Ibid., 84.

20. Ibid., 169.

21. Ibid., 135.

22. Whiting, *You Gotta Have Wa*, 66.

23. For a lighthearted, but educational portrayal of American baseball players in Japan, watch *Mr. Baseball*, a film starring Tom Selleck as Jack Elliott. Elliot is an individualistic American whose actions as a player are continually colliding with the cooperation and group oriented approach so prevalent in Japan.

24. Whiting, *You Gotta Have Wa*, 71.

25. Haidt, *The Righteous Mind,* 225.

26. Tavris, *Anger,* 28.

27. Haidt, *The Righteous Mind*, 32-34.

28. Blackburn, "To Feel and Feel Not," 35.

29. May, *Will and Spirit*, 211-12.

30. Childre, *Transforming Anxiety,* 48.

31. McCullough, *Beyond Revenge*, 13-15; Buller, "Four Fallacies", 78.

32. Seligman, "Positive Psychology: An Introduction," 12.

33. De Waal, *Age of Empathy*, 5; McCullough, *Beyond Revenge*, 12-13; Harris, *10% Happier*, 185.

34. McCullough, *Beyond Revenge*, 127.

35. Ibid., 155.

36. Ibid., 190.

37. Doi, *The Anatomy of Dependence*, 50.

38. Goldsmith, *What Got You Here*, 83-86.

39. Tannen, "The Power of Talk," 140.

40. McCullough, *Beyond Revenge*, 162-3.

Chapter 14

1. Shingon Buddhism, one of the mainstream forms of Buddhism in Japan, is a version of Vajrayana Buddhism. Just as Christianity comes in many forms,

i.e., Catholic, Lutheran, Baptist, Methodist, Mormon, Pentecostal and so on, the Buddhist world also contains a wide variety of different lineages and traditions that vary from country to country.

2. Langer, *Science of Mindlessness and Mindfulness.*

3. There are many different forms of meditation. Based on my own experience and research, practicing mindfulness is valuable for developing mindsight and widening one's window of tolerance. I am not suggesting all forms of meditation or mind training are equally valuable or efficacious.

4. Caveat emptor! If this chapter makes you curious and you would like to explore mindfulness meditation more, there are many good books and audio programs available. Be careful when choosing a teacher—while there are many good ones who are competent and have great integrity, many so-called spiritual teachers turn out to be charlatans. Such teachers are probably suffering from more self-deception than the students they take advantage of. Simply developing more mental powers and charisma is no guarantee a person will not also be looking for gullible students on which he can build his ego and personal empire.

5. Harris, *10% Happier*, 167-179.

6. Creswell, "Neural Correlates," 560; Harris, *Waking Up*, 8.

7. Langer, *Science of Mindlessness and Mindfulness.*

8. While it is true that many people get caught up in negative thoughts, identifying with them and replaying them over and over in their minds, this is the result of a conditioned response or unresolved traumatic experience, not the mind's more natural reaction, which is to simply recoil.

9. Mindfulness meditation is sometimes referred to as insight meditation because of the number of insights we get about our minds and identities. Both of these terms, mindfulness and insight, are English translations of the original Pali word, *vipassanā.*

10. Siegel, *Mindsight*, xii.

11. Creswell, "Neural Correlates," 561.

12. Wenner, "Brain Scans Reveal Why Meditation Works."

13. Goleman, *Emotional Intelligence*, 268.

14. Killingsworth, "The Future of Happiness Research," 88-9.

15. In 2005, I was looking for ways to help me better manage my anxiety and stress and heard about mindfulness meditation. When I learned there was to be a ten day mindfulness training at Sunrise Ranch near Loveland, Colorado, I decided to participate. That was where I first met Shinzen Young. Because the results were so encouraging, I attended a second ten day retreat, again with Shinzen, at Sunrise Ranch in 2006. Since then I have been meditating regularly, sometimes with local groups of other meditators, but mostly on my own.

16. In addition to his residential trainings, Shinzen uses internet and telephone conferencing to stay connected with his students around the world. Each month he offers a training in mindfulness meditation via phone conferencing. For more details, see www.BasicMindfulness.com

17. Harris, *10% Happier*, 168.

Chapter 15
1. Arye, "Transforming Conflict into Community," 112.
2. I first met Lane and Arlene in Switzerland in the late 1980s, when I attended several Process Work workshops led by Dr. Arnold Mindell. When I recently read the journal article that reported their experiences in Croatia, I was inspired by both the poignancy and the amazing transformations that were occurring in the groups they were working with.
3. Mindell, *Leader as Martial Artist*, 5-6.
4. Wilber, *Integral Psychology*, 2.
5. Patterson, *Crucial Conversations*, 21.
6. Wilber, *Integral Psychology*, 38-43.
7. Ibid., 44-46.
8. Ibid., 93.
9. Some people refer to this as the ethnocentric stage. Because ethnocentric has such a negative connotation for many people, I have chosen the more neutral term, sociocentric. In the way I am using these terms, they are roughly synonymous.
10. Wilber, *Kosmic Consciousness*, CD 5, Track 3.
11. Wilber, *Integral Psychology*, 44.
12. The original Latin quote, *Homo sum, humani nihil a me alienum puto* appeared in the play *Heauton Timorumenos*.
13. Mindell, *Sitting in the Fire*, 42-3.
14. Arye, "Transforming Conflict into Community," 4.
15. Levine, *In An Unspoken Voice*, 52.
16. Audergon, *The War Hotel*, 173-207.
17. Levine, *In An Unspoken Voice*, 31-37; Van der Kolk, *Restoring the Body*.

Chapter 16
1. These were Croatian Serbs, i.e., ethnic Serbs who had been living in Croatia for generations and who possessed Croatian citizenship.
2. Mindell, *Sitting in the Fire*, 89.
3. Tomasello, *Why We Cooperate*, 111.
4. Damasio, *The Feeling of What Happens*, 30.
5. Arye, "Transforming Conflict into Community," 118.
6. Ibid., 119.
7. Similar forums are still being facilitated to promote further healing and reconciliation. For more details on this, visit www.cfor.info
8. Tomasello, *Why We Cooperate*, 13.

REFERENCES

Argyris, Chris. "Teaching Smart People How to Learn." *Harvard Business Review*, May-June 1991, 99-109.

Arye, Lane and Arlene Audergon. "Transforming Conflict into Community: Post-War Reconciliation in Croatia." *Psychotherapy and Politics International*, Volume 3, Issue 2, June 2005, 112-121.

Audergon, Arlene. *The War Hotel: Psychological Dynamics in Violent Conflict.* London: Whurr Publishers, 2005.

Barabási, Albert-László. *Linked – How Everything Is Connected to Everything Else and What It Means for Business, Science and Every Day Life.* New York: Plume, 2014.

Barnlund, Dean C. *Public and Private Self in Japan and the United States.* Tokyo, Japan: The Simul Press, 1975.

Baron-Cohen, Simon. *Mindblindness: an Essay on Autism and Theory of Mind.* Cambridge, MA: MIT Press, 1995.

Beck, Aaron T. *Cognitive Therapy and the Emotional Disorders.* New York: International Universities Press, Inc. 1976.

Becker, Ernest. *The Denial of Death.* New York: The Free Press, 1973.

Belt, Don. "Sweden in Search of a New Model." *National Geographic*, August 1993, 8-34.

Benkler, Yochai. "The Unselfish Gene." *Harvard Business Review*, July-August, 2011, 77-85.

Benko, Jessica. "The People Who Walk with Reindeer." *National Geographic.* November 2011. 62-81.

Blackburn, Simon. "To Feel and Feel Not." *The New Republic.* December 24, 2001. 34-38.

Blass, Thomas. "Understanding behavior in the Milgram obedience experiment: The role of personality, situations, and their interactions." *Journal of Personality and Social Psychology.* 60 (3) 398-413, 1991.

Briggs, Jean L. *Never in Anger: Portrait of an Eskimo Family.* Cambridge, MA: Harvard University Press, 1970.

Brooks, David. *The Social Animal: The Hidden Sources of Love, Character, and Achievement.* New York: Random House, 2011.

Buller, David J. "Four Fallacies of Pop Evolutionary Psychology." *Scientific American,* Vol. 300, No. 1, (2009) 74-81.

Burgoon, Judee, David Buller and W. Gill Woodall. *Nonverbal Communication: The Unspoken Dialogue.* New York: Harper and Row, Publishers, 1989.

Canton, Naomi. "Cell phone culture: How cultural differences affect us." Updated CNN online report of Sept 12, 2012. www.cnn.com/2012/09/27/tech/mobile-culture-usage/index.html

Carneiro, Robert L. "The Role of Warfare in Political Evolution." In, *Effects of War on Society.* Ausenda, Giorgio (Ed.). San Francisco: Center for Interdisciplinary Research on Social Stress, 1992.

Childre, Doc and Deborah Rozman. *Transforming Stress.* Oakland, CA: New Harbinger Publications, 2005.

———. *Transforming Anxiety.* Oakland, CA: New Harbinger Publications, 2006.

Cialdini, Robert B. *Influence: Science and Practice.* Fifth edition. Boston: Pearson, 2009.

Covey, Stephen R. *The 7 Habits of Highly Effective People.* New York: Simon & Schuster, 1989.

Cozolino, Louis. *The Neuroscience of Human Relationships: Attachment and the Developing Social Brain.* New York and London: W. W. Norton & Company, 2006

Creswell, J. David, Baldwin Way, Naomi Eisenberger, and Matthew Liebermann. "Neural Correlates of Dispositional Mindfulness During Affect Labeling." *Psychosomatic Medicine* 69: 2007, 560-565.

Csikszentmihalyi, Mihaly. *Flow: The Psychology of Optimal Experience*. New York: Harper Perennial, 1990.

Damasio, Antonio. *Descartes' Error: Emotion, Reason, and the Human Brain*. New York: G. P. Putnam's Sons, 1994.

———. *The Feeling of What Happens*. San Diego and New York: Harcourt, Inc. 1999.

———. *Self Comes to Mind: Constructing the Conscious Brain*. New York: Pantheon Books, 2010.

De Becker, Gavin. *The Gift of Fear*. New York: Dell Publishing, 1997.

De Waal, Frans. *The Age of Empathy*. New York: Three Rivers Press, 2009.

Diamond, Jared. *Guns, Germs, and Steel: The Fates of Human Societies*. New York: W. W. Norton & Co, 1999.

Doi, Takeo. *The Anatomy of Dependence*. Tokyo: Kodansha International, 1971.

Doidge, Norman. *The Brain That Changes Itself*. New York and London: Penguin Books, 2007.

Douglas, Mary. *Purity and Danger*. London and New York: Routledge Classics, 2004.

Ekman, Paul. *Emotions Revealed*. New York: St. Martin's Griffin, 2007.

Elias, Norbert. *On the Process of Civilization,* Volume 3 of *The Collected Works of Norbert Elias*. Dublin: University College Dublin Press, 2012.

Fine, Cordelia. *A Mind of Its Own: How Your Brain Distorts and Deceives*. New York and London: W. W. Norton & Company, 2005.

Fischhoff, Baruch and Ruth Beyeth. "I Knew It Would Happen: Remembered Probabilities of Once-Future Things." *Organizational Behavior and Human Performance*, 13, 1975, 1-16.

Flannery, Kent and Joyce Marcus. *The Creation of Inequality*. Cambridge, MA: Harvard University Press, 2012.

Frankl, Viktor. *Man's Search For Meaning: An Introduction to Logotherapy*. New York: Washington Square Press, 1963.

————. *Auf dem Weg zu einer Psychotherapie mit menschlichen Anlitz.* Speech at European Evolution of Psychotherapy Conference, Hamburg, Germany, July 27-31, 1994. Program G 207, Audiotape #75.

Gazzaniga, Michael S. *Who's in Charge: Free Will and the Science of the Brain.* New York: HarperCollins Publishers, 2011.

Geertz, Clifford: *The Interpretation of Cultures.* New York: Basic Books. Republished in 2000.

————. *Local Knowledge: Further Essays in Interpretive Anthropology,* Third Edition. New York: Basic Books, 2000.

Gilligan, James. *Violence.* New York: Vintage Books, 1996.

Gladwell, Malcolm. *Blink: The Power of Thinking Without Thinking.* New York, Boston and London: Little, Brown and Company, 2005.

Goldsmith, Marshall. *What Got You Here Won't Get You There.* New York: Hyperion, 2007.

Goleman, Daniel. *Emotional Intelligence.* New York: Bantam Books, 1995.

————. *Social Intelligence: The New Science of Human Relationships.* New York: Bantam Books, 2006.

Guns, Germs, and Steel. DVD produced by Lion TV for National Geographic Television and Film. 2005.

Haidt, Jonathan. "The Emotional Dog and Its Rational Tail: A Social Intuitionist Approach to Moral Judgment." *Psychological Review,* Vol. 108, No. 4 (2001): 814-834.

————. *The Righteous Mind: Why Good People Are Divided by Politics and Religion.* New York: Vintage Books, 2013.

Hall, Edward T. *The Silent Language.* New York: Doubleday, 1959.

————. *The Hidden Dimension.* Garden City, NY: Doubleday, 1969.

————. *Beyond Culture.* Garden City, NY: Anchor Books, 1976.

Hanson, Rick and Richard Mendius. *Buddha's Brain: The Practical Neuroscience of Happiness, Love & Wisdom.* Oakland, CA: New Harbinger Publications, 2009.

Harris, Dan. *10% Happier.* New York: HarperCollins Publishers, 2014.

Harris, Sam. Waking Up: *A Guide to Spirituality Without Religion*. New York: Simon & Schuster, 2014.

Haslam, S. Alexander and Stephen Reicher. "Tyranny: Revisiting Zimbardo's Stanford Prison Experiment." In Smith, Joanne R. and S. Alexander Haslam (eds.). *Social Psychology: Revisiting the Classic Studies*. London: Sage Publications, 2012.

Hess, Melissa Brayer and Patricia Linderman. *The Expert Expat*. Revised edition. Boston and London: Nicholas Brealey Publishing, 2007.

Hofstede, Geert. *Culture's Consequences*. Newbury Park, CA: Sage Publications, 1980.

Hofstede, Geert, Gert Jan Hofstede, and Michael Minkov. *Cultures and Organizations—Software of the Mind*. New York: McGraw-Hill Books, 2010, Third Edition.

Jenkins, Mark. "Last of the Cave People." *National Geographic*, February, 2012, 127-141.

Johnson, Barry. *Polarity Management: Identifying and Managing Unsolvable Problems*. Amherst, MA: HRD Press, Inc. 1992.

Jones, Edward E. and Victor A. Harris. "The Attribution of Attitudes," *Journal of Experimental Social Psychology*. 3 (1967): 1-24.

Kandel, Eric R. *In Search of Memory*. New York: W.W. Norton & Company, 2006.

Killingsworth, Matthew. The Future of Happiness Research." *Harvard Business Review*. January-February, 2012. 88-89.

Kipnis, Laura. *Against Love: A Polemic*. New York: Pantheon Books, 2003.

Kohls, L. Robert. *Learning to Think Korean: A Guide to Living and Working in Korea*. Yarmouth, ME: Intercultural Press, 2001.

Kluckhohn, Florence. and Fred .L. Strodtbeck. *Variations in Value Orientation*. Evanston, IL: Row, Peterson and Company, 1961.

Kluger, Jeffrey. *The Sibling Effect: What the Bonds Among Brothers and Sisters Reveals About Us*. New York: Riverhead Books, 2011.

Koutlaki, Sofia A. *Among The Iranians*. Boston: Intercultural Press, 2010.

Kuhl, Patricia K. "Born to Learn: Language, Reading, and the Brain of the Child." Paper presented at the Colorado Early Learning Summit, Denver, Colorado, May 21, 2003

Langer, Ellen J. *Mindfulness*. Reading, MA. Perseus Books, 1989.

———. *Science of Mindlessness and Mindfulness*, an interview with Krista Tippett on NPR, May 29, 2014. Available at www.onbeing.org

Levine, Peter A. *In An Unspoken Voice: How the Body Releases Trauma and Restores Goodness.* Berkeley, CA: North Atlantic Books, 2010.

Matsumoto, Michihiro. *The Unspoken Way*. Tokyo and New York: Kodansha International, 1988.

May, Gerald G. *Will and Spirit.* New York: HarperCollins Publishers, 1982.

McCullough, Michael E. *Beyond Revenge: The Evolution of the Forgiveness Instinct.* San Francisco: Jossey-Bass, 2008.

McEwen, Bruce. *The End of Stress as We Know It.* New York: Dana Press, 2002.

Milgram, Stanley. *Obedience to Authority*. New York: Harper and Row, 1974.

Mindell, Arnold. *Dreambody: the Body's Role in Revealing the Self.* London: Routledge, Kegan Paul, 1982.

———. *The Leader as Martial Artist: An Introduction to Deep Democracy.* New York: HarperCollins Publishers, 1992.

———. *Sitting in the Fire.* Portland, OR: Lao Tse Press, 1995.

Mr. Baseball. Universal Pictures. 1992. Directed by Fred Schepisi.

Nathanson, Donald L. *Shame and Pride: Affect, Sex, and the Birth of the Self.* New York: W. W. Norton & Company, 1992.

Navarro, Joe. *What Every Body Is Saying.* New York: William Morrow, 2008.

Nees, Greg. *Germany: Unraveling an Enigma.* Yarmouth, ME: Intercultural Press, 2000.

Ost, James, Aldbert Vrij, Alan Costall and Ray Bull. "Crashing Memories and Reality Monitoring: Distinguishing between

Perceptions, Imaginations and False Memories," *Applied Cognitive Psychology* 16: (2002) 125–134.

Parsons, Talcott. *The Social System.* Glencoe, Illinois: The Free Press of Glencoe, 1951.

Patterson, Kerry, Joseph Grenny, Ron McMillan, and Al Switzler. *Crucial Conversations: Tools for Talking When Stakes Are High.* New York: McGraw Hill, 2002.

Pearce, W. Barnett. *Interpersonal Communication: Making Social Worlds.* New York: HarperCollins College Publishers, 1994.

Porges, Stephen W. *The Polyvagal Theory.* New York: W. W. Norton & Company, 2011.

Putnam, Robert D. *Bowling Alone.* New York: Simon & Schuster Paperbacks, 2000.

Rabinowitz, Christina Johansson and Lisa Werner Carr. *Modern-Day Vikings.* Boston and London: Intercultural Press, 2001.

Rousseau, Jean-Jacques. "A Discourse on the Origin of Inequality." In, *Great Books of the Western World,* Volume 35, Mortimer J. Adler, (Ed.) Chicago: Encyclopedia Britannica, Inc., 1952.

Sapolsky, Robert M. *Why Zebras Don't Get Ulcers.* Third edition. New York: St. Martin's Press, 2000.

Schulz von Thun, Friedemann. *Miteinander Reden 1: Störungen und Klärungen.* Hamburg, Germany: Rowohlt, 1994.

Schwartz, Jeffrey M. and Sharon Begley. *The Mind & The Brain: Neuroplasticity and the Power of Mental Force.* New York: Harper Perennial, 2002.

Searle, John, *Speech Acts.* London: Cambridge University Press, 1969.

Seligman, Martin and Mihaly Csikszentmihalyi. "Positive Psychology: An Introduction." *American Psychologist, 55,* (2000), 5-14.

Siegel, Daniel J. *The Developing Mind: Toward a Neurobiology of Interpersonal Experience.* New York and London: The Guilford Press, 1999.

———. *The Neurobiology of "We"—How Relationships, the Mind, and the Brain Interact to Shape Who We Are.* Compact disc. Boulder, CO: Sounds True, 2008.

————. *Mindsight: The New Science of Personal Transformation*. New York: Bantam Books, 2010.

Shaules, Joseph. *The Intercultural Mind—Connecting Culture, Cognition and Global Living*. Boston and London: Intercultural Press, 2015.

"Spirit of the age." *The Economist*, December 19, 1998, 113-117.

Tannen, Deborah. "The Power of Talk: Who Gets Heard and Why." *Harvard Business Review*, September-October 1995, 138-148.

Tavris, Carol. *Anger: The Misunderstood Emotion*. New York: A Touchstone Book, 1989.

Tavris, Carol and Elliot Aronson. *Mistakes Were Made (but not by me)*. Orlando and New York: Harcourt, 2007.

Thomann, Christoph and Friedemann Schulz von Thun. *Klärungshilfe*. Hamburg, Germany: Rowohlt Taschenbuch, 2001

Tomasello, Michael. *Why We Cooperate*. Cambridge, MA: The MIT Press, 2009.

Tremayne, Soraya. "Change and 'Face' in Modern Iran." *Anthropology of the Middle East*, Vol. 1, No. 1, Spring 2006, 25-41.

Trompenaars, Fons and Charles Hampden-Turner. *Riding the Waves of Culture*, 3rd edition. New York: McGraw-Hill, 2012.

Van Berkum, Jos J.A.; Bregje Holleman; Mante Nieuwland, Marte Otten and Japp Murre. "Right or Wrong? The Brain's Fast Response to Morally Objectionable Statements." *Psychological Science*, September 2009, Vol. 20, Issue 9. 1092-1099.

Van der Kolk, Bessel. "Foreword" in Porges, Stephen A. *The Polyvagal Theory*. New York: W. W. Norton & Company, 2011.

————. *Restoring the Body: Yoga, EMDR, and Treating Trauma*, an interview with Krista Tippett on NPR, October 30, 2014. Available at www.onbeing.org

Wenner, Melinda. "Brain Scans Reveal Why Meditation Works." Special report to LiveScience on June 29. 2007. www.livescience.com/7306-brain-scans-reveal-meditation-works.html

Wexler, Bruce E. *Brain and Culture: Neurobiology, Ideology, and Social Change*. Cambridge, MA: The MIT Press, 2006.

West, Richard and Lynn H. Turner. "Communication Accommodation Theory" in *Introducing Communication Theory: Analysis and Application*, 4th edition. New York, NY: McGraw-Hill Higher Education, 2010.

Whiting, Robert. *You Gotta Have Wa*. New York: Vintage Books, 1989.

Whitmore, John. *Coaching for Performance*. Second edition. London: Nicholas Brealey Publishing, 1996.

Wilber, Ken. *Integral Psychology: Consciousness, Spirit, Psychology, Therapy*. Boston & London: Shambhala, 2000.

———. *Kosmic Consciousness*. Compact disc. Boulder, CO: Sounds True, 2003.

Wilson, Timothy D. *Strangers to Ourselves*. Cambridge, MA: Belknap Press of Harvard University press, 2002.

Zimbardo, Philip. *The Lucifer Effect: Understanding How Good People Turn Bad*. New York: Random House, 2007.

INDEX

ABOUT THE AUTHOR

Greg Nees, Ph.D., is an interculturalist, coach, and consultant. He earned his B.A. in psychology from UCLA, worked and traveled in West Africa, and then took up residence in Europe. In Germany he worked as an English teacher, translator, and college instructor. While leading intercultural communication seminars at the Johannes Gutenberg University, he discovered the joy of promoting understanding between the different peoples of the world.

He returned to the U.S. in 1990 to complete his doctorate in communication studies. Today he works with expatriates, multicultural teams, and international organizations that want to improve their global competence. His seminars and coaching sessions focus on the interaction of culture, mind, and communication style to help his clients raise their awareness and develop the skills needed to achieve their goals. For more on Greg and his work visit **www.gregnees.com** or **www.talkingtogether.com**

If you liked this book and want to support its message, please take a minute and write a short review to help spread the word. Thank you!

Made in the USA
San Bernardino, CA
08 August 2016